Moral Responsibility
and Persons

Moral Responsibility and Persons

Eugene
Schlossberger

TEMPLE UNIVERSITY PRESS

Philadelphia

Temple University Press, Philadelphia 19122
Copyright © 1992 by Temple University. All rights reserved
Published 1992
Printed in the United States of America

The paper used in this publication meets the minimum
requirements of American National Standard for Information
Sciences—Permanence of Paper for Printed Library
Materials, ANSI z39.48-1984 ⊗

Library of Congress Cataloging-in-Publication Data
Schlossberger, Eugene, 1951–
    Moral responsibility and persons / Eugene Schlossberger.
      p. cm.
    Includes bibliographical references and index.
    ISBN 0-87722-879-5 (hard)
      1. Responsibility. 2. Agent (Philosophy) I. Title.
BJ1451.S33 1992
171'.3—dc20   91-11848

By permission of Oxford University Press,
much of the text of Eugene Schlossberger,
"Why We Are Responsible for Our Emotions,"
Mind 95 (January 1986) is incorporated into this volume.

For my parents, Kurt and Else

My father died while this book was in production. He was the most affectionate man I have ever known, a puppy-hearted man, full of love and frisky joy. I always think of him laughing. He told us often, in those last months when he knew he was not well, that we should not feel sorry when he died, because he had had a good life. He lived for his music, his family, and his students, and all three he served with delight. He was loved and knew he was loved: what more can one ask? Everything that is good in me came from him. I cannot remember a single time when my father let me down. We played sonatas together, cut roses together, went on walks in the wet woods humming from *Fidelio*. One day, when I was twelve, I took my oils and painted a mountain scene on my bedroom wall. Most parents, I suspect, would have been aghast. My father nailed a frame around my mountain and told me he was proud of me. If ever once I make someone feel the way my father made me feel all my life, I will count my life a happy one.

Contents

Acknowledgments

DURING THE YEARS that this work was in progress, I have bene-fited immensely from criticisms and suggestions from, and conversations with, a large number of people. Special thanks are due Joel Feinberg, Peter van Inwagen, Myles Brand, Alan Donagan, Irving Thalberg, Ronald Moore, Robert Richman, Richard Eldridge, Hans Oberdiek, Holly Smith, Hugh LaFollette, Joan Callahan, Judith Andre, Larry Stern, Alan Fuchs, Noel Carroll, Robert Hoag, Richard Galvin, Sara Ketchum, Danny Nathan, and Robert Evans.

I wish also to thank my colleagues and students at Swarthmore College and at Louisiana State University for their encouragement, interest, and help. I am also indebted to Lawrence Falkowski and Kelly Hite, with whom I profitably discussed much of the manuscript at great length. And although much of this work is directed toward overturning traditions, I take pleasure in adhering to at least one tradition by expressing my gratitude to my wife, Lynn, for her extensive editorial and substantive criticisms and suggestions. Finally, I should like to thank the NEH for its kind support, and the editors and readers at Temple University Press for their assistance.

Moral Responsibility
and Persons

I

Approaching Responsibility

OVERVIEW

THIS BOOK talks of many things (although kings receive barely a mention, and cabbages appear not at all). It attempts to provide a systematic and illuminating picture of some of our most important moral concepts and practices. Among the topics that arise in the course of these discussions are not only moral responsibility, the nature of personhood, and the problem of determinism, but also insanity, punishment, the mind-body problem, the moral status of computers, the character of emotions (particularly gratitude and resentment), the nature of psychological explanation, identity over time, moral luck, negligence, duress, and wrong acts done from good motives.

My task begins, as does so much in philosophy, with the self. Persons have a very special place in the world as we see it. We do not worry about respecting the aims of corkscrews and geraniums or about hurting the feelings of Mount Rushmore. We need not try to be fair to termites, as we must to our fellow persons. And, despite the fondness we might have for a favorite chair or an oft-used pipe, we do not feel gratitude, comradeship, resentment, or moral respect toward them. We cannot have personal relationships with our furniture.

Perhaps the most striking difference between persons and nonpersons is that we hold persons morally accountable. True, we sometimes assign obligations, of a sort, to house pets. The family dog must not bite children or eat the begonias. And pets are generally "punished" (subject to sanctions) for disobeying these rules. But we do not hold dogs, earthquakes, and computers morally responsible for the damage they do. We do not speak of morally tainted dogs or saintly computers. By way of contrast, moral accountability is at the heart of our personal interactions and relationships. As P. F. Strawson points out, to treat someone as a person is, in large part, to treat her as subject to praise or blame. Moral responsibility lies at the heart of "gratitude, resentment and forgiveness; of all reciprocated adult loves; of all the essentially personal antagonisms."[1] One cannot, after all, be grateful (in the fullest sense) to a rain that ends a drought. For the rain did not fall with an understanding of our plight in mind; it was not moved by pity, friendship, or a sense of justice. In short, the rain, however welcome, is not praiseworthy.

This book has its origin in the belief that moral accountability is closely tied to what it is to be a person. It seemed to me that to understand ourselves as persons, we would have to understand the nature of moral responsibility. Conversely, fundamental disagreements about responsibility could be settled only by appealing to a deep and illuminating account of the roots and nature of moral responsibility. By looking carefully at what it is to be a moral person, this book presents an alternative to deeply entrenched, traditionally held views about moral responsibility.

By the "traditional view" I do not really mean a single view, but any view that makes two assumptions: the first assumption is that one is morally responsible only for acts or deeds that are caused or brought about in the proper manner (for example, actions that are brought about by the exercise of free will or actions that result from one's intentions and desires). The second claim seems a natural addition to the first: no one, traditional views maintain, can be held responsible for something "beyond her control."[2] Thus many writers have pledged their allegiance to the "principle of alternate possibilities"; one is not morally responsible for an act unless one could have done or chosen otherwise.[3] Both claims, I will argue, are wrong.

Many of my claims may seem somewhat surprising. So I would be surprised if most readers did not, at least initially, take strong exception to several of my theses.[4] Indeed, the traditional claims I attack have often been taken as truisms, and much of our moral discourse is based on them. It is difficult to imagine an argument that would convince the traditionalist that neither the causes of our actions nor whether something is within our control is directly relevant to moral responsibility. For instance, traditionalists claim that someone cannot be responsible for having done something if he could not have done otherwise than he did. A minority disputes this claim. What could settle the issue? One might try to imagine an act for which the actor seems to be responsible, even though he could not have done otherwise (such as Harry's slapping of his landlord, discussed later in this chapter). But the traditionalist is more likely to say "he must not have been responsible after all" than to change her deeply held convictions. So this kind of argument is unlikely to persuade her that we can be responsible for doing something even if we could not have done otherwise. Suppose, however, we give the traditionalist a compelling account of what it is to be morally responsible, an account that explains, in a fundamental way, why it is reasonable to hold persons but not goldfish morally accountable. And suppose we show that our account stems from the very notion of what it is to be a person. And suppose we then use our account to explain cases that have puzzled moral philosophers and jurists, and to justify and clarify the practices and institutions (such as punishment) to which moral responsibility is crucial. Suppose, in addition, that our view sheds light on several perennial philosophical problems, such as the problem of personal identity. Finally, if we can also answer the traditionalist's objections, and show that the "odd" or "counterintuitive" aspects of our account are not so strange when seen in the right perspective, then we have given the traditionalist a powerful reason to change her mind. That is what this book hopes to achieve.

It follows that although the book contains its fair share of specific arguments, the ultimate test is not the persuasiveness of the individual claims and arguments I make, but the explanatory power and cohesiveness of the book as a whole. Much of what I say consists in putting my claims in the proper perspective, so that they appear natural rather than odd. And, ultimately, the strength of my position comes from the way it unites considerations from a variety of areas into a single and, it is hoped, illuminating account. It is both the strength and the peculiar vulnerability of my project that unless the general picture of moral agency I present is illuminating and compelling, many readers will remain unpersuaded. So it is with considerable trepidation as well as hope that I offer this work.

The basic intuition motivating my view is that moral agency and responsibility alike have their roots in the fact that we, unlike pebbles and tape recorders, approach the world with an evaluative framework. We make sense of our experience in terms of a network of concepts, goals, aims, standards of excellence, and so forth. We have, in the widest sense of the word, a moral outlook. The reason we do not praise or feel gratitude to the drought-relieving rain is not that the rain could not help but fall, had no choice, but that it has no moral outlook. What is crucial to responsibility, I suggest, is having a moral outlook upon the world. In order to feel pity, establish friendships, or have a sense of justice, one must have a moral framework, a set of moral attitudes and understandings one uses in making sense of and responding to the world about one. Unless one has such a moral framework, a "worldview," one cannot make moral choices, one cannot perceive choices in moral terms. I suggest that all and only moral persons are held morally responsible because moral persons are those organisms who understand the world in moral terms; persons view the world in such a way that moral predicates are applicable to the world as they see it. And so the lives of moral persons— their actions, decisions, relationships, feelings, and perceptions— have a moral dimension. It is also this capacity for moral perception that grounds our resentment, blame, praise, gratitude, and even love of persons.

This chapter introduces the problem of moral responsibility and gives some reasons for wanting an alternative to the traditional view along the lines of my account.

That account begins with a detailed explanation of what it is to be a person, the subject of Chapter II. "Person" is a status term, and there are several conceptions of personhood, each of which plays a different role. Questions concerning legal status invoke legal personhood, while questions concerning rights and responsibility depend on moral personhood. Moral personhood is explained in terms of what I call a "worldview," the network of attitudes, beliefs, dispositions, goals, values, and judgments, both specific and general, fleeting and enduring, that one uses in making sense of and responding to the world about one. Much care is given to explaining what it is to "express" one's worldview. Briefly put, an act expresses someone's worldview if we can "make sense" of the person's behavior in terms of her beliefs, values, and so forth (if we can give what Daniel Dennett calls an "intentional explanation"). The character of emotions and the status of computers receive some attention. Full and partial personhood are distinguished, and an explanation is given of why moral persons, as I define them, can be morally evaluated and merit rights. Finally, my concept of personhood is used to resolve some of the traditional puzzles about personal identity.

Chapter III gives an account of moral responsibility in terms of this conception of personhood. It begins by defining a very limited sense of "responsibility," a sense that is similar to what we might call "moral worth," or "moral evaluability." To say that someone is responsible for x, in my sense, is just to say that she is morally evaluable on the basis of x. "Jones is responsible for x," in my special sense, means that Jones is morally flawed to the extent that x is morally undesirable and lustrous to the extent that x is morally salutary. Since moral evaluation is important to many of our practices, this limited sense of "responsibility" is an important one. It is not, of course, the only way in which we use the word "responsibility." It may not even be the "ordinary" way in which "responsibility" is used. But I will argue later that it does most of the *work* we want the notion of responsibility to do.

Indeed, one way to put my view is that we should *eliminate* the ordinary notion of moral responsibility, and *replace* it with the notion of moral evaluability. I find it less misleading, however, to say that I am using a stricter notion of moral responsibility. After all, I want to show why it is proper and fitting to praise and blame people, to resent and feel gratitude toward people, and to insist that evil people merit punishment. Since this is the point of saying that people are morally responsible for what they do, it would be seriously misleading to say that I wish to eliminate moral responsibility. Moreover, my special sense does capture *one* of the ways we ordinarily use the word "responsibility." Richard Brandt points out that "when philosophers say that human beings are 'morally responsible' for their actions, what they apparently mean . . . is that it is right and proper, sometimes, to engage in blaming and praising. . . . People are sometimes fittingly, deservedly, praised and blamed."[5] I am not sure I agree that this is what *most* philosophers mean by "morally responsible." But it is certainly a legitimate use of the term. According to the *Oxford English Dictionary,* "worth" is defined as "the relative value of a thing in respect of its qualities or of the estimation in which it is held."[6] So if Jones has a morally lustrous or odious quality that shows something about her as a moral agent, her moral worth is affected. Now one standard meaning of "to blame" is "to find fault with, to censure."[7] Hence to find moral fault with Jones is (morally) to blame her, and so to find her "morally responsible" in Brandt's sense.

In any case, the reader should keep in mind (1) that when I talk about moral responsibility, I am talking about being morally evaluable for something, and (2) that (I show later) when I am morally evaluable for x, I am thereby subject to whatever praise or blame, resentment or gratitude, or punishment or reward x merits.

The rest of Chapter III is concerned with developing a detailed account of responsibility in this special sense. Traditional accounts of responsibility center on how our acts are caused. We are responsible, they claim, for acts caused in a certain way, by our choices, intentions, or desires. I hold that one is responsible not for one's acts as such, but for instantiating certain *traits.* Now by a trait I mean simply any property or feature we can ascribe to an agent. Some of my traits are very closely related to actions. It is, after all, a feature of mine that I have sung "Nessun Dorma," and so *having sung "Nessun*

Dorma" is a trait one can correctly ascribe to me. Other traits, such as *being a habitual liar,* involve many actions, while *being a citizen of the United States* and *believing in astrology,* although traits, involve no particular actions at all. So my view, unlike the traditional view, does not limit responsibility to actions or choices.

I further deny that responsibility is a causal notion. What is important is not that we cause something to happen in the right way, as the traditional view requires, but that the traits we instantiate express or fit with our worldviews. In other words, we are morally evaluable for those properties we instantiate that show something about us as moral agents, that reveal, reflect, or express our attitudes, judgments, beliefs, values, and so on. A person is blameworthy insofar as the moral stance reflected in those beliefs and values is incorrect.

Moreover, we are responsible only for properties that are sufficiently specific. In particular, someone is responsible only for traits that include all the information required by the moral theory used to evaluate her.

In sum, a "full moral person" is responsible for the sufficiently specific traits she instantiates that reflect or express, in the appropriate manner, her worldview.

This account is used to analyze and resolve traditionally puzzling cases, such as responsibility for emotions, wrong acts done from good motives, negligent acts, and acts performed under duress. Several striking conclusions are reached: for example, that we are responsible for our emotions even if we could not help having them, and that having acted under duress does not diminish one's responsibility one whit (although it may modify what one is responsible *for*). My account is then defended against various objections (for example, Thomas Nagel's argument from moral luck). Many of these objections stem from an untenable view of the moral self as a kind of "pure chooser," a myth to which the traditional view is committed.

Chapter IV argues that, given my account of responsibility, determinism (the view that all our acts are caused in accordance with universal laws of nature) does not threaten or undermine moral responsibility.

It may appear that the disagreements between my view and traditional views are spurious, as I do not mean the same thing by "responsibility" that traditional views do. In a sense this is correct. However, my sense of "responsibility" is meant to *replace*, in many contexts, the more traditional sense. Chapter V discusses punishment and personal emotions such as gratitude and resentment. It is argued that my view of responsibility can be used to justify and explain the retributive aspect of punishment and the nature and appropriateness of gratitude and resentment. If I am right, there is no need to invoke the problematic traditional view of responsibility.

If my view is correct, some important consequences follow. A new criterion for legal insanity must be formulated. The conceptual bases of punishment and contract law must be rethought. Our conception of the self as a moral agent must be modified. The Principle of Alternate Possibilities is false. Determinism does not undermine moral responsibility. We can be responsible for things for which the traditional view does not hold us responsible (such as things we would have done had we had the opportunity). Most of the generally accepted analyses of acts of negligence, omission, and the like are incorrect. So if I am right, much of our moral discourse needs revision.

PROBLEMS WITH THE TRADITIONAL VIEW

Since the traditional view is both widely held and deeply entrenched, one must have good reasons for rejecting it. So it seems appropriate to begin by sketching a few reasons for seeking an alternative to the prevailing view. The remainder of this chapter will list some of the reasons for preferring my view to the traditional view, even though most of them will be discussed in detail only later. This "catalog" of grievances will help orient the reader as the various issues arise.

Counterexamples

Sometimes the traditional view gives wrong results. We are responsible, I will argue, for some things that are neither done nor chosen. We are responsible for some things that are "beyond our control." And there are some things for which we are responsible although we could not have done otherwise. So the traditional view, which insists that responsibility is for actions or choices and that control and the ability to have done otherwise are prerequisites for moral responsibility, is mistaken.

Here I will discuss three sorts of cases (more will arise later). The first case concerns acts one would have performed had one had the opportunity. The second example concerns character traits, such as being wise, which are neither acts nor choices. The third is a counterexample to the Principle of Alternate Possibilities (that is, the claim that one is not responsible for doing something unless one could have done otherwise).[8]

The first counterexample to the traditional view concerns things one did not do or choose, but would have done or chosen had the opportunity arisen. Let us imagine that William is the sort of person who would use a public office for illicit gain. He never attains public office, and so he never abuses the public trust. So William has done no wrong.

Nonetheless, this feature of William's character reveals a moral failing of his. It counts against him that he would abuse public office. Indeed, it counts against him even if he never seriously considers the possibility of becoming an officeholder, and so gives no thought to what he would do were he to become a public official. (Hence he never even "hypothetically" chooses to abuse public office.) So although William has not *done* anything that is morally offensive, it seems evident that William is less laudable, more subject to moral disapprobation, less morally worthy, than is someone otherwise similar who would not have abused public office. Conscientious Clarence, who would not abuse public trust, is (other things being equal) morally superior to William. Yet Clarence's moral superiority does not rest upon any acts he performed or choices he made. So a theory of responsibility that evaluates only deeds and choices must deny that Clarence is morally preferable to William. It must deny that Clarence is more morally deserving or more morally lustrous than William. And that is surely wrong.

True, we tend to judge William less harshly than we do corrupt public officials. This is due to a variety of factors. For example, we have limited confidence in our judgments about what people would do. We might wonder whether achieving high office would change William's dispositions. Moreover, William's moral standing is not the only factor. We tend to be distressed by damage actually done, quite apart from moral culpability. So it is not surprising that we are often more perturbed by culpable harm than by harmless dereliction. In addition, it may be morally worse to be corrupt *and* seek public office than merely to be corrupt, since the former contains an additional element of deceit and hypocrisy. In sum, we may feel less inclined to blame the potential felon than the actual felon. He may even be less *blameworthy*. But he is no less *responsible* for his felonious disposition.

So the moral superiority of Clarence to William seems to be a counterexample to the traditional view of moral responsibility. By way of contrast, this case presents no problem for my view, for William's disposition to abuse public office is a trait of his that (as we will see) helps constitute his personhood. On my account, William is responsible for his morally unsavory disposition.

Dispositions to act and to choose are not the only sticking points for the traditional account. One can be responsible for character traits that are not merely dispositions to act or choose. *Contra* behaviorism, being wise requires more than being disposed to perform acts appropriate to one's circumstances. One must also have certain kinds of knowledge and understanding to be counted wise.

For example, suppose that Hilary decides to follow the prescriptions written in a book he has found lying in a dark and rain-swept alley. He has not as yet read the book. He simply likes the cover, perhaps, or is following some sort of casual impulse. Now as it happens, Hilary is a lucky fellow. The book was written by a wise philosopher, and so Hilary's actions in the years thereafter are, by and large, appropriate. Hilary is clearly disposed toward performing wise acts, that is, acts that are in accordance with the dictates of wisdom. But Hilary is not wise; indeed, he is a fool for following the dictates of a book simply because he likes the cover. He is a lucky fool, no doubt, but a fool nonetheless.

Thus to praise someone for her wisdom is not to praise her for an act, a choice, or even a disposition to act or to choose. It is rather to praise her for a trait that depends essentially upon internal states such as knowledge and understanding. To be wise is to live a life of deep understanding of the human condition. This means two things. First, one's judgments, attitudes, values, ways of thinking about things, and so forth show appreciation of the deeper moral and human features of the world we inhabit. Second, those judgments, attitudes, and the like are properly reflected in one's choices, actions, circumstances, emotions, relationships with others, and so on.[9] So wise people express and realize their wisdom in deeds and choices. Acting wisely is part of being wise, because it is foolish to act in ways that violate one's deepest understandings. Thus it makes no sense to attribute wisdom to someone whose acts are unrelievedly inappropriate. And it may be that we *know* someone to be wise only by attending to her acts, choices, and assertions. But apt acts, choices, and assertions do not, all by themselves, *constitute* wisdom. So in praising a wise person, we are not, as such, praising her actions or choices, but praising what she is. Indeed, if knowledge is valuable in itself, as many would hold, then it would seem to be important to *be* knowledgeable, not just to perform acts of erudition. Similarly, if knowledge is intrinsically valuable, it is good not only to strive for knowledge, but to succeed. In general, although deeds and choices are the primary *signs* of what one is like as a moral being, they are not the only things that are of moral significance.

It is useful to put this point in a broader context. The history of ethics contains two sorts of normative judgments. Some moralists have attempted to articulate rules of conduct, while others have attempted to adumbrate virtues based on a conception of what constitutes a good human life, a life that has *eudaimonia* (to use the term Plato and Aristotle would use). Lon Fuller, for example, distinguishes between what he calls the "morality of duty," that is, rules of conduct to which we owe it to others to conform, and the "morality of aspiration," judgments about what it is to lead a good life.[10]

The traditional view seems to be ill-equipped to handle judgments about the morality of aspiration.[11] The traditional view evaluates only wise *acts,* rather than the trait of being wise. Consider, for a moment, the ethical stance expressed in the *Iliad* and the *Odyssey.* Homeric ethics seems to consist in identifying traits of character deemed worthy of emulation (such as valor, hospitality, and loyalty) and, to a lesser extent, traits to be shunned. What is important, to the Homeric mind, is not simply to act in accordance with certain rules, nor merely to perform valorous acts, but to *be* valorous, to *be* loyal. Indeed, it is not uncommon in early epics for a hero to wish for opportunities to *display* his valor. And insults often take the form of aspersions upon another's valor, rather than unflattering claims about his acts. The hero's wish and the opponent's insult make sense only if acts have significance as *signs* of what one *is,* if the ultimate object of moral evaluation is one's character itself and not merely the acts that express that character.

My view, with its emphasis on traits that express personhood, evaluates traits attributing both actions and character. It is responsive to the demands of the morality of duty and to those of the morality of aspiration. The traditional view, however, fails to recognize the moral importance of being wise (and not merely acting wisely), being loyal (and not merely acting loyally), and so on.

Of course, the traditionalist might reply that the cases of Clarence and Hilary show only that the traditional view needs to be supplemented: we are responsible for our acts as well as for some other things. In other words, the traditionalist may say that we need two accounts of responsibility, the traditional account of responsibility for actions *plus* a second account of responsibility for traits and things we would have done. This response, however, will not do. After all, every act-description has a corresponding trait-description. (For example, the act of scratching my head corresponds to the trait of having scratched my head.) Thus, if we accept an account of responsibility for traits, we no longer need an account of responsibility for acts: once we add the supplementary account of moral responsibility needed to handle the cases of Clarence and Hilary, the traditional account becomes superfluous.

Counterexample three is an attack on the Principle of Alternate Possibilities, or PAP for short.

The main argument for PAP is its purportedly universal acceptance. So it is worth noting that PAP has come under attack in recent years.[12] Even more telling are two sorts of counterexamples to PAP. One sort is somewhat artificial but relatively sharp, namely the "Frankfurt" counterexamples (as Peter van Inwagen calls them),[13] the first of which was presented by Harry Frankfurt in 1969.[14] The other sort of counterexample is exemplified by the case of Milbur.

Milbur is a gentle, compassionate man. For years Milbur has visited the sick each Saturday, bringing them joy and comfort. He has never considered changing this pattern. One day the legislature passes a law requiring citizens to spend one day a month visiting the sick. From now on, Milbur could not do otherwise than visit the sick once a month.[15] Does this mean that Milbur is suddenly no longer praiseworthy for doing what he has always done? (That would indeed be a piece of bad moral luck.) Which of his four monthly visits no longer counts? The point is that Milbur remains responsible for visiting the sick, because the passage of a law requiring sick visits does not diminish the fact that Milbur places a high value on humane acts. And it is because Milbur values humane acts, not whether he could have done otherwise, that we praise him.

Milbur's case helps us see the point of asking whether someone could have done other than he did. When we are assessing responsibility, the point of the question is not, as Dennett suggests,[16] prediction of future action. Nor is the ability to have done otherwise necessary for responsibility. Rather, in some kinds of cases, my inability to do other than I did means that you may not attribute to me the values and attitudes you otherwise would. Usually, for example, walking smack into a closed door shows haste and preoccupation. But if you learn that my contact lenses just fell out and I could not see the door, you will no longer attribute haste and preoccupation to me. My reporting Jones to his superiors might ordinarily indicate meanness and envy, since I am inflicting a gratuitous harm on Jones. If you learn that I had no choice but to report him, my act takes on a different meaning: it is no longer reasonable to assume I acted out of envy. In short, learning that someone could not have done otherwise often alters our assessment of the attitudes and values that person realizes in the way she lives her life. Since this is not true in Milbur's case, the fact that Milbur was not free to avoid paying sick visits is irrelevant. By contrast, if Evans would never consider visiting the sick but for his legal obligation to do so, then his visits do not reflect a commitment to compassion, but rather a commitment to staying out of jail. So it would be a mistake to praise Evans for his compassion, since Evans's visiting the sick is not a reflection of compassion. (Of course, we might legitimately praise him for his prudence.) It is in this sense that the question "Could she have done otherwise?" helps determine, as Dennett says, "what meaning we should attach" to someone's actions. And that is why the ability to have done otherwise is not a precondition for moral responsibility, even though "I could not have done otherwise" is sometimes an absolving excuse.

The second set of counterexamples to PAP, the Frankfurt-style counterexamples, have the following form: A decides to do x, and does so. Unbeknownst to A, something would have made him do x, even had he decided not to. So, like it or not, A had to do x. Here A is morally responsible for having done x, even though he could not have done otherwise.

The example I will give goes a step further, for it shows that one can be morally responsible for having performed a bodily movement that one did not cause at all. And so one could hardly have done otherwise.[17] Suppose that Harry decides to slap his landlord at 6:02 this morning. He begins to do so. At that moment, unbeknownst to Harry, Bill presses a button on a mechanism, which first blocks Harry's neural impulses and then swings Harry's arm, resulting in a resounding slap. Harry, who mistakenly believes that the slap was caused by neural impulses generated by his brain, is quite satisfied. Now it is quite clear that Harry could not have done otherwise than slap his landlord. Moreover, the movement of Harry's arm was not a result of any choice of Harry's. It was not even causally related to Harry's intentions, desires, beliefs, or decisions. Rather, the movement of the arm was caused entirely by Bill's machine.[18] Harry, of course, is blithely unaware of the intervention of Bill's machine. He is pleased that the slapping he intended for his landlord has been loudly consummated. As far as Harry is concerned, he slapped his landlord.

Does Harry escape responsibility for slapping his landlord? The answer must be a resounding "no." After all, it seems perverse to maintain that Bill's intervention cleared Harry of moral blame. (That would be a case of extraordinary moral luck indeed.) Must Harry's landlord, if he is to be reasonable, absolve Harry of guilt? And suppose that Harry, after learning of Bill's intervention, said, "You can't blame me. True, I intended to slap you, I thought my slapping you was caused by that intention, and my intention would have caused the slap had Bill not pressed the lever. And I am happy that your face was slapped. But as a matter of fact I did not cause the slap. Hence I am free of responsibility." Would we be morally bound to accept this and absolve Harry of all blame?[19]

It might be objected that Harry is guilty only of *attempting* to slap his landlord. Usually, however, we use the language of attempt to indicate that the intended result did not occur. It marks a discrepancy between the intended state of affairs and the actual event. "Attempted murder" means that the intended victim did not die. The notion of "attempt" is useful, because we are often concerned with the harm done as well as the state of mind of the perpetrator. In this case, however, the harm was actually done. Surely it would make no morally relevant difference if Bill's machine failed to function (and so the slap *was* causally related to Harry's intention).

Finally, it might be said that Harry did not "slap" anyone, since slapping is an action, and Harry performed no actions. Perhaps there is a sense of "slap" in which this is true. But there is also a sense of "slap" in which "A slapped B" simply describes a bodily movement of A's. (Consider, for example, "the waves slapped against the rocks.") In this sense of "slap," Harry clearly slapped his landlord, did not cause the slap, and is responsible for having slapped his landlord.[20]

Harry's case is not a mere technical difficulty for PAP and its variants. Rather, Harry's case demonstrates two important points, and suggests another. First, it is at least plausible to hold Harry responsible. Even those prepared to absolve Harry must recognize the existence of contrary intuitions. So the Principle of Alternate Possibilities cannot be considered unproblematically true; PAP, in other words, must be argued for, not merely invoked as a truism. Second, one must be careful in describing what an agent is responsible *for*. I suggest that Harry is responsible for instantiating the trait *having slapped his landlord* (where "slapped" just describes a bodily movement), rather than for an intention, an act or act-type, or a state of affairs (for example, his landlord's having been slapped) or type of state of affairs. This trait Harry could not have helped but instantiate. Finally, Harry's case strongly suggests that what is important for responsibility is not so much the causal link between one's intentions and one's deeds, but whether one's deed "fits" (for example) one's intention. If the deed expresses, or fits, the intention, one can be responsible even if no act was caused by the intention, and even if no *action* (in the strong sense) was performed. (Since the notion of "fit" is central to my account of responsibility, I discuss it in considerable detail in Chapter II.)

Harry's unusual plight suggests that we are not really concerned, when making moral evaluations, with the *causes* of an agent's actions. We are concerned rather with the moral character of the agent. As a rule, when a person has no alternative to doing x, his doing x reveals little about his moral character. Thus PAP has a certain surface appeal. But the appeal is illusory. Although we often seem to appeal to inability as an excuse, the inability is not *itself* the reason we excuse the offender, but merely an indication that some other excuse is appropriate, some other exculpatory condition obtains. For example, suppose that I say, "Don't blame me for wrecking your car; I couldn't help it. The brakes failed." We recognize this as a valid excuse. But its validity rests not so much upon the fact that I could not have done otherwise, I argue, as it does upon the fact that no attitude, belief, value, or morally significant disposition of mine is revealed by or reflected in the damage done to your car.

Indeed, Harry's case suggests that one can be responsible for something one did not cause at all. Harry's hand struck the face of his landlord without any assistance from Harry himself; the slap occurred quite independent of any desire, intention, or decision on the part of poor Harry. True, what made Harry responsible was his intention to perform the slap. But what is significant hcre is not the *causal* relation of the intention to the slap (there was none), but what having that intention shows about Harry's moral attitudes, dispositions, and so forth. Harry is culpable, I will suggest, because his worldview, that is, the sum total of his attitudes, beliefs, and so on, fails to fit the requirements of morality. One must not be misled by the fact that actions and the causal stories we tell about them are what generally *reveal* attitudes. What is relevant is that one *has* morally unsavory attitudes.

In sum, there are good reasons to think that PAP is incorrect. Even if the above-mentioned considerations do not *prove* the falsity of PAP, enough has been said to shift the burden of proof to the holder of PAP.

Practical Advantages

When Jones shoots Smith, he performs but a single act.[21] So the traditional view, which evaluates acts, is limited to a single judgment about Jones's shooting of Smith. All it may say about this case is that Jones is responsible or is not responsible for shooting Smith. And if shooting Smith is all Jones can be held responsible for, it is all he can be praised or blamed for. The traditional view gives only four options, no matter how complex the case may be. We can say that Jones is not responsible for shooting Smith. Or, if he is responsible for shooting Smith, we can say that he is praiseworthy for shooting Smith, blameworthy for shooting Smith, or neither.

By contrast, when Jones performs the single act of moving his finger on the trigger, he evidences a great many traits. He may evidence disrespect for the law, concern for his wife's well-being, hatred of Smith, and so forth. Thus a theory that evaluates traits has many more options. Jones may be morally responsible for some properties he instantiates by pulling the trigger, though not for others. He may be praiseworthy for a few of them, and blameworthy for several others. So if we evaluate each of Jones's many traits, rather than his single act, we can give a more flexible and precise account of his moral standing. We may praise him for his concern for his wife, blame him for disobeying the law, and so on. If he meant only to wound Smith, we may blame him for negligence (that is, for failing to pay sufficient heed to the risk to Smith's life), blame him for countenancing bodily injury to Smith, while, perhaps, praising him faintly for preferring to wound Smith rather than kill him. If he did not realize that shooting Smith might prove fatal, we may blame him for not having deemed the matter worthy of further investigation before pulling the trigger. If he did investigate, but his research was faulty, we might blame him or absolve him of negligence, depending on whether his efforts were reasonable ones, given the circumstances. Each of these factors can be expressed as a separate trait, and so evaluated. Thus our analysis can be as complex as we like.

As we will see, this added flexibility yields more exact and satisfying moral evaluations in some otherwise problematic cases. So trait analysis has a practical advantage over act analysis. It is more precise, more accurate, and less cumbersome. With trait analysis, as we will see, it is much easier to make moral judgments about complex cases. For now, a single illustration will suffice.

If people are responsible only for their acts or choices, then "acts of omission" raise some puzzling questions. There are two sorts of omissions. One may make a decision not to perform a particular act at a particular time. Marjorie may ask me, on Tuesday, January 4, at 6 P.M. to give five dollars to a particular charity, and I may refuse. This kind of omission is not troublesome for the traditional view. But omissions need not be like this. An omission may simply be the fact of nonperformance over a period of time. Suppose, for example, that

Teri has not given money or time to a charitable cause for the last twenty years. She has had the means to give and knew that a reputable charitable agency was located just next door to her (she has had the opportunity to give). To her shame, however, Teri is quite parsimonious. Now clearly Teri is morally responsible for her uncharitableness, for her failure to give to charity. After all, if being charitable or giving to charity are good things, given Teri's circumstances, then she is morally flawed to the extent that she does not give (is not charitable). That is, someone otherwise quite like her, but who did give to charity, would be her moral superior. And it is undeniable that we would regard a change in Teri's uncharitability as a moral improvement in her.[22]

So if we are responsible only for our acts or choices, as the traditional view would have us believe, then it follows that failing to give to charity for twenty years must be an act or choice of Teri's.[23] But this seems somewhat puzzling. Is her failure a single, continuous deed that takes twenty years to perform? Or does Teri perform a new act of not giving to charity at every moment she is not engaged in giving money? If so, then I perform the act of, for example, failing to visit a sick relative every time I brush my teeth, sleep, or save a drowning child. In fact, I would be guilty of indefinitely many failings to give to charity even if I gave regularly every afternoon. So there are serious problems with saying that not giving to charity for twenty years is an act of Teri's. Saying that her failure was a choice of hers is also problematic. Teri may never have chosen not to give money to charity. She may, for example, simply not have devoted attention to the subject. If so, she is morally inferior, other things being equal, to someone who does think about it and does donate. Thus it is difficult to explain Teri's moral flaw in terms of her acts and choices. Acts and choices are done and made in particular places at particular times. Indeed, if Davidson is right, an action is a particular bodily movement. And it is hard indeed to pinpoint the particular bodily movement that constituted Teri's not giving to charity.

By way of contrast, traits or features need not be linked to particular bits of "mental" or physical behavior. A trait is merely a feature one can ascribe to an agent, a property (in the widest sense of the term). Some traits, of course, will involve or center upon actions (such as the trait of having lied). Others, however, will reflect *states* of an agent or thing (such as being fragile or strong). And whereas an action must be performed at a particular time and place, one can instantiate the trait of being physically strong even when one is fast asleep or supine with fatigue. Again, traits may characterize an agent's behavior over long stretches of time. *Being unreliable* and *being inconstant,* for example, are not particular actions one performs. Rather, inconstancy and unreliability are general features of one's behavior over a lengthy period. And surely one can be held responsible for being unreliable or being inconstant. But neither of these is an act or a choice.

To summarize, then, it is hard to point to a particular act or even set of acts that constitute Teri's failure to give to charity or someone's being inconstant or unreliable. Thus it is hard to see how act or choice analyses can account for responsibility for failure to give to charity, for inconstancy, or for unreliability. In contrast, there is no difficulty in ascribing to Teri the traits of having been uncharitable, inconstant, or unreliable during the last twenty years.[24]

This is not, of course, an insuperable objection to the traditional view. Perhaps one could, with sufficient ingenuity, provide an act or choice analysis of responsibility for failing to give to charity and for being inconstant.[25] My discussion of acts of omission and long-term traits is not meant to *refute* the traditional view, but to illustrate the ease with which traditionally puzzling cases can be analyzed if one adopts a trait analysis. Teri's case displays an *advantage* my account has over traditional accounts.

Nonetheless, it must be admitted that the claim that we are responsible not for actions as such, but for properties, will strike some as odd. I do not think it is. In fact, I think it suits our deeper conceptions of moral evaluation much better than the traditional view does. After all, no major moral theory evaluates actions directly; they all evaluate actions via specific properties that are of moral interest.[26] A finger movement, for example, is not, *qua* finger movement, of moral interest. What is significant about that finger movement is that, in making it, one instantiates some morally significant *properties,* such as, for example, being a murderer.[27] Now if the basis of moral evaluation is not my actions as such, but the properties I instantiate, then it seems natural, intuitively correct, to hold me accountable for instantiating those properties, rather than for my actions as such. If what is of moral significance about my finger movement on the trigger is the malicious disregard for human life it evidences, then what I am morally accountable for is that malicious disregard, not the finger movement by which I evidence it.

In sum, our habit of speaking of responsibility for actions is *merely* a habit and does not suit well our deeper conceptions of moral evaluation.

One final odd consequence of the traditional view is worth pointing out. If we accept the traditional view's claim that we are responsible only for freely chosen actions and we accept Plato's claim that people choose to do wrong only through error, it seems to follow that we are responsible for some of our good deeds but none of our bad deeds.[28] This is, at best, an uncomfortable consequence that my view avoids.[29]

Determinism and Moral Luck

Some deep difficulties have plagued the traditional view, difficulties that my view will enable us to solve. The most persistent and troubling of these thorns in the side of the traditional view is the problem of determinism.

Determinism seems to present a dilemma for responsibility. Any action of mine either is caused in accordance with universal laws of nature or is not caused to occur.[30] Now if it is not caused to occur, the alternative seems to be that it is a random event.[31] Surely I cannot be held responsible for a random event. So if there are uncaused actions, I cannot be held responsible for them. What of actions of mine that are caused in accordance with universal laws of nature? In an important sense, these acts are "beyond my control." If determinism is true, it seems, I could never have done otherwise than I did, and none of my acts is "free."

Thus, it seems, if the traditional view is correct, no one is ever responsible for what she does. Moreover, whether we are good or bad seems to be a matter of "moral luck"; some are lucky and have genes and upbringings productive of moral virtue, while others, the unlucky ones, have genes and upbringings that lead to an evil character and so to evil behavior. (And if some of our acts occur randomly, then it is a matter of luck whether these random acts are morally upright or morally heinous acts.) But surely we cannot be blamed for something that is a matter of luck. It is absurd to blame someone because his ticket did not win the state lottery. It is just as absurd, it is said, to blame someone because he drew, in the lottery of life, "bad" genes or a "bad" environment.

Traditionalists who want to avoid this result have tried to show that actions caused in accordance with the laws of nature, despite the fact that they are causally inevitable, are "within our control," "free," and/or "voluntary." Despite the fact that my stealing a jumping jack from the toy store was causally necessary, they say, I could have done otherwise than steal the toy off the shelf. Their efforts have met with less than universal acceptance.[32]

My view offers a simpler solution. Once causation is divorced from moral responsibility, as my view suggests, the standard arguments that determinism is incompatible with moral responsibility no longer apply. On my account, I can be responsible for things that are not chosen, freely or otherwise, and not within my control. So even if causally necessitated acts are beyond our control and even if we cannot do otherwise than we do, we can still properly be held responsible for what we do.

Since these are complex issues, they are discussed at length in Chapters III and IV. If my arguments there succeed, then my account of responsibility lays to rest the spectres of determinism and moral luck. And this is surely a major reason for preferring my account to the traditional one.

The Self as Moral Agent

Behind any theory of responsibility is a picture of the self as a moral agent. The traditional view (I argue) is committed to an untenable view of the self as moral agent, a view I call "the myth of the pure chooser." On the traditional view, the self becomes a kind of homunculus who is somehow "behind" all of our feelings, dispositions, abilities, and the like. My feelings and abilities, on this view, are not part of me, but external encumbrances that limit what I can choose. This is an unsatisfactory view of the self. My view, I argue, presents a more acceptable picture of the self as moral agent.

Applications

Since moral responsibility plays a large role in many of our beliefs and practices, one test of an account of responsibility is its fruitfulness in explaining those practices. My account of responsibility, I argue, may be used to construct an explanation of and a justification of much of our moral life. It sheds light on such questions as the insanity defense and has obvious implications for the morality of abortion and the nature of personal relationships. I am claiming, in short, that my account forms part of a powerful system of moral and legal explanations.

A Glance Forward

Having motivated a search for an alternative to the traditional view, I turn now to my own view. One is morally responsible, ultimately, for one's personhood. I am morally evaluable on the basis of the traits I instantiate, both general and particular, whose collective possession makes me a unique moral agent. I call such traits "traits that are partially constitutive of personhood." Specifically, I claim that one is morally responsible for instantiating those traits that are (1) partially constitutive of personhood, (2) sufficiently specific, and (3) instantiated while one is a full moral agent.

These conditions require considerable explication. Which traits are partially constitutive of my personhood? Are *being short* and *having been born in New Jersey* constitutive of my personhood? Furthermore, since any given act can be described in an indefinite number of ways, I instantiate an indefinite number of traits every time I act. For which of these am I responsible? (What, in other words, is the correct parsing of an act into traits?) What about traits evidenced by an infant or while under hypnosis?

In order to answer such questions, we need four things. We need (1) an account of what it *means* to say that A is responsible for x. We need (2) to know *on what basis* A may be held responsible for x (in that sense). We also need (3) to know how to apply that criterion to troublesome cases. These three needs are addressed in Chapter III. However, without a clear picture of personhood, talk of "traits constitutive of personhood" is empty. So we need (4) a rigorous characterization of personhood. Answering that need is the task of the next chapter.

II

Personhood

FOR WELL OVER three centuries philosophers have puzzled over the problem of personal identity. On what basis, they have asked, do we insist that a chunky, middle-aged accountant in 1986 is the same person as a bald, squealing infant in 1936? The two do not look alike, talk alike, or think alike; they do not even enjoy the same sorts of food (with the possible exception of apple sauce). Very little that is true of the accountant is also true of the infant.

Let me put the problem more precisely. Consider the accountant just as she is at a particular moment in her history, say 2:30 P.M., on May 23, 1986. Just as we can, in our imaginations, consider a (spatial) slice of a pie, I want to consider a temporal slice of the accountant. Let me call such a slice a "person-stage." A bit of imagining may help clarify the notion of a temporal slice. Suppose that, in some laboratory in southern California, scientists have created a human body replete with advanced brain states. As soon as the "power" is turned on, the body comes to life. It has apparent memories of having lived fifty years (for example, it seems to remember having been a small child). It has a full set of likes and dislikes, desires, goals, skills, and so forth. A split second later, the power is turned off. A temporal slice or person-stage is somewhat like that.[1] In other words, a person-stage is the collection of subatomic particles, arranged in a certain way, that comprise the accountant at a given moment in time.[2]

The problem is that, in some sense, the accountant and the infant are two very different person-stages. One may detest the one and find the other delightful.[3] On the other hand, it is crucial to our treatment of the accountant that she is the same person as the infant; her special relationship with her parents, her citizenship, and her inheritance all require identifying her with that infant. What is it, then, that makes them stages of the same person? We may call this the "problem of personal *identity*" and distinguish it from puzzles about how we can *tell* that they are the same, which we may call the "problem of personal *identification*." Now it may be possible to solve the problem of personal identification without a deeper understanding of what it is to be a person. That is, we may be able to describe how we *tell* which stages belong to the same "person" without worrying too much about what that means. And in fact many discussions of personal identity do not articulate a conception of personhood. But one cannot fully explain what *makes* two stages the same person without explaining what makes them *persons*.

Unfortunately, this point is often overlooked by philosophers, who sometimes seem to forget what is at stake. As a result, much of the philosophical literature concerning personal identity misses the point altogether.[4] Philosophical questions about the nature of personhood have important consequences, as the concept of personhood plays an important role in many of our social and moral concepts and institutions. For example, many antiabortionists claim that it is wrong to kill a fetus because a fetus is a person and so has a "right to life." Hence many discussions of abortion turn on what it is to be a person. The concept of "the self" also plays an important role in various psychological theories. Moreover, it is a fundament of our conception of just punishment that one person not be punished for the wrongdoing of someone else. True, my culpability may depend, to some extent, on someone else's misdeeds, as in a conspiracy. But it is for *my* role in the conspiracy that I may be punished.[5] Again, I have marital obligations in 1986 only because I can be identified with a person-stage who took marriage vows some time earlier.

So what one says about personhood must be compatible with the ways in which we treat (or ought to treat) persons; an explanation of what it is to be a person must take account of the role that the concept of a person plays. And so a satisfying account of what makes me now the same person as a graduate student in 1975 must explain, or at least make it possible to explain, why I may be punished for that graduate student's violations of the law, why I am married to (a later stage of) the woman that graduate student married, and so on. And it must explain, or at least make it possible to explain, why I have the rights and obligations that come with being a person.

Conversely, any satisfying account of moral responsibility must accord with a satisfying theory of personal identity.[6] What makes me responsible for having been rude to my mother in 1966 must be closely connected to what makes me the same person as that rude 1966 teenager, for it is the "myness" of the rude behavior that renders me answerable for it.

The object of this chapter, then, is to articulate a conception of personhood that can answer perplexities about personal identity and that can also serve as the basis for the institutions and concepts that rely upon the concept of personhood. In particular, the aim is to develop a conception of personhood that can help explicate moral responsibility.

THE GENERAL CONCEPT OF A PERSON

If we look closely at the range of uses to which the word "person" is put in fields as diverse as law, ethics, medicine, and psychology, it begins to become clear that there is not just one conception of personhood but many. Sometimes we use the word "person" to mean those who belong to the species Homo sapiens. Other times we mean by "person" those with the ability to initiate lawsuits, inherit property, and so on. Or we may mean by "person" those who have certain rights and duties. And psychologists who speak of "persons" may mean something quite different from any of these.

I want to suggest that personhood is a "status" term; to be a person is to achieve a certain status. And there are several different concepts of "person," each corresponding to a different sort of status. To be a biological person, for example, is to attain a certain biological status, and to be a legal person is to have a certain legal status. Legal persons, in other words, are those things that, for example, possess legal rights, are able to advance legal claims and enter into contracts, and are liable for certain sorts of legal obligations. The meaning of "biological person" is rather different from that of "legal person"; the two terms point to rather different features. To say that our accountant is the same biological organism as an infant born some fifty-odd years ago is to point to the continuity of biological function between the two. To say that she is the same moral person as a twenty year old in 1956 is to say, for example, that she may be held morally accountable for the promises and misdeeds of that twenty year old. These are clearly rather different sorts of claims. Even if it should turn out that one entails the other, it is clear that the two assertions do not *say* the same thing.

But I want to make an even stronger claim. Not all legal persons are biological persons, nor need all moral persons be biological persons. And some legal persons are not moral persons. I argue that, in certain areas of law, corporations and cats count as persons, although neither can be said to be a (full) moral person. So it should come as no surprise that the criteria for being the same legal person as some infant born in 1936 are not necessarily the same as the criteria for being the same moral person as that infant.

I am claiming, in other words, that we employ several distinct concepts of "person," with different criteria for identity. Thus the question of whether this middle-aged woman is the same person as that infant of fifty years ago is, as it stands, unanswerable; it is quite possible that the accountant and the infant are the same person in one sense (for example, the same biological person) but not the same in another.[7]

In other words, the issues in which personal identity plays a role employ several distinct concepts, and the answer to a question about personal identity depends upon which concept is at stake. There is, of course, a subjective sense of self, and this sense will also be defined in terms of some sort of function. Continuity of subjective sense will then be continuity of the properties upon which this function is based. But questions concerning moral agency, such as responsibility and (retributive) punishment, will not depend on this but on continuity of moral agency. Questions concerning which stage should inherit under a will hinge not on sameness of subjective self but on sameness of legal personhood.

There are at least two reasons for thinking I am right about the nature of personhood. First, my approach has a certain explanatory power. It helps solve (I argue in the section entitled "Personal Identity") many of the standard perplexities concerning personal identity. It helps explain why persons have rights and are morally evaluable. In short, it forms part of what I hope will prove an enlightening and persuasive way of looking at a number of important issues. Second, I think it undeniable that we do employ the concepts I call "biological personhood," "legal personhood," and so forth, though we may refer to them in different words. Since those concepts, as we will see, do not employ the same criteria for identification, being the same "biological person" (as I use the term) need not entail being the same "legal person" (as I use the term). Of course, one could insist on restricting the use of the term "person" to but one of these concepts, using other terms (such as "legal agent") for the others. But my claim is not about terminology at all. Restricting the word "person" to biological persons would not change the fact that continuity of biological function (being the same organism) and continuity of legal standing are different, and that both are important to our practices and concepts. There are, whatever we choose to call them, several rather different types of continuities of "temporal slices" of individuals, which play different roles in our discourse about the world. And each employs different criteria of individuation. Thus my conclusion follows, to all intents and purposes, from the mere fact that the different conceptions of personhood I articulate are coherent, useful notions that use different criteria for identification.

Status Terms

I want to claim that there are different types of personhood and that my cat can be a legal person without being a biological person. Since this raises certain metaphysical questions, it is necessary to begin with a brief excursion into metaphysics. In particular, the first thing one must understand about personhood, I would suggest, is that the word "person" is both a status term and a composition term. So I will begin with a few words about status and composition terms.

It is easiest to explain what I mean by looking at a few examples. Consider the term "weapon." Nothing is a weapon *by nature;* to be a weapon is either to be used by someone in a certain way (for example, to attack someone else) or, by extension, to be an instance of a kind of thing that is often used in that way (for example, a knife), or perhaps to have been made by someone who intended the object to be used in that way. What makes something a weapon, in other words, is not its intrinsic properties, not the thing considered by itself, but rather the way that someone uses it, or the way that people typically tend to use things of that sort, or the intention of the person who made it. So "weapon" is a function term; it marks a use to which people put things, a role that some things happen to play in human behavior.

The word "weapon" is what I will call an "intentional" term. What the word "weapon" attributes essentially reflects human purposes, goals, ways of thinking about things, and so forth. In an important sense, the sentence "the thing in my hand is a weapon" says as much about us as it does about the thing in my hand. It asserts that we can or tend to use it (or things like it) in a certain way. It is not just that we could not use the word "weapon" in the absence of certain human purposes and customs. Rather, those purposes are part of the *content* of what the word "weapon" attributes.[8] Similarly, since anything with a certain social status counts as "gentry," "gentry" is an intentional term.

"River" (like "street") is also an intentional term. Whether the Ohio and the Allegheny are two rivers or one long river is a matter of custom, convention, and human purpose, not a fact of nature. It is, after all, the sort of thing we could change by fiat. A debate about whether the Ohio and the Allegheny are "really" two rivers is bootless; we could not commission a panel of experts to determine the truth of the matter, for the truth about these rivers is as we (collectively) say it is. The "brute" fact is that there are so many molecules of water in such and such locations. That we conceive of some of them as forming a river is a fact about us rather than a fact about the world.[9] So "gentry" and "weapon" are, unlike "quark," intentional terms. "Weapon" is a function term and "gentry" is a status term. Neither, however, is a "composition" term.

Composition terms are "count nouns" whose application is not parasitic upon the use of other count nouns.[10] For example, one can count the number of weapons in a room only by counting the knives, guns, and the like. Weapons are objects, *already defined in some other way*, that can be used in a certain way. Thus the identification of weapons is parasitic upon more primary terms, such as "knife," "gun," "fist," and "hat pin." And so "weapon" is not (and "knife" is) a composition term. Again, one does not count rivers by counting drops of water, nor does one count streets by counting bits of asphalt. "River" and "street" are primary identifying terms, primary ways of dividing the world up into objects. So "river" and "street" are composition terms. Some intentional terms, such as "weapon," are not composition terms. And some composition terms, such as "electron" and "quark," are not intentional terms. But some terms, such as "river" and "street," are both composition and intentional terms.

I do not mean to suggest that all intentional distinctions are arbitrary (nor that they are all reducible to nonintentional terms). For example, my claims about moral personhood are intentional assertions. Yet I think good reasons can be given for employing my account of moral personhood rather than some other account. In fact, I think my account is objectively correct. So I think that an intentional assertion can be true or false or at least correct or incorrect. But the criterion for its correctness is different from the criterion of correctness for "there are quarks."[11]

Now the term "person," I suggest, is like the term "river"; it is an intentional composition term. Were we to list the "fundamental" objects in the world, we might include quarks, electrons, and the like. Such things constitute the (ultimate) ontological furniture of the world. By contrast, to say that a river runs through Louisiana is to note a feature of certain collections of quarks, electrons, and such; one can perceive certain continuities in the passing caravan of subatomic particles. Similarly, to say that an infant in 1936 and an accountant in 1986 are the same person is to assert that two momentary bodies, or body-stages, belong to a series of body-stages and that the series has certain interesting features. (More precisely, it is so say that a temporal series of distinct collections of subatomic particles, one member of which existed in 1936 and another of which exists in 1986, exhibits certain continuities.) In a sense, there are no persons, only quarks, electrons, and the like, which collectively exemplify certain features. Just as the numeral "1" written in the sand is not a "thing," in some fundamental sense, but just a feature of the disposition of grains of sand, so persons are not "things," but features of subatomic particles. Of course, it is quite proper to talk about persons as "things," just as one is not wrong to describe the "1" etched in the sand as "the thing I just wrote in the sand." Only one must not be misled by this use of the word "thing" into thinking that persons have the same ontological status as quarks.

Two brief examples, biological and legal personhood, will help illustrate these points.

Biological Personhood

We often use the word "persons" to mean human beings, that is, members of our species. In any case, whatever words we use, we often single out members of our species. Let us call this use of the term "biological personhood." To be a "biological person" is to be a single, continuing, functioning organism of the species Homo sapiens. "Biological person" is a composition term; that is, "biological person" is a count noun, and we do not count human beings by counting droplets of protoplasm.

I will not spend a great deal of time on biological personhood. Little of what is said elsewhere in the book depends on adopting any particular account of biological personhood. Still, is it helpful to have several examples of different sorts of personhood. So I will make a few remarks about one way of analyzing biological personhood.

The concept of a biological species has received a great deal of attention, from the writings of Louis Agassiz—who thought that there is a set of "true" species distinctions, each of which is an idea in the mind of God—to the extensive contemporary literature. For Agassiz (and perhaps for Saul Kripke), "natural kinds" mark essential distinctions in nature. On this view, quite apart from human purposes, one classificatory system is right, the others wrong. Taxonomy is an attempt to capture something objective that is independent of human agency, such as God's thought (for Agassiz) or natural essences.[12]

Most contemporary biologists take a different (and, I think, preferable) view. The "ultimate facts" of nature concern microlevels (such as the behavior of subatomic particles), not large animals. How we categorize species depends on what we wish to explain. For example, one could consider the pond in which a frog lives to be part of the organism. Some ecologists have suggested that the entire earth should be understood as a single organism.

Such alternative biologies would not be incorrect; rather, they would point out different regularities in nature. A taxonomy that considers all the organisms in a given pond to be one organism, for example, is a taxonomy that clarifies the structure of ecosystems, whereas standard taxonomy clarifies the structure of genetics and reproduction. The latter is more useful in explaining mutation and natural selection, in applying biology to agriculture and animal husbandry, and so forth. The former might be more useful in explaining large-scale ecological processes. Thus one's choice of taxonomy reflects, to a large degree, one's purposes, what it is one wants to explain. One could easily describe the biological world with a different set of species concepts, based on a different conception of a biological system. However, once one selects a basis for taxonomy, such as the ability to mate, species distinctions become empirical. Two organisms do not (generally) belong to the same species if they cannot in fact mate and produce offspring. And this is a matter for empirical investigation. So taxonomy is partly an empirical matter and partly a matter of explanatory aesthetic. For the sake of simplicity, let us assume a standard taxonomy based on genetics.

My account of biological personhood is, in an important sense, an Aristotelian one. What makes this flesh and bone a human being is the way the molecules of flesh and bone function together over time, the fact that these molecules evidence human respiration, human digestion, human reproduction, and so on. That is, organisms over time evidence a variety of biological functions: they reproduce, ingest and process food, and so forth. Some of those functions will be common to many species: most species respirate, digest, and reproduce. Even so, there are many different ways of reproducing. What counts as reproduction varies from species to species. Some organisms lay eggs, and duck eggs are different from chicken eggs. Other organisms reproduce by mitosis. Fortunately for us, the mechanism by which human beings reproduce is quite different from that which replicates ferns. There is, in other words, a peculiarly human form of reproduction. I suggest that being a member of a species and being the same organism over time are both based on continuity of particular forms of reproduction, digestion, respiration, and so forth.

In particular, what makes something (biologically) human is that its stages over time exhibit the processes, such as human reproduction, human digestion, and human respiration,[13] that are central to membership in the species Homo sapiens. This author now and baby Eugene are stages of the same biological person, because we can see the stages leading from baby Eugene to the author of this book as evidencing human reproduction, human digestion, and so on, much as a series of snapshots of a ball at different heights with respect to a tower can be seen as shots of a single *fall* from the tower. Several stages are stages of the same biological person if the positions of their lungs, the states of their red blood cells, the positions of their sperm cells or ova, and the like can be seen as "snapshots" of an instance of human respiration, an instance of human reproduction, and so on. More generally, if two "temporal slices" are part of a series of slices that shows continuity of those functions central to membership in a species, then they are temporal slices of the same biological organism.

So identity conditions for biological persons differ somewhat from identity conditions for amoeba or jellyfish. And there may be cases in which a biologist is unsure about whether two temporal slices belong to the same organism. (Insect metamorphosis provides a good example.)[14] Nonetheless, I think the basic logic of biological identity is clear. Species terms determine a set of specific biological functions whose continuity provides the grounds for identification of organisms over time.

To say, then, that A, B, and C are temporal slices of the same biological person is to say that the internal states of A, B, and C exhibit a certain pattern and that the differences between them can be described in terms of certain biological functions that are central to membership in the species Homo sapiens.

Since spatio-temporal continuity and/or contiguity is often cited as an important consideration in personal identity, it is worth pointing out that spatio-temporal continuity and contiguity do play an important role in biological identity. But they do so only because they tend to be key ingredients in the sort of causal stories we generally tell about biological phenomena. One could imagine, for example, an organism with spatially detached limbs whose movements were controlled electromagnetically. For such an organism, spatial contiguity would not be an important factor in determining identity over time. So, were it the case that the biological processes on which our species concepts are based typically involved discontinuous fields, then spatio-temporal continuity and contiguity would not be very important in determining biological identity.

Legal Personhood

Legal personhood is strikingly different from biological person-hood. In some areas of law, nations, corporations, and even cats count as persons. So I will say just a few words about legal person-hood and about what we can learn by contrasting legal with biolog-ical personhood. My remarks will be quite sketchy, since legal per-sonhood is rather complex and varies from one area of law to another.

To be a legal person is to have a certain legal status: persons, in law, are parties to legal transactions. Since the law covers very differ-ent sorts of transactions, there is more than one type of legal person-hood. A few examples should help illustrate my point.

In inheritance law, a legal person is anything that can inherit under a will, contest a will, and so forth. For anything that can inherit, contest wills, and so forth has full legal standing, is a full party to the relevant legal transactions. Cats and other pets, for example, can in-herit under a will, contest a will (that is, a challenge to a will may be mounted in their behalf), and so on. So, for the purpose of inherit-ance, cats count as persons. Indeed, they have the same standing in inheritance law that infants do.

In contract and tort law, persons are entities that can be held liable or can advance legal claims. Roughly, they can sue or be sued for damages. (I say "roughly," because persons sometimes enter into contract and tort law as "third parties." For example, A slanders B by making a slanderous remark to a third party, C. Presumably I have not slandered my lawyer if I say to my cat that my lawyer viewed the movie *Jaws* as a family history.) So legal persons in tort and contract law include corporations, classes of individuals (as in class-action suits), organizations, and local and national govern-ments. For they all have the status of full participants in the legal process. The Ford Motor Company and Joe Smith have the same legal standing; they have the same sorts of rights, obligations, and so on.[15]

The same cannot be said, however, of marital law; one cannot marry a corporation (much to the distress of certain hard-working businesspersons). Thus corporations are not persons with respect to marital law. Similarly, one cannot marry a cat, and so cats do not count as persons in marital law. Thus a cat is an inheritance person but not a marital person. Since full parties to inheritance law might not be full parties to contracts, it is sometimes useful to speak of "inheritance persons" and "contract persons."

Traditionally, neither cats nor corporations have counted as persons in criminal law. The fact that in 1979 the Ford Motor Company found itself the defendant in a criminal case suggests that the concept of criminal personhood is undergoing some alteration. Legal personhood results in some curious anomalies. One can sue the mayor of a city without suing John Smith, even though John Smith is the mayor. Indeed, in a class-action suit, John Smith might find himself included as a party to both sides of the suit.

Given this account of legal identity, it is not hard to explain what it is to be the same legal person over time. Continuity of legal identity means continuity of legal standing. For example, two stages, A and a later stage B, are the same inheritance person when B is (prima facie) entitled to inherit goods (properly) willed to A, can revise a will written by A, and so on. Similarly, A and B are the same person for criminal law when B may be punished for the punishable offenses committed by A, when B's act of killing is premeditated if A meditated it, and so forth. In general, to say that A and B are the same legal person is to say that A's legal position (A's rights, claims, obligations, liabilities, and the like) is applicable to B.[16]

Once again, I think it clear that what I am calling "legal personhood" plays an important role in our practices and concepts. It is also undeniable that, in some areas of law, cats and corporations are within the extension of the concept I am calling "legal personhood," although neither cats nor corporations are biological persons. One could, of course, take issue with my terminology. One might deny that the law sometimes considers corporations and cats *to be* persons. Rather, one might say, the law sometimes treats cats and corporations *as if they were* persons. But it is not clear what point this distinction serves. If indeed tort law gives John Smith and the Ford Motor Company the same status, treats them as parties to a legal transaction in precisely the same way, then it is not clear what point one is making when one denies that, as far as the law is concerned, corporations are persons.

It is worth taking a moment to compare biological and legal personhood. For the contrast between biological and legal personhood suggests some interesting points. Legal personhood is accorded to anything with a certain legal status, to any full party to the relevant legal transactions. Similarly, biological personhood is accorded to anything that fulfills a certain biological role, namely exhibiting certain functional traits that are useful in explaining evolution. So it is not surprising that being the same biological person depends on continuity of biological function, while being the same legal person depends on continuity of legal role.

One can summarize this point more generally. For any type of personhood, X, to be an X-ical person is to attain a certain X-ical status. X-ical status is defined in terms of particular properties or processes. And being the *same* X-ical person depends on continuity of those properties or processes.

The second point that our discussion of legal and biological personhood suggests is that two temporal slices might be the same biological person but not the same legal person, or vice versa. (Indeed, one of the slices could be a legal person, yet fail to be a biological person at all.)

Our primary interest in this book, of course, is not in legal or biological personhood, but in moral personhood. So whereas a few rough remarks about the former two are adequate here, moral personhood requires close attention. It is to moral personhood, then, that we now turn.

MORAL PERSONHOOD

An explanation of moral personhood has several levels. The first thing to be explained is what it means to say of a thing that it is a moral person. So much is easily done. Moral persons, as I use the term, are those things that have full moral standing. To say that something is a moral agent is to say that it is a participant in the moral enterprise; it has rights and obligations, can be praised or blamed, and so forth. (I will use the terms "moral agent" and "moral person" interchangeably.) Anything that plays this moral role, that achieves this moral status, I will call a "moral person." So moral personhood, at least in principle, is not limited to human beings (members of the species Homo sapiens). Conversely, it may turn out that some human beings are not moral persons.

The second level of explanation is more difficult. What is it about us, one wants to know, that gives us this status; on what basis is it proper to praise, blame, and assign rights to something? The answer to this question I call an "account" of moral personhood. A satisfying account explains when, under which conditions, something counts as a moral person and why something that meets those conditions ought to be given rights and duties. So "moral persons are those organisms with opposable thumbs" will not do as an account of moral personhood. For even if all and only organisms with opposable thumbs are moral persons, there is nothing about having an opposable thumb that justifies moral evaluation and the granting of rights. Similarly, an account of moral personhood over time explains when, under which conditions, two stages belong to the same moral person, and also explains why, if A and B meet those conditions, it is reasonable to blame B for A's failings.[17] Much of this chapter is dedicated to providing an account of moral personhood.

The third level of explanation concerns what might be called a "regulative ideal" or "normative account" of personhood. What is it, one might ask, to live a full human life, to lead a life that fully expresses the moral potential of personhood? This is the question Aristotle addressed when he spoke of the virtues and of human beings as rational animals. It is the question that Mill addressed, as I understand him, when he claimed that happiness is the ultimate end of human conduct.[18] Although many philosophers have dismissed this question as unintelligible, I would urge that a normative picture of personhood is at the heart of normative ethics. Moreover, the second level of explanation takes full shape only when the third level is complete. For example, the difference between a full person and a partial person, on my account, is that a full person has a conceptual framework rich enough to be able to make sense of the ideas, concepts, practices, and so forth that are called for by the correct normative picture of personhood. For example, suppose forgiving one's enemies is a crucial aspect of the good life. To be able to forgive, one must have some sense of what an affront is. So in order to be a full person, one must be capable of feeling affront. Thus I cannot give a rigorous definition of full personhood without detailing the correct normative picture of personhood.

Unfortunately, a detailed normative account of personhood would take a work at least as long as this one. Thus my account of personhood will have to remain somewhat sketchy in certain important respects. I will, however, include a few remarks about how a normative picture of personhood would fill out my account of moral personhood.

My account of moral personhood is somewhat complex and raises some difficult questions. Put briefly, to be a moral person is to have a (more or less) coherent evaluative outlook on the world, which I call a "worldview," and for that worldview to be properly embodied in and expressed by one's interactions with the world about one. In turn, one has the beliefs, emotions, and such that make up one's worldview to the extent that a certain kind of story can be told about one's behavior, circumstances, and experiences. My moral personhood is the instantiation or embodiment of my worldview in my dealings with the world. In a phrase, a moral person is a worldview in operation, an agent whose thoughts and actions reflect a worldview. One is a moral agent because one's inner and outer life (occurrent feelings and behavior) can be understood as the working out of a complex moral stance (in the widest sense of "moral"). And so traits or features that constitute one's moral personhood are those features of one's states, activities, and attendant circumstances that express, embody, and/or instantiate one's worldview.

The task of the next several pages will be to make these somewhat vague remarks considerably more clear and precise.

Worldviews

Moral persons judge, evaluate, and understand the world about them. We make sense of the sights, smells, sounds, and tastes we encounter, the optical irradiation patterns (to use Quine's phrase) to which we are subject; our experiences occur within a framework of expectations, goals, values, attitudes, and so forth. This framework, this tenuously connected network in terms of which the world as we find it has meaning and significance, I will call a "worldview." A person's worldview, in other words, is his attitudes, beliefs, dispositions, emotions, expectations, goals, desires, and understandings, both general and particular, fleeting and enduring. It is his distinctive manner of regarding and interacting with the world about him. It consists, at any given moment, not only of his articulated convictions about reality, but also of specific and transitory perceptions, dispositions and desires, expectations, and assumptions. My anxious disposition, my enjoyment of a certain shade of blue, my finding humor in a sign that reads "I. Yankum, Dentist," and the value I place on honesty all help shape what Wittgenstein might have called "the world as I see it." It is this evaluative framework that I call a "worldview."

A few examples might prove helpful in clarifying what I mean by a "worldview." Let us begin with something quite ordinary. I enter my study and, sliding on a pile of papers scattered across the floor, think "this room is not very neat." Now each of the objects in my study has some definite spatial location (quantum physics aside). And the disposition of mass throughout the room does not depend on how I regard it (again ignoring quantum indeterminacies). But my study's being messy is not just a matter of physics; whether a room is neat is not determined only by the spatial configuration of the objects within it. In deciding that my study is not neat, I rely on my notion of domestic order. And the concept of "domestic order" is intentional; it depends essentially upon human purposes and dispositions.

Consider what is involved in calling a room "neat." Since we place some value on accessibility, we call a room "neat" only if we can readily locate certain sorts of objects. A room is not neat if no one can find anything in it. But not everything in a neat room is easy to locate. Some things just do not count. For example, we generally do not care which piece of blank paper we put in the typewriter, but we do care which book we read. So we must be able to locate a particular book, but not a particular piece of blank paper. This is one way, then, that neatness depends essentially upon our purposes and aims. Again, a neat room must not violate our aesthetic sense of proper display. Things intended to be seen, such as wall hangings (but not a pile of handkerchiefs in a drawer), must be presented to the viewer's eye in a pleasing way, in a manner suited to our conception of proper exhibition. For example, things we regard as "clashing" should not be too close together. Things we regard as belonging together, such as a collection of Babushka dolls, must exhibit a pattern that is both pleasing to and easily discerned by members of our society. (Other cultures, after all, may be disposed to see different sorts of patterns.)

These are but a few of the criteria for being a neat room. Yet it is already obvious that our expectations, desires, and dispositions to perceive are essential to what it means to call a room "neat." The very meaning of the term "neat" (and not just its application) invokes a rather complex network of expectations, values, and habits that human beings in our society happen to share. Thus perceiving a room to be neat reflects my worldview for it evidences the expectations, values, and the like that I employ in making sense of, giving significance to, what meets my eye.

Similarly, actions often express one's worldview. And so traits that predicate or reflect particular actions (such as having lit a pipe on October 17, 1981) partly constitute moral personhood. After all, my actions reveal a variety of underlying beliefs and values. For example, suppose I light my pipe, knowing that tobacco is carcinogenic. My act reflects my attitudes toward pleasure, self-discipline, health, and the relation between present and future benefits. My desire to smoke might also reflect a belief that smoking a pipe makes one appear distinguished and that appearing distinguished is valuable. And my wish to appear distinguished is itself indicative of what I want from others, how I expect them to interact with me, what I think is important to them, and so on. Thus even so simple an act as lighting a pipe reflects a wide range of values, attitudes, and beliefs.

Most of what we do and feel shows something about our worldview. Sometimes the connection between choices and values is very clear. A great many of our choices are what I call "proclamative choices," that is, choices that affirm a value, choices that one views as exemplary. For example, a dog might choose bones over biscuits. But he is not, one presumes, taking himself to be setting an example that others, under the appropriate circumstances, ought to follow. By contrast, a chef who omits oregano from a dish might well be saying "this is how ratatouille ought to be made." The chef's choice is proclamative, while the dog's is not. In omitting the oregano, she gives voice to her values, expresses her commitment to a standard to which she thinks the world should conform. In general, a proclamative choice is a paradigmatic instantiation of a principle, a general moral or aesthetic insight. Indeed, Jean-Paul Sartre went so far as to claim that in choosing, a person chooses for all mankind; a choice is always an assertion that this is how a human being should act.[19] Now I do not think this is true of every choice; there are nonproclamative choices. Nonetheless, which choices I regard as proclamative and which I do not is itself an important component of my moral framework. For example, suppose that I believe that listening to the music of Beethoven provides the sort of experience that is part of the good life (*eudaimonia*), while I attach no moral significance to the taste or enjoyment of strawberries. Then for me, listening to Beethoven rather than the local popular radio station is a proclamative choice, while choosing strawberry over cherry pie is not. And that fact about me is part of my worldview.[20]

Even nonproclamative choices are not, as a rule, independent of the values implicit in our worldviews. My choice of an Indian vegetable curry over sugar-coated peas may reflect my attraction to complexity and subtlety. (It is worth noting that the unity in diversity that I find attractive in Indian cuisine is also a standard of excellence, in my eyes, of works of art.) My preference for a "brooding" deep blue bedroom over a "cheerful" yellow one may reflect a host of attitudes about the proper role of bedrooms, about what qualities are most important in a life (reflectiveness as opposed to cheeriness), and so forth. I do not mean, of course, that I think about these things when selecting paint for my bedroom walls, but rather that my choice does not occur in a vacuum—it reflects, is informed by, my framework of values and attitudes. These color preferences are not neutral; they express values, what one thinks it important to seek. They reflect, to some extent, one's conception of a successful or good life.[21]

I am suggesting that, in an important sense, most of our choices are moral choices. This may seem a surprising claim. It is clear enough that when I choose death rather than dishonesty because I believe it wrong to lie, my act expresses a moral conviction. But it may be less clear that when I choose to read Plato rather than sleep on the beach, I am also expressing a moral vision. And it seems distinctly odd to say that buying a yellow rather than a blue dress is a moral choice.

My claim seems odd because we tend to think of morality as the rules of conduct that specify our obligations to others.[22] This is certainly an important part of morality; we do have moral obligations to others. But I am using the world "moral" in its widest sense. In general, a "moral" judgment, as I use the term, is a judgment about how one ought to be or live, based on values, a conception of the good, or a conception of human excellence. So a moral perspective also includes a conception of what a good human life is, of what is good and valuable in the world and what is not. It includes what Peter Glassen calls "charientic" judgments, that is, disapprobation of "the things thought to be vulgar—like chewing gum, making scenes, picking one's nose, etc."[23] It includes judgments about taste and style, since perceptions of beauty, style, and the like are subject to moral evaluation. (Note that I not saying that *being beautiful* is morally evaluable, but rather that *judging x to be beautiful* is.) Many things we might not ordinarily call "moral" nonetheless express evaluative judgments and so are "moral" in my sense. So my choosing to read Plato voices a moral judgment. It expresses, for example, a belief that understanding is of greater value than pleasant sensations. And that is a moral judgment.

Of course, human actions are generally complex, and in fact my decision to read Plato might reflect any of a variety of things. Perhaps my pursuit of philosophy is the result of a belief that understanding is one of the major things that makes human life of value, makes human life a good thing. As a result, I may well think that others who do not value or exhibit understanding are deficient human beings; they are less good according to the standard of excellence appropriate to human beings (to use Platonic language). Of course, there are other reasons why one might choose to read Plato. I might simply be a hedonist who dislikes heat and sunshine. Nonetheless, hedonism is a moral view. Again, I might read Plato because I want to impress the philosopher I am dating. But here again, my opting to impress her rather than enjoy the sunshine reflects my conception of what is important in life. How it does so depends on what it is about impressing her that appeals to me. Am I am seeking approval, a loan, thoughtful conversation, or sex? If the latter, do I regard sex as an opportunity for demonstrating my efficacy, abandoning my inhibitions, giving pleasure to another, or sharing a deeply personal experience? Whatever the psychological story to be told about my reading Plato, it attributes to me attitudes about what is of value, about what one ought to seek in life.[24]

The kind of psychological story I am telling about us is usually complex. Sometimes we do not recognize our own propensities. I may have a tendency, of which I am quite unaware, to dislike anyone named Sally. That too is a part of my worldview, even though I would sincerely (and mistakenly) state that I have no particular attitude about the name "Sally." Sometimes we do not perceive the values and attitudes implicit in our behavior. For example, suppose that I shun various people, none of whom can appreciate the difference between fine craftsmanship and shoddy work. Perhaps I value the appreciation and pursuit of excellence. I may, as a result, regard people who are indiscriminate as, to some extent, morally flawed; they lack something that is of importance in leading a good, full human life. But I may be quite unable to say why I shun those people; all I can say, perhaps, is that "they are not my sort of person." If asked "What sort is that?" I may well be unable to say. Again, many in our society value daring and excitement. They regard a conservative, deliberate accountant as a deficient human being. It is not only that they would not be happy living the life of a conservative, deliberate accountant, nor that they would not choose such people as friends, although both these things may be true. Their judgment is stronger; they regard the accountant as a flawed human being, as someone whose life does not measure up. For it lacks what they consider of importance in a human life.[25] So in laughing derisively at a cautious character on the movie screen, they do not express only a preference or personal predilection. They also express a moral judgment, a conception of the good human life, of how people ought to lead their lives. But they may quite unaware of why they look down on certain coworkers or fictional characters. So the ways in which our behavior expresses an evaluative framework may be complex, varied, and unacknowledged by us.

So far we have discussed some of the ways in which actions and judgments evidence one's worldview. Two other aspects deserve special attention. My worldview also includes or is revealed by my emotions and my "intelligence." I should like to say a few words about these two rather interesting (and potentially problematic) components of a worldview.

Most human emotions, I suggest, express one's worldview. Emotions do not come over us like measles: they are wedded to the way we view the world.[26] I am not alone in this belief. Robert Solomon, for example, claims that "we live . . . in a world that is populated with objects of value and objects of fear, gains and losses, honors and justices, intimacies and inequalities. It is our passions—and our emotions in particular—that set up this world, constitute the framework within which our knowledge of the facts has some meaning, some 'relevance' to us."[27]

I am not going to argue, as many philosophers have done, that emotions *are* judgments.[28] I need to argue only that many human emotions are inconceivable apart from the judgments they express.[29]

I will begin with a paradigmatic case of an emotion that expresses a moral viewpoint. If I become angry when I hear that a gang of terrorists has killed a group of innocent children, my anger is an expression of a moral stance. For these actions violate my moral convictions so flagrantly that anger, moral outrage, is the only appropriate response. I may even feel that anyone who does not share my ire is morally defective. After all, what could we make of someone who said he thought acts of terrorism were morally heinous and professed to value the well-being of others, but felt happy and gay-hearted when hearing that terrorists had killed seventeen innocent bystanders? We could only assume that his professed disapproval of terrorism is insincere. Conversely, were I to become convinced that acts of terrorism are not immoral, or that those who do them act wrongly but in a laudable, if mistaken, attempt to do good, I would no longer feel anger, or at least not the same sort of anger. (I would have a rather different feeling.)

Feelings of moral outrage are not the only emotions that express worldviews. If Rolfe feels pleasure when an attractive stranger smiles at him while walking down the street, it is not because he delights in the sight of small lip movements. It is because, for example, he sees in that tiny motion of the lips a sign that he is sexually attractive. And he takes pleasure in his attractiveness because he has certain views about the value of sexual attractiveness in leading a life. For example, he may equate sexual attractiveness with self-worth. Of course, he may value attractiveness only because it enables him to have sex with women. But then his pleasure at the smile depends on the value he places on sex. And this, too, depends on a variety of moral judgments.

Because the thesis that most human desires and activity are value-laden is so important to my view, it is worth pointing out that we rarely feel "pure lust" in the sense of desire for the simple physical sensations of intercourse. It is misleading to speak of adult sexual desires as "pure lust." There are many different sorts of lust, and each involves a different complex of attitudes. For example, in our society, sexual success is a potent indicator of personal worth, and so, for many, sexual desire is, at least in part, the desire to enhance one's standing as a person. Again, for many, sexual acts are pervaded by the notions of conquest and surrender, and so sexual desire is in large part tied up with attitudes about conquest and surrender. For others, the ability to excite another person sexually is a particularly significant form of efficacy, and for them sexual desire is bound up with attitudes and feelings about personal efficacy. Fortunately, there are other ways of regarding sex. The nature of sexual desire varies from individual to individual. But sexual yearnings in adults are always heavily attitudinal. Sex is such an emotionally powerful subject largely because it is so heavily laden with attitudes about fundamental values.

We do not have to do sociology to show this. Studies of human sexuality show that manual stimulation of the genitals is generally a more effective method of producing the appropriate physical sensations than is intercourse (since manual stimulation allows for greater control). Thus, were those who desire sex primarily seeking the appropriate physical stimulations, manual stimulation would be preferable to intercourse. Thus the fact that most people prefer intercourse to masturbation shows that most people's sexual desires are heavily value-laden. Indeed, even those who employ prostitutes generally prefer that the prostitutes simulate sexual interest or assume postures or guises that have heavy psychological overtones (for example, being "naughty" or "degrading"). In short, even those who frequent prostitutes are generally more interested in the psychological aspects of sex than in the purely physical ones (to the extent that this distinction between the psychological and the physical makes sense at all). In turn, these psychological attitudes are powerful only because of the patron's moral framework (for example, a sense of enhanced self-worth through power over the prostitute or a delight in the "wickedness" of having sex with a nun). Thus even the pleasure most users of prostitutes feel reflects their moral framework. (One important consequence of this point is that the true amoralist cannot even feel such "low" pleasures as those typically felt by "johns.")

So it is clear, I think, that in the absence of a variety of attitudes toward and judgments about sexuality, there would be nothing about the lip movements of the stranger to please or displease Rolfe. And so Rolfe's pleasure at the smile of a passing stranger reflects several attitudes, goals, and beliefs.

Now it is true that under emotional stress we often act in ways we ordinarily would not. The force of saying that Herbert acted in anger when striking his mother may be to suggest that Herbert would not strike someone when he was not angry. Nonetheless, Herbert is not a hapless victim of his anger. Our emotions are not elemental rivers that wash over us and bandy us about on their currents. True, Herbert may normally believe that violence is wrong. He may later regret having hit his mother and may even feel that he "was not himself." But Herbert's striking his mother does express his worldview, his evaluative framework. He was, perhaps, guilty of a kind of selfish indulgence, viewing his emotions as a kind of transcendent imperative that overrides ordinary consideration for others. If so, this is a moral failing, though not, perhaps, as evil as sheer sadism is. It is an incorrect moral judgment. Herbert may have felt frustrated and inefficacious and hit his mother to allay his feelings of inefficacy. Here Herbert's act of violence reveals a fundamental immaturity and lack of respect for others. He valued relieving his distressing state of mind more highly than he valued his mother's right not to be hit. Again, this is a moral shortcoming: he holds an incorrect moral view, incorrectly ranks competing values. Indeed, the point at which his need to relieve his anger overcomes his respect for his mother tells us something about the relative strengths of the value he places on these two. Given Herbert's attitudes and values, he could not help but strike his mother. And it is precisely his inability to refrain from hitting her that tells us something about his values and attitudes. So although, in one sense, Herbert was "out of control" and acted despite his ordinary moral beliefs, in a deeper sense his angry act was in accord with his moral viewpoint. Herbert simply has conflicting attitudes. (Or, more accurately, attitudes that sometimes demand conflicting responses.)

Put another way, both before and after his outbreak of anger there is something in his worldview, his attitudes, values, and the like, that accords with reacting to trying circumstances by striking his mother. One can, as it were, "read off" from his pre-angered worldview what he would do if certain ire-provoking conditions obtained.[30] In other words, Herbert's wrathful response is not divorceable from his state of mind when he is not angry. Anger is not like demonic possession. Despite his usual gentleness, Herbert's act of violence stems from a flaw in the mental framework he brings to the world on all occasions. The immaturity and lack of respect Herbert shows by hitting his mother to relieve his frustration does not suddenly sprout into being when an irritating event occurs. They are aspects of the way he regards the world, even when he sits, knitting contentedly, before the cheerful fireplace.

In short, Herbert's anger should not be understood as akin to an electrical surge that causes a computer to crash, but as a kind of "bug" in the programming that shows up only under unusual circumstances. After all, others can get very angry indeed without ever hitting anyone. The difference between Herbert and those others is not due to a faulty switch in Herbert's brain, but reflects a difference in their values and attitudes.[31]

Of course, "emotional disturbance" may result from a host of physiological conditions, such as a chemical imbalance in the brain. But the important question here has little to do with brain physiology. We can describe Brutus's stabbing of Caesar as "so much steel moving so many inches," or as "an act of betrayal." Similarly, we can describe what is going on in Herbert as enzymatic activity or as an expression of certain values. Granted, there may be *some* cases in which a fit of anger is a kind of "short circuit" in the brain, akin to a muscle twitch. The angry behavior's occurrence was entirely independent of any values or attitudes the agent has. If this is what happened to Herbert, then his striking his mother tells us nothing about his worldview precisely because his act was entirely independent of any attitudes or values he might have.[32] Needless to say, such occurrences are rare. In all but these rare cases, emotional outbursts reflect our underlying attitudes.

These are but a few examples, of course. But if we think about the emotions that adult human beings tend to feel, it becomes clear that virtually all of them are inextricably embedded in a background framework of values and judgments. Almost without exception, our emotions reflect, to some appreciable degree, our worldviews. As Charles Taylor points out, we are self-interpreters. Our feelings, whatever else they are, are characterizations of our situation. "Human life is never without interpreted feeling: the interpretation is constitutive of the feeling."[33]

Of course, I have shown only that such attitudes and goals are necessary conditions for many emotions, not that they are part of the emotions themselves. Further remarks on the latter claim can be found in Appendix E. However, my claim that emotions express attitudes does not require me to claim that attitudes and judgments are *part* of the emotion itself; all that is needed is that the emotion *reflects* (is intelligible in terms of) attitudes and judgments. My point is that one's feelings embody one's general way of regarding and responding to the world. Thus emotions, whatever their causes, are partially constitutive of personhood.

One final case is of special interest. Is one's intelligence part of one's moral personhood? The answer is "yes and no." For there are two things one might mean by "intelligence." One might mean by saying of someone that she is intelligent that her worldview is enlightened, insightful, and penetrating rather than dull and benighted. That is, one might be characterizing someone's actual manner of conducting her life (that is, her thoughts, dispositions, acts, attitudes, and reactions). In this sense, to be intelligent is simply to have a keen worldview, and so intelligence (in this sense) is partially constitutive of moral personhood. However, people often mean by "intelligence" a great physiological *capacity* or *potential* for learning. Now one's physiological potential is not, per se, constitutive of personhood. Rather, it is an important causal factor governing the development of one's personhood. In this sense of the word, intelligence, if it exists at all, is not partially constitutive of moral personhood.

Careful attention to this last point will help remove some potential misunderstandings. For we often employ traits that are not themselves constitutive of personhood as a way of indicating the presence of traits that are. When we say, for example, that Bertrand is the sort of person who comes from a broken home, we are attributing to Bertrand certain *other* features that are partially constitutive of moral personhood (for example, a certain sort of insecurity or distrust of others), which are often *caused by* or *associated with* coming from a broken home. Again, being short might influence my personality. Here being short, though not itself constitutive of personhood, results in my having traits that are constitutive of personhood. That is, being short is not part of and does not reflect my worldview, though it might be a *cause* of my having the worldview I in fact have. After all, I do not change my worldview by growing taller (although a change of worldview might *result* through the normal operations of causality). So being short is not part of or an expression of my worldview, even though being short is often associated with certain personality characteristics. It is the set of personality characteristics, not being short, that is partially constitutive of personhood.

So my worldview is to be found in my behavior, my emotions, my judgments, and my intelligence. This is not an exhaustive list. My worldview consists of all the attitudes, perceptions, beliefs, values, goals, propensities, and so forth, the framework of evaluations and concepts that constitute my way of understanding and responding to the world around me. And the world as I see it is a world of values;

my feelings, thoughts, and actions reflect, in a variety of ways, what I deem good and what I deem bad, what I deem important and what I deem unimportant, what I value and what I do not.

A few final words of clarification may avoid some misunderstandings. By one's "worldview" I mean much more than one's articulated beliefs, more than the sentences with which one would agree. For one can have attitudes and values of which one is unaware. Also, one's worldview is not limited to large-scale, important beliefs. My belief that you are at this very moment licking your lips is part of my worldview, even though it is a belief about a very small portion of the world. Finally, I mean more by one's "worldview" than what is sometimes called one's "character." A cowardly person who performs a single brave deed is sometimes said to have acted "out of character," that is, uncharacteristically. In this sense, the brave deed does not express her "character." But it does express her worldview. For the fact that she acted bravely shows something about the way in which she understands and responds to the world; her act reveals some of her beliefs, values, and so on.

In other words, we sometimes use the word "character" to denote someone's long-term, general characteristics. Being cowardly, for example, may be a "character trait." Now when we say of someone that she is cowardly, we are stating a rough generalization about her. She is cowardly, in other words, in virtue of the way she weighs moral against prudential considerations, in virtue of her felt desire to run on numerous occasions, and so on. (We are attributing to her a general trait that she instantiates by virtue of instantiating a host of more specific traits.) So she does not fail to be cowardly because, on rare occasions, she acts bravely. Her personhood, on the other hand, includes very specific as well as quite general features. For her personhood includes not only her being cowardly, but also the particular judgments reflected by her felt desire to run on a particular occasion and the rather different judgments reflected by her unusual brave act. Moreover, her worldview includes judgments and beliefs (such as judging a room neat) that we do not ordinarily associate with the word "character." The belief that two plus two equals four does not reveal one's "character," as we usually use the word. But it is a part of one's worldview. So one's "character," in this sense of the word, is a proper part of one's personhood.[34]

There are still some important questions about worldviews that remain unanswered. In particular, I have made heavy use of the notion of "expressing" one's worldview in an action, emotion, and so forth. This is a crucial concept. And so the next section is devoted to a rather detailed examination of what it is to express one's world-view.

Expressing Worldviews

It is clear enough that actions, emotions, and so forth often express our beliefs and attitudes, but important questions remain about the relation between actions and beliefs, emotions and attitudes. This section explores that relationship.

It is easiest to begin with four things I *do not* want to say.

Suppose that my smoking reflects the belief that pipe smokers appear distinguished. I do not want to say that my belief *caused* me to strike the match. To say that an act expresses a belief is not to make any claim at all about the causes of that act. (This point will prove central to my account of responsibility.)

Nor do I want to say that I performed a sort of moral *calculation* before I lit my pipe. Perhaps I did. More likely I did not. But no such calculations are necessary for an act to express a moral belief or value.

Moreover, although it may be tempting to think of my worldview as my *dispositions* to behave, it would be wrong. Many of our dispositions, such as our unfortunate propensity to fall off cliffs when pushed over the edge, do not reflect our worldviews, since not every behavioral disposition is linked to a belief, attitude, or value. It is not part of my worldview, for example, that my knee is disposed to jerk when struck in a certain place by a rubber mallet. The point is not that I "cannot help" having this bodily response. The point is just that the jerking of my knee when struck is unrelated to any attitude or belief I might have. You learn nothing about my values by tapping my knee. So some dispositions to behave are not part of a worldview. Many plants, after all, are disposed to follow the sun. Yet we do not regard a plant's heliotropism as a belief that sunlight is desirable. And there are reasons other than custom or convenience why we do not. There are reasons for not seeing an autumn leaf's disposition to fall to earth as a desire to get closer to the ground. Conversely, there is no straightforward way to define attitudes and values in terms of dispositions to act.[35] So it would be a mistake to summarize my notion of "worldview" as the "dispositional set" a person has.

Finally, I do not want to suggest that a belief or attitude is a *discrete mental entity* that bears some mysterious relation to our actions. In some sense, beliefs and attitudes just are their expressions in action and thought. On the other hand, we cannot make moral sense of human beings except by viewing what they do in terms of their attitudes and values.

This last point is important. If we have a misleading picture of what it is to have a belief or a value, we will misunderstand the way in which actions express attitudes. Thus, in order to explain how our behavior expresses our beliefs, values, and so forth, we must look more closely at what beliefs and values *are*.

Once again, it is easiest to begin by saying what beliefs are not. Although we sometimes talk this way, we do not "have" a belief in the same way that we have legs and arms. My beliefs are not little pieces of my mind or brain. There is no particular reason to believe that a given belief or attitude is a particular physiological state, much less that it is a particular nonmaterial, mental object floating somewhere in my mind. And my believing something is not, as a rule, a particular event.

True, we sometimes voice our beliefs to ourselves and to others. And so I might, at some point, say to myself "Aha! So smoking *is* dangerous." We may call such episodes, when we voice a conviction to ourselves, "occurrent thoughts." Granted, we frequently have occurrent thoughts. But most of our beliefs are not and have never been occurrent thoughts. I have believed for many years that radishes are edible without saying, to myself or to others, any such words. And I may never have *heard* words to that effect either; the mere presence of radishes on my plate coupled with the sight of others eating them might have been enough to produce my belief that radishes are edible. Moreover, I may be unable to articulate some of my beliefs and attitudes. I may be surprised to discover that I have had them for years. And I may even be wrong about my beliefs. For example, I think I believe that Julia is trustworthy. Yet I scrupulously avoid placing her in a position of trust. I do not tell her things that I do not want bruited about. When Julia is due to visit, I "tidy up," removing small valuable objects from view. When my going to the bathroom would leave Julia alone in a room full of valuables, I remain in the room until my discomfort becomes acute. And I have a tendency to look around the room carefully after she leaves. Someone familiar with my actions could then convince me that, in fact, I did not trust her.

In short, although occurrent thoughts are evidence that I have a certain attitude or belief, they are not conclusive evidence. And so, although having an occurrent thought may indicate that one has the relevant belief, beliefs are not themselves mental episodes or occurrences of thought.

Nor are my beliefs simply those sentences to which I am disposed to assent. For example, suppose that I believe, mistakenly, that George Washington was born in 1802. However, I remember seeing, in an Italian edition of the *Encyclopedia Britannica,* the words "Giorgio Washington era nato in 1732." I do not speak or read Italian and do not understand the sentence. However, the words stick in my mind. Since I have great faith in the *Encyclopedia Britannica,* I would assent to the sentence "Giorgio Washington era nato in 1732," though I do not believe what the sentence says, namely that Washington was born in 1732. And so my beliefs and the sentences to which I am disposed to assent may not coincide.

Finally, my beliefs need not be causes of my acts. To say that my smoking reflects a belief is not to make a straightforward, efficiently causal claim about the origin of my act. There need be no causal gear connecting my belief with the movement of my arm as I strike the match. As we will see, there are many, quite different ways in which my striking the match could reflect the belief that smokers appear distinguished.[36] Some explanation seems desirable, then, of why my smoking a pipe does and a plant's seeking the sun does not express a belief. Unfortunately, space permits but a few remarks.

THE NATURE OF BELIEFS. I wish to suggest that a belief is a feature of the whole of one's acts, circumstances, and occurrent thoughts and feels. My having a belief means that a certain kind of story can be told about (the whole of) my behavior, inner experiences, and circumstances. Let me explain.

Most of the time, we make sense of people's acts by talking about their beliefs, attitudes, emotions, and so forth. Suppose that my niece walks in while I am watching *La Boheme* on television and asks me "What's going on?" I could answer her, quite accurately, by saying "now he moves his foot, now he opens his mouth, and now he moves his lips." My answer, however, would not make the proceedings on stage any more intelligible to her. She wants me to tell her a story about Rodolfo's acts in terms of goals, beliefs, desires, values, attitudes, and so on. That kind of story would explain, make sense of, render intelligible, the movements of the actor on stage. And most of the time we can do that. Usually, there is what Daniel Dennett calls an "intentional explanation" of our actions.[37] That is, it is possible to "explain" my actions by attributing to me certain values, goals, beliefs, and the like. One can show the purpose of, reason for, or justification of my acts, make predictions about my future acts, and so forth, by attributing to me a certain worldview.

To illustrate this point, it is useful to look at something a bit simpler than human beings. Consider a chess-playing computer. As Dennett points out, it is hard to beat a good chess-playing computer by examining its circuitry or even its program. You will probably fare better by pretending the computer is a "real" player, with beliefs, goals, and strategies. One can oppose a good chess-playing computer more successfully by treating its moves as indicative of beliefs and strategies than one can by trying to predict its behavior on the basis of principles of electronics or by studying its program. It pays, in other words, to take what Dennett calls the intentional stance, to treat the computer's responses as reflecting, as explicable in terms of, beliefs.

For example, I might take the computer's move to indicate a belief that I am about to mount a queen-side attack. This tells me something about how the computer is likely to respond; I can make predictions about the computer's future moves. Moreover, it allows me to "make sense of" the computer's move; I can understand the computer's move not just as the inevitable result of certain circuits' being closed, but as the realization of a certain strategy and as a step toward certain goals. As a result, I might decide to "fool" the computer by launching a king-side attack. Here I am not assuming any particular picture of how the computer works. And I may have only some very rough ideas about how the computer's "belief" will affect its play. (The computer, after all, may not be a perfect player, and its moves might not be the best way to act on its belief. In any case, there may be several "reasonable" ways to respond to a threatened queen-side attack.) Explaining the computer's move as due to a belief that its queen side is threatened is not like explaining the move as a result of a certain switch's being closed.

Note that there is no address in memory that holds the computer's "belief" that rooks are more valuable than pawns; that belief is implicit in the variety of decisions the computer makes, in the various kinds of calculations it makes, and so forth. The belief that checkmating is winning is manifested not only in the "check-for-checkmate" routine, but in *every* decision the computer makes. They are all made, in some sense, with a view to avoid being checkmated or to checkmate the opponent.

That belief, in other words, is a feature of the whole of the computer's operations. Of course, some beliefs may be localized in the sense that the "automotive principle" of the car resides in the engine. One may say so if speaking loosely. But cars are not automotive without wheels, axles, and so on. Strictly speaking, being automotive is a feature of the whole car's operations.[38] Similarly, speaking loosely, a given computer belief may be localized in a particular piece of the program. But, strictly speaking, the computer's belief is not a particular piece of the computer and not an efficient cause of its behavior. The belief that checkmate is winning does not *make* anything happen; rather, it is a *feature* of what *does* happen.[39]

Now I do not want to say that the computer actually has beliefs, but just that the computer's "pseudo" beliefs help shed some light on what beliefs are. We can attribute a (pseudo) belief to the computer without knowing anything about how the computer operates, without knowing what makes the computer act as it does. When I say that the computer believes I am about to launch a queen-side attack, I am trying to make sense of the computer's moves, to tell a certain kind of story about what I see on the screen. Thus "the computer believes p" is an intentional assertion; it says that the computer's acts can be understood in a certain way. The same point applies to persons. Saying that Jones has a certain belief is saying that one can explain Jones's acts and so forth in a certain way.

CONDITIONS FOR BELIEF. Let us be a bit more precise. Person A has the belief that p if and only if

1. there is a coherent story to be told about A, a story that explains, in the appropriate sense, most (or at least a good part) of A's bodily movements, verbal behavior, and inner mental life (occurrent beliefs, feels, sensations, and the like),
2. that story attributes to A the belief that p,
3. that story, as a whole, is not inconsistent with (at least most of) A's bodily movements, verbal behavior, and inner mental life, nor with A's circumstances, including the "way of life" of his society, and
4. that story is consistent with a general pattern of storytelling that applies to others as well as it applies to A.

This somewhat dense sentence requires some explication.

Intentional explanation. The first thing to note is that Jones's having a belief does not depend upon what anyone knows about Jones. The requirement is that there *be* a story of the right sort, not that anyone in fact knows or even could know it. So Jones's having a belief does not depend on anyone's knowing that Jones has that belief.

Second, something must be said about what it means to "explain" Jones's behavior, circumstances, and occurrent feels. Again, a few general comments must suffice.

A successful explanation has several features. It has some predictive value. This does not mean that it tells us exactly what Jones will do. It is enough if the explanation provides a useful guide to Jones's future conduct. We have *some* sense of what to expect from someone who is angry with us, even if we cannot predict exactly what she will do. It is this sense that allows us to understand others to the extent that we do, have some sense of what to expect from them, and have some idea of how to respond to and interact with them. After all, we generally have no access to the physiology or brain states of others; biochemistry is useless to us in dealing with landlords, lovers, and lounge lizards. Yet we have at least a rough idea of how to elicit praise, gratitude, anger, clenched fists, or physical assault from others.

In addition, a good explanation makes a phenomenon intelligible, allows us to say "now I understand." That is, it is enlightening in some important way. An explanation clarifies the nature and/or structure of a phenomenon, points out which of its features are significant, allows us to relate it in important ways to other phenomena, and so forth. And an explanation often provides the reasons for something, gives a basis for evaluating it. In other words, the theory must both conform to and illuminate, make understandable, what human beings actually do. The more comprehensible human behavior seems when viewed in terms of the theory, the more successful the theory is (other things being equal). So the criterion of success for an intentional psychological theory is, in some sense, "subjective," in much the same way that exegesis of a literary text is subjective. There is evidence that supports or undermines a theory, but the ultimate test of a theory is its explanatory power. And explanatory power should be understood not only in terms of the predictions the theory makes, but also in terms of how insightful it is, of how much it helps us understand the nature of what it explains.[40] (Similarly, it is a criticism of an exegesis of a literary text that it provides a shallow or trivial or uninteresting reading of the text.)[41]

Finally, a successful explanation satisfies the canons of induction. For example, the explanation should not, as a rule, employ arcane mechanisms or mysterious entities that rival explanations, equally successful in other ways, do not require. Hence "the devil made him do it" is usually not a satisfying explanation. Again, the "principle of charity" must be observed; an explanation that makes Jones's behavior rational or standard is preferable, other things being equal, to one that makes Jones's behavior irrational, bizarre, due to a physiological malfunction (and so beyond the pale of intentional explanation), and so on.

The third point to be noted is that the story we tell about Jones must cover the whole of Jones's behavior and inner occurrences. Beliefs do not come singly; to have a belief is at the same time to have a network of beliefs, attitudes, values, feelings, and so forth. You cannot have just one belief.[42] For example, in order to have a bona fide belief that the glass is full of water, one must also have beliefs about what a glass is, what water is, and so forth. And one must have some way of relating beliefs to one another. For example, the glass's being full of water entails that it is not empty and not full of helium gas. Now people are sometimes illogical and can have contradictory beliefs. But I am not sure what it means to say that Jones believes the glass is full of water, yet that he is just as likely as not to believe that the glass is empty, that there is no glass, and that the glass is full of helium. You cannot have beliefs but make no connections at all among them. You might have a variety of occurrent thoughts. But they would not be beliefs. For what makes an occurrent thought a belief, as opposed to a passing fancy or fantasy, is not an accompanying sensation of truth. How often, after all, do you experience a *feeling* of conviction? No, what makes an occurrent thought a belief is the way it fits with our responses to the world, our acts, thoughts, and feels. (That is why we can be mistaken about our beliefs.) So to have a belief, one must also have canons, implicit or explicit, rough or precise, for relating beliefs to one another, canons for assessing beliefs, and so on. One must also have a notion of truth, of the difference between entertaining a notion and thinking it true.

So what we must attribute to Jones is not, really, a single belief, but a belief system, a network of beliefs. Moreover, we cannot justifiably attribute to Jones the belief that Sally is trustworthy if most of Jones's actions indicate distrust of Sally. So it is reasonable to say that Jones believes Sally is trustworthy only if there is a comprehensive story that covers most of Jones's behavior.

Of course, few people are perfectly rational. Most people have at least some inconsistent beliefs. And so some of Jones's acts might not suit the belief that Sally is trustworthy. But the principle of charity requires that we view others, if possible, as generally rational. An explanation should attribute conflicting beliefs to someone, for example, only if no story otherwise as good attributes consistent beliefs to him. And, ideally, acts that ill-suit the beliefs we attribute to Jones should be explicable in terms of other aspects of the story we tell about him. Thus we might explain Jones's imposing a curfew on Sally, despite his belief that Sally is trustworthy, as indicating anger at Sally or a need to assert his authority.

In practice, of course, our information is limited. We often attribute beliefs to people we know little about. Indeed, if Smith says, "I think there is life on Mars," I might reasonably say that Smith believes there is life on Mars on the basis of just a single action of his. But when I do so, I am making a fair number of assumptions about what he will do in other circumstances, what he cares about, what else he believes, and so forth. And for my attribution to be *correct*, there must be some psychological story to be told about most of Smith's actions and inner occurrences, a story that includes his believing there is life on Mars. The story need not explain everything about him, but it must at least be consistent with (almost) everything about him. (Again, I do not mean that his beliefs must be consistent; a person may well have conflicting beliefs. But in that case the story to be told will attribute conflicting beliefs. And it must "make sense of," explain, the conflict.)

The fourth point to note is that the story about Jones must fit into a general theory of human psychology. That is, although individuals are different, there are important patterns to be discerned in human activity. There may be no psychological "laws," in the sense of simple but powerful regularities that have no exceptions. But there are at least general patterns of explanation. An explanation of Jones's behavior that makes Jones radically unlike everyone else is, at best, suspect.

Occurrent feels, free will, and machines. The last requirement for the claim that Jones believes p is that the story to be told about Jones must be consistent not only with his behavior, but with his occurrent feels and thoughts. This is not to say that any special thoughts must pass through Jones's mind. But saying that Jones has the belief that stoves are hot does mean that he not only avoids putting his hand on the stove, but also has internal experiences appropriate to having that belief. He may feel queasy, for example, when he imagines his hand on the stove. There may be no specific occurrent feel or thought that justifies us in saying Jones believes that stoves are hot. But can we say that Jones believes that stoves are hot, that hot things burn, and that burns are painful if he feels relaxed when picturing his hand on the stove, mentally pictures ice cubes when he hears the word "stove," and so on? The point is that in order to ascribe correctly any beliefs to Jones, Jones must have *some* appropriate occurrent thoughts or feels. And those thoughts or feels must be consistent with the belief ascribed to Jones.

This is why (and here I differ from Dennett) current computers do not really have beliefs and why heliotropic plants do not really believe that the sun is to the left. That is, plants and computers do not have beliefs in the sense that matters for moral personhood. In order to have a bona fide belief, one must care about truth. Unless truth is valued, there would be no point to judging and deciding. But computers and plants do not *care* about truth. True, we could, if we so chose, call what the computer does "deciding" and "judging." But computer "decisions" and "judgments" would not play the role that human decisions and judgments play.

This is an important point. Unfortunately, given the history of the mind-body dispute, it is hard to express my claim. For a rather bootless pattern characterizes the recent history of the mind-body debate. Dualists use a given term to point to what is lacking in the materialist picture, and materialists respond by changing the meaning of that term. For example, to answer the charge that physicalism cannot account for sensations, the "ouch quality" of pain, if you will, J.J.C. Smart defined the sensation of red as the brain process occurring in a normal perceiver standing in front of, for example, a fire engine. ("Normal" is defined behaviorally; a normal perceiver puts Winesap apples in one pile and Granny Smith apples in another.) But of course dualists were not saying that materialists cannot explain how we sort apples. They were trying to point to something of which anyone who opens his or her eyes is immediately aware. The same game has been played with "experience" and "consciousness." The current dualist term is "missing qualia." No doubt materialists will soon define away the problem of "qualia."[43] But whatever term one uses, human beings, unlike chess-playing computers, are not "dark inside."

Now in some sense, of course, a chess-playing computer "cares" about whether Q-7 is empty, just as a thermostat cares about maintaining the temperature. That is, it behaves in the appropriate way. But it does not have the occurrent feelings and thoughts that make its "concern" morally or explanatorily important. I do not mean that caring *is* a thought or sensation. But at least some occurrent feels of tension, anxiety, elation, and so forth, on at least some relevant occasions, are, in certain circumstances, prerequisites for caring. One does not care, in the relevant sense, for one's life if, for example, the visual experience of a dangerous sea does not have a dark and menacing quality, and one feels no relief when one's life is saved nor any fear when it is threatened, and there is no extra vividness to one's occurrent sensations on joyful occasions, and one never experiences the ache of longing for things one will never have, and so forth. There are many different ways in which caring for something might manifest itself in one's inner life. But if one never has *any* of these feelings, or any others like them, it is not clear what it could mean to care about one's life.[44]

True, we could define a special sense of "caring," caring$_1$, in a way that allows computers or plants to care$_1$. (For example, to care$_1$ for x is for x to be assigned a high number in a program that calculates moves in a game according to a weighted set of goals.) But caring$_1$ is not relevant to moral personhood. A computer that cared$_1$ about winning chess would direct its activity to winning. But it would have no investment in whether it succeeded or not. It would lack "commitment" in the crucial sense that it would experience no distress when its activities failed to bring about the goal to which they were directed. There is, in the relevant sense, no "way the world is" for the computer; the computer lacks the full-blooded concepts that make "good" or "bad" applicable concepts to what its sensors indicate is going on, since it lacks the inner life of feels and sensory experience that turn behavioral preferences into values.

It is for this reason that a computer cannot make a mistake. Obviously, the computer can malfunction, so that what it prints out is not what we want it to print. Suppose, for example, I am running a simple adding program. I type in "2 + 2," and the computer prints "3." Since I want the computer to add correctly, I might call this "a mistake." And certainly the computer is operating nonstandardly. But a nonstandard operation is a "mistake" only if one is engaged in an activity with a point, and an activity has a point only if one has goals and values one cares about. If most people sneeze once and I sneeze twice, I have not made a mistake, though my sneeze is nonstandard. Similarly, the computer's printing a "3" on the screen is not a mistake, since the computer does not care about arithmetic. Imagine, for instance, that the patterns the ocean waves carve in the sand look like "2 + 2 = 3." Has the ocean made a mistake in arithmetic? Of course not. We are not even tempted to say this, because we do not usually use the ocean as a tool for arriving at arithmetic truths. Since we do use computers to add, we might well say "the computer made an adding error." Yet the computer is no more committed to or aware of arithmetical truth than is the ocean. It feels no horror or frustration at the "3" on the screen. It feels no resolve to do better. The "3" on the screen does not look out of place or mocking. Since the computer has no real point of view, "3" is "as good" an answer to the computer as "4." True, the computer might have a "check for mistakes" routine. But, ultimately, what makes this routine a "check for *mistakes*" routine, rather than simply another configuration of high and low voltages, is that the user or the programmer cares about whether the number the computer prints is truly the sum of two and two. So even if we define a special sense of "belief" in which computers can have beliefs, computer "beliefs," in this special sense, would not matter in the way that "real" beliefs do.

Pain is an even clearer example, so it deserves a brief look. Suppose we define "pain" in a way that does not require ever having any occurrent feels, so that computers can "feel pain." My point is that computer "pain" would not play the role that human pain plays. Without occurrent thoughts and feels, there would be no *reason* to avoid pain (even if there would be *causes* of avoidance behavior).

Imagine, for example, a computer with an enormous memory. Every possible input is cataloged as "painful" or "okay." When a "painful" input is encountered, the machine chooses its responses from an immensely long list. Such a machine may well exhibit pain-avoidance behavior. If the list is complete enough, the machine may even pass the "Turing test" (that is, its responses are indistinguishable from those of a human being). But there would be no *point* to avoiding pain. And there would be no moral onus to generating a "painful" input.

The problem here is not that in my example the computer's response is not "calculated"; the problem is not that the program is boring. The problem is rather that what makes causing pain *wrong* is missing. Even though the machine could produce the sounds "please do not do that, it hurts," could answer the question "why do you not like that?" and could act appropriately (say by administering shocks to those who cause a "painful" input), the machine does not "care" in any sense that justifies us in feeling concern for it. We may wish to avoid the shocks the computer produces, but it is absurd to feel sympathy for the machine or to feel guilty about causing it to print out "that hurt." The point here is that no one worries about stopping a game of computer chess because the computer might feel frustrated. And we should not start worrying even if the computer were programmed to let loose a shockingly verisimilitudinous howl when a finger lights on the reset button.

Note that it will not help to have the computer simulate a broader range of behavior. Suppose that if I turn off the computer in the middle of the game, the computer will "refuse" to play next time I turn it on. Then I do have to worry about "offending" the computer. But my worry is purely instrumental. All I care about is getting the desired output. A friend who told me "do not turn off the computer during a game" would be giving me operating instructions, not moral guidance. It would be foolish to worry about whether the computer "really" likes me, as I might worry about whether a purported friend really likes me, to feel embarrassment about how the computer regards me; or to feel moral concern that, even if no human beings are adversely affected, my computer's feelings might be hurt. My relationship to the computer remains instrumental, like my relationship to my car and unlike (it is hoped) my relationship to my friends. In short, no matter how well the computer simulates human behavior, it is not a person. It does not have beliefs and emotions in the sense that matters to moral personhood. Again, I do not mean that machines could never have real beliefs and emotions. But they would not come to have real beliefs simply because they simulated more behavior, or simulated it more accurately. They would need to have occurrent thoughts and feels.

Thus one cannot, *pace* Dennett, give an intentional explanation of the thermostat's behavior, except as a convenient expository or predictive device. Speaking of the desires and beliefs of thermostats commits one to a view of thermostats that is not, in general, supportable by thermostat behavior. The ascription of a belief requires not only the appropriate behavior, but the appropriate mental experiences ("raw feels" or whatever).[45] Indeed, it is useful to think of the chess-playing computer as having beliefs, only because the range of our interactions with the computer during the game is so limited.

It is crucial to see that it does not matter that the machine's responses are caused. After all, if the computer had truly distressful pain feels, even if causally induced, it would be wrong to cause the computer unnecessary pain. The computer fails to feel pain or have beliefs because it lacks occurrent experiences, thoughts, and feels, not because it lacks free will.

Still, the reader might object that my account of a worldview implicitly depends on free will. Why, one may ask, do we not attribute to people pushed off a cliff the desire to hit the ground below? Is it not precisely because they cannot *help* but fall? And if this is the reason, then Mike's belief that there is life on Mars depends on his ability to believe otherwise.

There is something right about this argument, and something wrong. It is true that the spectacle of poor Adalbert plummeting earthward after being pushed off a cliff by the jealous Werther does not lead us to say that Adalbert desired to hit the ground. The reason that we do not attribute this strange desire to Adalbert is that we have a better explanation. We can explain Adalbert's fall by gravitational attraction without attributing any desire at all to him. The point is not that Adalbert could not help but fall, but that a story that attributes to Adalbert the desire to hit the ground does not satisfy the canons of induction. It explains nothing that the law of gravity, which we accept in any case, does not adequately explain. Conversely, there are strong reasons for *not* attributing to him the desire to hit the ground. Presumably, a story that attributes to him the desire to hit the ground will poorly suit his occurrent feel of anxiety, his screaming and clawing at the cliff wall, and so on. And since most of us desire to avoid falling off cliffs, there is a presumption against his having that queer desire. So attributing to Adalbert the desire to hit the ground violates the canons of explanation: it is simply a poor explanation.

What is right about the argument, then, is that a purely causal explanation of someone's behavior sometimes (but not always) makes attributing a belief or desire or value superfluous. It does not follow, however, that beliefs must be freely chosen. The causal story we tell about Adalbert might make his desiring to hit the ground not superfluous but plausible. It is easiest to see this point with a different example.

Suppose we say that Quincy drank because his body lacked water and that lack activated a complex biofeedback mechanism that resulted in his going into the kitchen, pouring water into a glass, and drinking. This causal story makes it plausible that Quincy desired to drink and that he believed that drinking would satisfy his desire. In this case it is hard to give a satisfying account of his complex acts and his occurrent feels without attributing those beliefs and desires to him. What makes it plausible to attribute beliefs and desires to Quincy is that, unlike the case of Adalbert's falling from a cliff, a story attributing a desire to Quincy sheds additional light on his behavior and occurrent feels. We gain additional understanding if we view Quincy as having a desire. And that additional understanding need not be causal. Whatever the causes of his drinking, his desire to drink makes his drinking *reasonable.*

Thus an IBM PC is not a person, not because its behavior is caused (so, *ex hypothesi*, is Quincy's), but because when the computer prints, for example, "murder is okay," in an important sense the computer "does not *mean* it." The computer is not, of course, being insincere. Rather, the computer lacks the character of inner life that constitutes commitment and so lacks bona fide values and beliefs. It has no worldview. A computer programmed to print out moral judgments would not, on that account, possess a worldview, any more than a copy of *Principia Ethica* has a worldview. Both, of course, *represent* worldviews. But neither (itself) *possesses* a worldview. The computer no more believes that murder is wrong than a vinyl phonograph disc and a strip of magnetic tape believe the information they carry.

Of course, there may, someday, be artificial machines that do have beliefs. There is nothing magic about carbon that silicon lacks. But such machines would not have beliefs simply because they have a more-complicated program. They must also have occurrent thoughts and feels.[46] The acts and feels of such a computer would be caused, but its pain would be no less real, its distress at witnessing a murder no less powerful. And it would be as wrong to cause such a computer pain as it would be to beat up a Boy Scout.

To summarize, then, current computers and plants cannot have true beliefs, because they do not care about truth. And they cannot care about truth, because they have no occurrent thoughts or feels.

CONCLUSIONS. This discussion of worldviews suggests three important points. First, in an important sense, worldviews *are* their expressions; I do not have beliefs *apart from* the emotions, actions, occurrent thoughts, conversations, and so forth that reflect them. Thus, when I speak of properties that "reflect" a worldview, I mean, strictly speaking, properties that express, partially constitute, and/or embody worldviews.

Second, it is clear that, strictly speaking, it is generally incorrect to speak of beliefs as efficient *causes* of actions. My beliefs are not independent of and prior to my actions; my actions, in part, *constitute* my beliefs.[47] Of course, what I did in the past may justify ascribing a particular belief to me. And so in some sense my belief could precede an act that expresses it. Still, a belief is not a brain state or a mental item that could cause a muscle contraction. It is rather a feature of the whole of my brain states, inner occurrences, and actions. Saying that a belief (efficiently) caused an action is a bit like saying the layout of my library (efficiently) caused my new book to be where it is. Strictly speaking, this is nonsense. Loosely speaking, it asserts that, for example, my books were ordered alphabetically by author, and I put the new book where it belongs. So although it is often useful to speak of a belief as the cause of an action, one must remember that one is speaking loosely.

Third, the efficient cause of my act is not what is important in morally evaluating me. Rather, what counts are the attitudes, beliefs, and judgments that can be reasonably ascribed to me on the basis of those acts. After all, morality is concerned not with neural firings as such, but with moral judgments, values, and attitudes. And if those judgments, values, and attitudes are not causes of actions, then it is not causes of actions, it would seem, that morality should judge. If I am right, then attitudes, beliefs, values, and judgments are not causes of actions. They are not discrete entities, but rather ways of characterizing the behavior and occurrent feels and thoughts of certain organisms. So morality should judge not the causes of action, but the worldview of the agent.

But suppose I am wrong about the nature of beliefs and values. It remains true that if I instantiate a trait that is conversant with and intelligible in terms of my attitudes, values, and judgments, that fact does demonstrate something about my moral worth, about whether I am a morally good or ill human being. After all, the efficient causes of our deeds are often opaque to us. Suppose that I believe that adultery is wrong and so do not honor the sexual request of Leila, my wife's best friend. Let us further suppose that although Leila is attractive to me, I tell myself that it would not be right and have strong feelings about the moral impropriety of accommodating her desire. Given this background, my choice is rationally explicable in terms of my belief about adultery. But even if beliefs could be causes, could anyone know that it was in fact my belief about adultery that *caused* me to deny her? After all, my saying, "sorry old bean, I'm married, don't you know" is a physical act, a bodily movement. The mere conjunction of an occurrent conviction and a bodily movement does not show that the bodily movement was caused (even in the loose sense) by the physical analogue of the conviction. Perhaps some other physiological occurrence intervened between my decision and my vocal behavior so that had I not, fortunately, had spinach for lunch, I would have found myself, much to my chagrin, making the sounds "my place or yours?" The point is that although my decision is *intelligible* in terms of my conviction, I cannot be certain that the conviction, however, genuine, was the *cause* of my decision.

None of these worries about the causes of my speech are particularly relevant to a moral assessment of me. I had the conviction, I thought about the decision in terms of the conviction, and I acted in accordance with it. I had, in other words, all the right sorts of mental and behavioral properties in order for my action to be fully comprehensible in terms of my conviction. What more is required in order for my action to show me to be, to that extent, not morally unworthy? Need we have recourse to the actual, complex causal mechanisms that brought about my refusal in order to make a moral judgment? Thus there are several reasons for preferring to speak of "reflecting" one's worldview instead of, as most philosophers have done, seeking the *causes* of one's acts and choices.

In sum, then, moral persons are organisms about whom a certain kind of story can be told. As a rule, their bodily movements and inner occurrences can be explained (in the sense given above) as manifestations and embodiments of a worldview. Their actions and their inner lives are comprehensible when viewed as expressions of beliefs, attitudes, goals, values, desires, understandings, judgments, and perceptions to which they are committed, in the sense that they (fullbloodedly) care about achieving those goals, care about the extent to which the world about them conforms to those values, and so on.

Moral Persons over Time

So far we have been concerned with what makes something a moral person. Moral persons, we have said, are organisms about which we can tell a certain sort of story.[48] Their behavior, circumstances, and occurrent feels and thoughts can be (justifiably) explained, understood, as expressing beliefs, attitudes, values, goals, and so forth. That is, we can tell about moral persons a story that attributes to them a fully developed set of beliefs, values, and so on. The story is enlightening; suits much of their behavior, circumstances, and occurrent thoughts and feels; and is inconsistent with little of it. And the story does not violate the canons of induction (it explains as many phenomena in as much depth as possible, as simply as possible, as charitably as possible, and so forth). This account tells us which things are stages of moral persons. But it does not tell us when two stages are stages of the *same* moral person.

In a sense, I am not going to answer this question. For I think we have only a rough sense of when two stages are the same moral person. Our rough sense is serviceable enough for most cases. But sometimes we are genuinely perplexed. Consider, for example, a vicious juvenile delinquent who later becomes a surgeon. To what extent should we hold the fifty-year-old surgeon morally accountable for the cruelties of the delinquent she was some thirty-five years ago? It is not clear how we should go about deciding such a case. And I do not have an easy answer. Instead, I am going to talk about what an answer would look like.

The first point to note is that, in an important sense, sameness over time raises no new problems. We identify stages over time in the same way we attribute beliefs and emotions. After all, beliefs, emotions, and so forth are not momentary items one can have, like twinges, since having a belief depends on the viability of a story that covers much of one's life. The reason I have the belief that two plus two equals four, even while playing tennis, is that the way I acted and felt in the past, and will act and feel in the future, justifies regarding me as knowing arithmetic. So you cannot attribute a belief to me unless you already identify my present stage with certain past stages.[49] In other words, moral persons are collections of temporal stages about which a certain kind of psychological story can justifiably be told. The very same things that justify a story saying that, at this moment, I believe that tigers have spots (for example, simplicity and charity) also make it justifiable to treat me now as the same moral agent as some twenty-year-old college student.

Still, sameness over time does raise an interesting problem. Our stories about persons must allow for psychological change. I no longer believe many of the things I believed as a college student. The fact that in 1970 I majored in philosophy, despite being told that jobs in philosophy were scarce, may be good evidence that I did not value job security then. It does not necessarily show that I do not value job security now. Values and beliefs change. Yet, despite these differences, we say that the fearless college student and the worried professor are the same person. Which changes result in new moral persons, and which do not?

It is easy enough to say, in very general terms, when A and B are stages of the same moral agent. Two conditions must be met. First, one must be able to tell a plausible psychological story that makes B's worldview a development of A's. Second, there must be a "personality core" common to all the stages in a temporal series of stages S.[50] A bit more strictly, my claim is that A and B are stages of the same moral person if and only if A and B belong to a temporal series of stages S such that S can justifiably be viewed as a causally continuous, evolving worldview in operation, and such that every stage in the series evidences the "personality core." Thus we identify the professor and the student because we can tell a convincing story about the evolution of his beliefs and values, and we recognize in the professor many of the traits of the student.

Note that *both* conditions must be met for the student and the professor to be the same moral person; one is not enough. Suppose, for example, that we can tell a convincing evolutionary story about the beliefs, values, and goals of the college student and of the worried professor. But the result of this evolutionary process is that the beliefs, values, goals, attitudes, and judgments of the professor are as different from those of the college student as it is possible for human worldviews to be. In that case, we would still identify, psychologically, the student and the professor. But it would not be reasonable to hold the professor morally accountable for the invidious beliefs (and acts reflecting those beliefs) of the college student. We are supposing, after all, that all the evil beliefs, values, judgments, propensities, and such that infected the college student have been purged. So no vestige of the evil reflected by the college student's misdeeds remains in the sedate professor. On what basis, then, can we deem the college professor, who is reasonable, altruistic, kind, wise, and generous, to be morally unworthy? Thus moral agency is not the same as what we might call "psychological personhood." Being the same "psychological person" requires only a convincing evolutionary story. But sameness of moral agency requires certain sorts of similarities as well. In sum, sameness of moral person over time requires two things. It requires a convincing evolutionary story, and it requires certain sorts of similarities, enduring features.

It is important to understand that a personality core is not like an apple core. It is not a part that remains unchanged. It is more like what Wittgenstein called a family resemblance. Any stages of mine will have "enough" of a group of characteristics. How much is "enough" varies with circumstances. Moreover, some characteristics count more than others. And the degree to which a stage has a core characteristic must be balanced against the number of core characteristics it evidences. Characteristics may be clustered, in the sense that combinations of characteristics may count more than the characteristics considered separately. Moreover, the characteristics may be quite general or quite specific. The characteristics may be disjunctive: having x or y, where there is a psychological "kinship" between x and y, may be a core characteristic. So the notion of a personality core is quite complex and somewhat elastic. What counts is that we can "recognize" the moral personality of one stage in the others.

Intuitively, then, A and B are the same moral person if we can "recognize" B's worldview in A's. Although this is undoubtedly somewhat vague, to make it rigorous and explicit is to provide an adequate psychology for human beings. Unfortunately, we are very far away from being able to do that. It is precisely because we lack such a psychological account that we cannot give rigorous conditions for sameness and perhaps cannot decide some of the difficult cases. Fortunately, as noted above, we all have a robust, if unsystematic (and even, in some respects, contradictory), view of human psychology. It is this intuitive sense of intentional psychology that grounds our everyday judgments of sameness of moral persons over time.

Lacking both a powerful psychological account that can be used to decide when stages are stages of the same psychological person and a moral psychology that determines what sorts of similarity moral accountability requires, we muddle on as best we can with our everyday notions.

I will conclude with a few hints about the missing psychological theory.[51] In many cases of personality change, the later trait, though different from the earlier one, is a natural outgrowth of it. I will mention two ways in which this can occur. First, an attitude or disposition can be a natural reaction to the problems caused by an earlier one. Consider someone who naively believes that justice prevails in the operations of the world around her and who has a strong sense of justice and an emotional commitment to seeing that justice is done. When she discovers how little justice has to do with many human activities and institutions, she may become depressed and then cynical and bitter. Here the later trait is a response to the earlier trait. An adequate intentional account of human psychology will contain a mechanism or structure that allows us to see one attitude or disposition as an outgrowth or development of the other. Again, I am not asserting that the first attitude is the *cause* of the second. It is possible, for example, that both attitudes are causally linked to biochemical states of affairs. The point is rather that the frustration of the first belief makes having the second attitude intelligible.

Second, someone who has the generic property of being attracted to fanatical panaceas and of ignoring evidence of their inadequacy may leave one cult and join another. The beliefs are different, but they are manifestations of the same more general tendency. So a specific attitude or disposition may be replaced by a new attitude or disposition that, although different, is an example of the same more general attitude or disposition. Some other examples may be useful. Consider the kind of insecure, intellectually arrogant person who needs to feel intellectually contemptuous of others but is sufficiently uncertain of his own brilliance that he needs constant reaffirmation of his own superiority. He is likely to be averse to subtle or complex evaluations that do not distinguish between the superior few and the inferior many. He is also likely to be averse to intellectually honest criteria of evaluation, since honest criteria always allow the possibility that he may fail to measure up. Such a person may have been a contemptuous and simple-minded behaviorist in the 1950s, treating other approaches with dismissive posturing, confidently and narrow-mindedly running rat experiments without examining the conceptual problems and limitations of his approach. Anyone who presented him with an argument against behaviorism was written off, with a sweeping gesture, as an old-fashioned obscurist. In the 1980s, he may have become a smug and condescending deconstructivist, arrogantly dismissing other views as blind to the obvious truth of relativism, again without examining the possible problems or shortcomings of his view. When equivocations or fallacies in his thinking are pointed out, he dismisses his interlocutor as hopelessly ignorant of the fact that reason is just another game that he too could play if he so chose: indeed, his logical errors are really marks of his superiority. Although his deconstructivist views of 1980 are quite different from his behaviorist views of 1950, a clear pattern emerges. (I am not, of course, saying that all behaviorists and deconstructivists fit this pattern.) Another example is provided by the former Nazi, discussed in Chapter III. Typically, to have been a Nazi, one must have been willing to let oneself be blind to reality: intellectual honesty and Nazism are incompatible.[52] This willingness to ignore reality rarely goes away, though it might show itself in very different ways.

Of course, *any* two attitudes will be instantiations of *some* more general property. (Quite trivially, for example, both attitudes are samples of the more general property *attitudehood*.) Only some general properties count toward being the same person. One of the jobs of an intentional account of human psychology is to indicate which general properties count and which do not.

In general, an adequate intentional account of human psychology articulates structures and mechanisms that render human behavior intelligible (whatever the efficient causes of that behavior might be). The comments made earlier about intentional explanations are relevant here. An adequate account has some predictive value, explains and illuminates most (or at least a good deal) of human activity and is consistent with (almost) all of it, obeys the canons of induction and the principle of charity (for example, it strives for simplicity and renders human activity as rational and consistent, as feasible), and so forth.

Any adequate intentional psychological theory must yield at least most of the following conditions for sameness:
1. There must be a subjective feeling of self. That is, B's recollections of deeds done by A must contain an element of self-recognition (for example, B feels shame about the misdeeds of A and not about the misdeeds of other stages contemporaneous with A). To some extent, this is a requirement that B be able to tell a story about her life history. B must see herself as having a past to which she feels attached and a future to which she is committed. In addi-

tion, there must be continuity of social role. B must see A's relationships and culture as relevant to her own relationships and
culture, as partly defining her place in the world.

2. Psychological change must be either gradual or explicable as a
   result of some discoverable trauma that is linked, by the relevant
   psychological laws[53] or patterns, to that sort of change.

3. There must be a set of relevant generic psychological properties.
   This enables us to determine which specific changes preserve psychologically important general traits and which do not. In general, sameness of moral agency requires that B's worldview be
   seen as "implicit" in A's and that all the stages contain enough
   common elements of a worldview, whether specific or general.

To some extent, then, sameness of moral personhood is a matter of
psychological theory. But it is also a matter of normative ethics. If
concern for others is a primary duty or a prime virtue, then a continuing concern for others will be important. If concern for others is
morally insignificant, then whether A and B both evidence concern
for others will not loom large in deciding whether B is morally accountable for A's sins. So ethical theory plays an important role. Of
course, there are many ways of showing concern for others. Perhaps
a particular sort of concern must be preserved for B and A to be the
same moral agent. Here too ethics plays a role. Are the different sorts
of concern morally significant? If so, then whether A and B have the
same sort of concern for others is likely to be important in deciding
whether A and B are the same moral person.

Moral Evaluation and Rights

Moral personhood plays a key role in our moral thought. For example, most of us agree that moral persons have a right to life, and
so my aunt Sophie has a powerful claim against me. I may not kill
her, even if her continued existence consigns me to a life of poverty.
The moral visions, aims, and needs of moral persons command respect in a way that the needs and desires of gnats do not, and moral
persons, unlike earthquakes, are blameable for the harm they do.
Now insofar as rights, obligations, and moral evaluation play any
role in our practices and in our judgments, we must be able to explain why it is reasonable to evaluate, grant rights to, and assign
duties to some things and not others.

Now unless an account of moral personhood casts some light on
what it is that makes moral persons so special that I must endure
poverty rather than kill one, and on what about me makes me sub-

ject to blame and worthy of respect, it is simply not an account of the relevant sense of "moral personhood." After all, I could, if I wanted, say that by a "moral person" I will mean anything that has five fingers. But then nothing important will rest upon being a moral person. We would still need to explain why some things have rights and others do not and why it makes sense to judge me, but not a pebble (morally) good or bad. So unless an account of moral personhood explains why those things it counts as "moral persons" have moral standing, it leaves this central problem untouched.

Antiabortionists who equate moral personhood with having human chromosomes are guilty of this error. As several writers have pointed out, there is no special moral cachet to human DNA as such.[54] No one would say "of course I must drown rather than throw Jones out of the lifeboat—just look at Jones's chromosomes!"

It is almost never pointed out, however, that most discussions of personal identity also ignore these questions. Yet it is a major virtue of my account that it casts considerable light on these questions, while many of its competitors do not. It is not clear, for example, why A should go to jail for B's misdeeds just because they have the same body or because they remember the same things. If free will is the crux of personhood, as I will soon suggest the traditional view of responsibility must say, then it must be the special moral beauty of free will that makes it heinous to kill a moral person. Yet it is far from clear why the ability to make uncaused choices, *as such,* is so terribly valuable.[55]

Space permits me to touch on but a small part of these topics here. In future works I will provide accounts of natural rights, punishment, contract law, and the authority of law generally, based on my notion of personhood.

MORAL EVALUATION. Normal adult human beings have a special moral status precisely because their choices, acts, feelings, and thoughts are *moral* choices, acts, feelings, and thoughts; they express a moral perspective. To the extent that this moral perspective accords with the *correct* moral perspective, her attitudes are good ones.[56] And because she (*qua* moral agent) just *is* those attitudes (actualized in a life), *she* is good. Conversely, when a moral person (as I have defined one) kicks a dog, his act reflects a variety of attitudes, perceptions, and the like, some of which are (presumably) incorrect (they conflict with the correct set of moral assertions and moral values). To the extent that the attitudes, and so on, reflected by the person's kicking the dog conflict with the correct moral outlook, his kicking the dog can be deemed bad. Because he (*qua* moral agent) just *is* those attitudes, and so on, actualized in a life, if those attitudes are bad, *he* is bad.[57]

In sum, persons are morally evaluable, on my account, because their conduct, dispositions, feelings, and thoughts reflect a worldview, a moral outlook, that is either correct or incorrect. Worldviews can be deemed good or bad on the basis of the extent to which they conflict with the correct moral view. The conflict may be direct; the correct view may deem hunting deer for pleasure wrong, while A believes hunting for pleasure to be virtuous. Or the conflict may be a second-order one. Our values and beliefs may themselves reflect yet other values and beliefs. For example, a belief that being rude is morally permissible may show unconcern for the welfare of others, whereas the correct moral view demands concern for the welfare of others. Conversely, anything that lacks a worldview might be able to display behavioral preferences (much as a heliotrope follows the sun). But its preferences and dispositions to act would have no moral significance.

The reason, then, that A may be judged adversely for his finger's movement on the trigger is that his muscle contraction in firing the gun embodies and expresses moral views that are incorrect, conflict with the moral truth (or, if relativism is right, with moral theory T). Moreover, those incorrect moral views are not incidental features of A, like having freckles; his embodying those incorrect views *is* (to a large extent) his moral personhood.

Of course, in some sense I may "believe" that murder is wrong but commit one anyway. In "yielding to temptation," however, I nonetheless manifest morally incorrect beliefs. For example, my killing Sally may show that I believe my own comfort is more significant than her most basic rights. And that is surely an incorrect moral view. I am suggesting, in other words, that in an important sense there is no such thing as "weakness of the will." My "weak" act reflects my other values and beliefs, often unacknowledged, often second-order (that is, beliefs about beliefs and values about values). Donald Davidson gives an interesting example. As she is about to fall asleep, "Ann" (not her real name) realizes that she has forgotten to brush her teeth. Although she realizes that sleep is more important, she gives in and gets up to brush her teeth. Here one wants to say that Ann's compulsion reflects other beliefs, attitudes, or values, say an abhorrence of personal slovenliness, or a desire to feel that her life is ordered by a regimen, the absence of which would make life seem uncontrollable and threatening. The point is that whatever the story to be told about Ann, there *is* such a story.[58]

Again, suppose Bill asks John to tell him one of Mike's secrets.

John does so, despite his belief that he is betraying Mike. Later he says, "I knew it was wrong, but I could not help myself." Here John's "weak" act shows, perhaps, that he values not offending Bill more than he values respecting Mike's trust, or that he values the thrill of being a newsbearer more than he values being trustworthy. Perhaps John just "could not assert himself," despite his desire to be more assertive. Here John may be afraid that being assertive would result in disapproval. Or he may have a deeply seated belief that the best kind of person is not assertive, a belief that conflicts with his more recently acquired belief that he ought to be more assertive. And so when John says, "I know I should have been more assertive, but I just could not," he is expressing a conflict of values, attitudes, and beliefs.

So one can sometimes be blamed for doing things that, in some sense, violate one's moral beliefs. For those acts may embody and express some of one's other, conflicting moral views.

It is also worth noting that if we are evaluable for the contents of our worldviews, then if A's behavior reflects a morally abhorrent worldview, if A made, all things considered, a morally objectionable decision or betrays a morally objectionable ranking of values, it seems reasonable to view A as a morally flawed person, however her behavior was caused.

In the next chapter, I will present and defend a detailed picture of moral responsibility along these lines. What should be noted here is that, if my account succeeds, what makes moral persons *evaluable* is precisely what makes them (on my account) *moral persons*. This is an important point. It strengthens both my view of moral person-hood and my view of moral responsibility. This is partly because the arguments given earlier apply here and vice versa. More crucially, it means that we have a unified picture of moral agency, a picture with great explanatory power, because it shows how moral personhood and moral responsibility are facets of what makes us moral beings in the first place.

RIGHTS AND THE VALUE OF PERSONS. When we say "A has a right to x," we may mean any of several different things. Most often we mean that A is morally or legally entitled to x, that others have a moral or legal duty to give x to A (if it is a claim right) or at least not prohibit A from pursuing x (if it is a permission right). Although a future work will provide a theory of natural rights of this sort, the topic is too large for this volume. However, natural rights rely on a less stringent notion, the notion of special respect. One thing we might mean by saying that A has a right to x is that A's desire for or pursuit of x merits special respect and concern. Whether or not one agrees with Bentham that talk of natural rights is "nonsense on stilts," only a complete amoralist would deny that some things deserve respect in a way that chairs and stones do not. Some things have a special status, as members of the moral community. It is those things we call "moral persons."[59] It is this sense of rights, the special respect due to the aims, goals, and lives of persons, that is the subject of this section. I will make no attempt to *prove* my view. Rather, I will show how my account of moral personhood leads to an account of rights (in this sense) and will try to make that account of rights plausible.

The core of my argument is that moral persons alone have a stake in the future based on a moral vision. This already distinguishes the aims of moral persons from the propensities of dandelions. But why must we respect those aims? The aims of moral persons deserve respect, I suggest, because those aims express and embody a moral vision. And such moral visions are the source of moral value. Thus to the extent that anything is valuable, moral persons are.

The first step, thus, is to show how the aims of moral persons differ from mere behavioral dispositions. Persons and persons alone have interests, because to have a moral vision is to have interests, and to have interests requires having a moral vision.

Just as a falling tree has no moral views that can be judged correct or incorrect, the tree has no set of goals or purposes that should be respected and no evaluative attitude about what happens in the world. It has no projects and no standards of excellence to which it wants the world to conform. It has no attitudes that would allow it to make evaluations. There is a real sense in which the tree has no "point of view." Thus it is fatuous to speak of respecting the tree's point of view, of protecting the tree's ability to pursue goals and/or to see its projects completed. In an important sense, the tree has no "interests."

Of course, there is a sense of the term "interest" in which the tree has interests. As Dennett puts it, "When an entity arrives on the scene capable of behavior that staves off, however primitively, its own dissolution and decomposition, it brings with it into the world its 'good.'"[60] But that sense of "interest" is of no moral significance. A tank that has automatic self-protection devices has "interests" in Dennett's sense. Yet surely it is not immoral, much less a violation of rights, to melt down the tank. Unless the tree cares about surviving, in a sense stronger than mere directed behavior, the tree has no morally important interest in surviving. After all, a suicide deems that survival is not in his interest. He may be wrong, but his view is not incoherent. Hence one's good cannot be defined as survival.

In any case, the fact that the tree acts to bring about its survival does not create any moral imperative, however weak, not to kill the tree, any more than it is wrong to destroy the tank. For the tree and the tank do not think it better that they survive, do not experience the agony of loss, and so forth.

This is not to deny that trees may be valuable and deserving of protection. It may even be that by destroying trees we would be violating the rights of future (human) generations, or that destroying the environment is evil. But we cannot, strictly speaking, violate the *tree's* rights or interests (in the morally important sense of the term).

To have rights, it is not even enough to feel wants. Nor is it enough to have free will.[61] Suppose we encounter an organism, the Wanter, that sometimes desires light and sometimes desires shade. It has no convictions, judgments, or general values; it simply feels a yen for light or a yen for shade. In other words, the Wanter has desires, not aspirations. So it is not committed to the world's meeting some moral standard. It does not have a general desire, for example, that the autonomy of organisms be respected. For if it did, the Wanter would have a moral value (it would believe that autonomy is valuable for its own sake). And, *ex hypothesi,* the Wanter has no general values or moral views. It merely wants to be in the light. In addition, let the Wanter's choice of shade or light be as free as you like. The Wanter has no general values, and so its choice will not be a principled choice. But it is free to choose shade or light as its whimsy suggests.

Now to the extent that it is, other things being equal, bad to cause pain, we do not want the Wanter to feel pain or frustration. But suppose it is convenient to fool the Wanter, or to anesthetize it, so that although its desires are not met it feels no pain or frustration. There is no reason not to do so. No one would think it immoral to fool the Wanter into thinking its desires are met. By way of contrast, it is at least plausible to say that fooling a person into thinking that her desires are met, in order to gain some advantage for oneself, is an immoral form of manipulation.

Of course, the Wanter has some minimal rights; it has a right, perhaps, not to be wantonly tortured. (That is, only a powerful benefit would permit Wanters to be tortured.) But this is because the Wanter *cares* about not feeling pain; if the Wanter did not mind feeling pain, it would not violate the Wanter's rights to torture it. Of course, in that case, we also would not be inclined to call what the Wanter feels "pain." In general, it is wrong wantonly to torture anything that is capable of being tortured. So the Wanter does have some minimal rights, but this is because the Wanter has, to some degree, the relevant characteristics of moral persons (it has the rudiments of a worldview). The Wanter, I would say, is a partial person and so has some of the rights of moral persons. The limits of its rights are the limits of its worldview. What the Wanter lacks is not free will or desires, but the kinds of values and attitudes that would make its choices and desires morally significant.

Thus the aims of the Wanter do not command respect the way that the aims of persons do. For persons, unlike Wanters, have standards they wish the world to meet. To a moral person, the world is not only a collection of events and objects. The world also instantiates or fails to meet values and standards. Events do not only occur. They have meaning, significance. This kind of significance is a precondition for caring, since, in order to care for something, I must see it as embodying or representing (or helping to bring about) important values, and I must consider some possible futures better for it than others. (That is why I cannot care for the law of gravity.) Thus persons care for and about the world and its future in ways that stones and snails (apparently) do not. It is in this sense that moral persons have a stake in the world and stones and snails do not.

Thus the first step has been accomplished. It now remains to be shown that moral visions are the source of moral value, and so if anything is of value, persons are.

Moral persons are central to morality; in a world without moral persons (human or nonhuman), no event would be good or bad, or even desirable or undesirable. I do not mean by this that there would be no one to *make* moral judgments, although that is certainly true. I mean something stronger. Imagine a universe forever uninhabited by moral persons. We can conceive of no event in that universe that *we,* the imaginers, can reasonably consider to be better or worse than any other event we can imagine occurring in that universe. (Except, of course, for events that might lead to the *creation* of persons. Moreover, animals, I will urge in the next section, are partial persons, and so a universe inhabited by dogs and cats is not wholly devoid of persons.) Quarks and electrical charges, considered as such, are morally indifferent; one quantum state is no different, morally speaking, from another. Similarly, there is nothing good or bad about the demise of a planet in an uninhabited universe. So in the absence of persons, the universe would be a meaningless clatter of subatomic events. Moral judgments are intelligible only with respect to persons. The conduct, welfare, and internal states of persons are themselves good or bad. Other things can be considered good or bad only insofar as they affect or relate to the conduct, welfare, and internal states of persons.[62]

Now I do not mean that only social goods are valuable. What I am saying is quite compatible with the claims that understanding is of value in itself and that justice and "the right" are of intrinsic value. Without persons there is no understanding, and in the absence of persons the concepts of justice and the right have no application. The stormy sea, after all, is not unjust to the cliffs it pounds against.

So the moral outlooks that constitute moral personhood are not only valuable, but the very source of value. Thus, to the extent that anything is of moral value, persons are.

Since this is an important point, I should like to suggest another way of arriving at this conclusion. A moral person, I have suggested, encapsulates a vision of the good (or, more likely, visions of goods) to which she is committed. And without such moral visions, morality has no application. Now if one takes morality seriously, as I do, one feels that the moral dimension is an important facet of human life. A human life bereft of a conception of the good is a stunted life; human beings who are not moral persons (for example, the "wild boy," perhaps) do not live satisfactory human lives. In other words, what I am saying is that morality is itself a good, and so a moral life, a life lived with a commitment to values, is preferable to an amoral life.

This is, of course, an assumption on my part, though an assumption that most of us cannot help making. After all, if I am right about the role that evaluative attitudes play in human emotion, a true amoralist has none of the complex emotions that characterize our lives. He has no real aspirations. He is merely inclined to act. Few of us, I trust, find this a satisfactory life, a life we would choose. So I will assume that morality is itself a good, that commitment to values is valuable. Since moral persons are characterized precisely by commitment to values, it follows that moral persons are valuable and that it is valuable that human beings lead lives in which they pursue commitments to morality. In other words, human *eudaimonia* or flourishing is good, and *eudaimonia* essentially includes the pursuit of a moral vision. So moral persons are valuable, and their pursuit of and commitment to moral standards deserves respect.

These remarks about the value of worldviews suggest another important point. Whatever else rights involve, they involve a recognition that the possessor of the right has a stake in the world equal to one's own. My remarks on worldview help explain why this is so. For what makes my own future valuable to me, what makes me care about anything, is equally present in others. Thus what makes me value my own future is equally true of others. So, whether I agree with their judgments or not, I must grant that, for the same reason that my future is important and valuable, other persons' futures (and those they envision for the world) are important and valuable. Perhaps not *as* valuable as mine, since I think mine are *right*. (If I thought other visions were as valuable, I could not really feel commitment to mine. It would be a matter of indifference which I chose.) But the importance of my own pursuit of a vision of how the world should be has the same *basis* as the importance of John's and Mary's pursuit of their moral visions. So recognizing the importance of my own stake in the future entails recognizing the importance of John's and Mary's stakes. And this recognition constitutes a basis for rights.[63]

Thus my account of moral personhood shows how personhood and rights are concomitant; having a worldview, a moral vision, is both the basis for rights and the essence of moral personhood. This is no small advantage. By way of contrast, bodily continuity and even memory theories seem misguided on this score; there is nothing about having a continuous body or even a continuous set of memories that justifies the attribution of rights. Hence my account of being a moral person, that is, being a worldview in operation, does seem to rest upon exactly those qualities that make rights and moral evaluation appropriate. Since what it is to be a moral person is to have rights and be susceptible to moral evaluation, this is a telling advantage of my account.

Partial Persons

I have said that to be a moral person is to have a certain sort of worldview that is reflected in one's dealings with the world. Now some worldviews are more developed than others, and some are more fully reflected in behavior than others. Having a fully developed worldview is a matter of degree. Is moral personhood also a matter of degree? Are there "partial persons," or is there a threshold below which nothing is a person and above which everything is?

This question is important for several reasons. Since both rights and responsibility hinge on personhood, troubling questions arise about the rights and responsibilities of those, such as animals, the insane, and the very young, who do not seem to be full moral agents. We need a rationale for absolving three-year-olds and the insane of moral responsibility for selfish behavior, without denying that the three-year-old and the insane have at least some rights. The notion of partial personhood will help us to do that. Partial personhood is also important for the abortion issue. If my analysis of personhood is correct, it follows that the fetus is not a person, since it lacks even a rudimentary worldview. But, as antiabortionists are quick to point out about such criteria for personhood, one-year-olds also lack developed worldviews. Does this make the killing of one-year-olds permissible? The answer, I want to suggest, is that one-year-olds, because they have rudimentary but not fully developed worldviews, are partial persons and so have some rights (though not the full set of rights adults have).

The nature of moral personhood, unlike, for example, the nature of legal personhood, suggests that there are "partial" moral persons. Being able to bring suit is an all-or-nothing matter. So there are no partial legal persons (at least in most areas of our law). By contrast, since having moral rights and obligations is not an all-or-nothing matter, we would expect that there are partial moral persons.

Moral persons can be "partial" in two senses. First, they may have some but not all of the rights, obligations, responsibilities, and such that constitute moral personhood. For example, a two-year-old does have a right not to be tortured but, unlike an adult, does not have the right to vote. It is a crime for one adult, acting on her own, to lock another adult in a room against his will. And it requires a lengthy, formal judicial procedure for a society to incarcerate an adult against his will. Yet in our society any parent may lock her child in his bedroom with not only impunity but authority. Animals also have some rights;[64] it is not only bad but unjust to torture an animal wantonly, though animals do not have the right to vote. Second, partial persons may have rights to a lesser degree. In many ways, a child's obligations are less binding upon him than his mother's are upon her. And, I would argue, the lives of chimpanzees deserve respect. We are obligated to undergo some inconvenience in order not to kill a chimpanzee, and so a chimpanzee has at least some right to life. However its right to life is not as strong as that of a normal adult *human being*. If forced to choose between letting die an ordinary, innocent adult human being and an ordinary chimpanzee, it would be wrong to let the human being die. So persons can be "partial" both in the scope of their standing and in the degree or strength of their standing.

Similarly, a partial person may not be responsible for some things that a full person would be responsible for. We do not blame a small child for making incorrect moral decisions about matters whose complexity is well beyond the ken of small children. It would be fatuous to evaluate a child adversely because of his stand on abortion or capital punishment. If children express a stand at all on these matters, we expect them to iterate what they have been told by their parents, whereas we would charge a normal adult in our society with intellectual passivity if she merely adopted whatever view on abortion her parents told her was correct. Furthermore, a partial person may be only partly responsible for a trait. By this I mean that although we do evaluate him on the basis of that trait, we do not give that evaluation the weight it would otherwise have. For example, a selfish five-year-old is not as good as a generous five-year-old. But whereas I might well refuse to befriend a selfish adult, it would be inappropriate to say to a five-year-old "you are selfish, and so I refuse to be your friend." The retribution earned by the misdeeds of small children is also greatly reduced. Whereas in some sense a generous five-year-old deserves a better fate than a selfish one, the kind of harshness earned by a selfish child is much less than that earned by a selfish adult. Nor does a three-year-old who, in a fit of pique, kills his younger sibling deserve the same harsh fate that an adult who murdered deserves. True, we might well "punish" a five-year-old for his selfishness, but punishment of small children is generally meant to be educational, not retributive. Little Johnny is punished for his lie in order to teach him not to lie, not because the badness of his lie deserves a bad fate.

Of course, the fact that we act as if we thought that animals and small children have rights does not establish that they *do* have rights. Our actions might be unjustified. What we need, therefore, is a rationale for according partial rights to animals and the very young.

Since to be a person is to be a worldview in operation, to be an agent whose activities reflect a worldview, there are two ways in which one can fail to be a full person. First, one's worldview may not be properly reflected in one's behavior. Consider the case of Riccardo, who shoots seven passers-by while believing himself to be rowing down the Thames on a balmy Sunday afternoon.[65] Riccardo has, perhaps, a fully developed worldview, a sophisticated set of beliefs, goals, and the like. But that worldview is not properly expressed in his response to the world. Riccardo fails to be a (full) person because his worldview is not "in operation."[66]

More important, for our purposes, is the second way one can fail to be a full moral person: one may lack the requisite sort of worldview. A full moral agent requires a fully developed worldview. It seems natural to suggest, then, that partial persons have partially developed worldviews. Dogs and cats, for example, appear to have rudimentary worldviews; it makes sense to speak of a dog's vision of the world. One must, of course, be very careful in speaking about the mental lives of animals; Wittgenstein's warnings about attributing features of human psychology to animals are worth heeding. It is not clear that a dog recently berated for digging in the garden feels shame, since feeling shame requires a variety of complex attitudes and social relationships. But the dog's behavior suggests that it has some sort of relevant attitude and that it participates in some sort of relevant social relationship with its owner. Again, it would appear that, in some sense, cats "recognize" people and places, have fairly complex individual preferences, and establish rudimentary social relationships. A cat "cares," in some important sense, about avoiding pain. (It feels genuine distress.) Now to the extent that a cat does have a point of view, does have some sense of how it wants the world to be, and if I am right that this is why persons are of special value, then a cat is of value for the same reasons (if not to the same extent) that full persons are. True, its aims are not on a par with our own. But this is not because cat chromosomes are somehow less prepossessing than human chromosomes. Rather, it is because cats do not have *fully developed* aims in the sense that we do. It would be fatuous to write a treatise on "cat morality." Nonetheless, they do seem to have aims of some sort, some sort of significant stake in the future. And the fact that they do have, at least to some appreciable extent, a particular way of regarding the world, as well as some investment in the future, indicates that their projects deserve at least some consideration.

These arguments apply even more forcefully to small children. It is absurd to inquire about a three-year-old's life goals, but a three-year-old certainly has a rudimentary point of view (has even a protopersonality), and there is much that she genuinely cares about. Thus the arguments in the preceding section concerning the value of moral persons also provide a rationale for treating animals and small children as partial persons.

This analysis of partial persons raises some interesting questions. First, when is a worldview "fully developed"? Surely Kant's worldview was more developed than my freshman college students'. Does this make college freshmen partial persons or Kant a "superperson"? The answer is that Kant and my college freshmen have the same moral status (both are full persons). This is because both Kant and Joan Student view the world in such a way that moral predicates apply to the world as they see it. Thus Kant and my student are both full moral agents, and their decisions, for good or ill, are properly termed moral decisions. (Presumably, Kant's decisions are better decisions than those of my students, but my student is no less morally evaluable for her decisions than is Kant.) For a partial person, this is only partially true.

In short, I want to say that there is a continuum of personhood, up to the threshold of full moral agency. Above that threshold, there are better or worse persons, but all are equally moral agents in the sense that they are fully evaluable for how good or bad they are. Below that threshold, organisms gradually approach full personhood. The child becomes more and more of a person as she develops. (A typical three-year-old is less of a moral agent than is a typical thirteen-year-old). This fact is reflected in the nature of our relationships with children: as the child develops, our dealings with him come gradually to approximate a full human relationship. You cannot have a full-blooded friendship with a three-year-old, though you can have a relationship that is to some degree, and in only some of the important ways, a personal one. As the child grows, this relationship may gradually develop, until at some point one realizes that it has become a true friendship. True, it is hard to pinpoint this moment. But there is a crucial difference between adult friendship and any relationship in which one of the parties is not treated as a full person. ("You cannot hold it against him that he was inconsiderate—he is only a child.") The threshold of full agency may not be a sharp line, but it is a real one nonetheless.

Still, the reader might expect a kind of "growth chart," matching characteristics with degrees of personhood (for example, the ability to imagine a future state makes one one-sixteenth of a person). Alas, I cannot give such a chart, because the answer requires a normative theory of human nature, a theory of what a full and satisfying human life consists in. I do not mean that a fully developed worldview is necessarily a good one; an evil person, after all, has a fully developed evil worldview. The connection is more subtle. For example, suppose that concern for others is an important constituent of the good life, *eudaimonia*. Then having a fully developed worldview requires understanding that there are other selves. And it requires having some conception of what it would be to experience concern for others. Without these concepts, one cannot evidence either concern or unconcern for others. That is, "Smith is unconcerned," in the relevant sense, means more than "it is not the case that Smith is concerned." Landslides do not show unconcern for the rights of innocent people and so do not violate morality by killing them. One can show unconcern only if one understands the world in a way that makes concern intelligible. So if concern is part of *eudaimonia*, then having a fully developed worldview requires having attitudes that make concern intelligible. On this view, someone who truly has no inkling that others have feelings, goals, and aims is not a full person but has the same status as a child or a deranged patient.

Again, if *eudaimonia* requires valuing, seeking, and, to some extent, obtaining insight into the world about one (as I believe it does), then having a fully developed worldview requires having some conception of truth. And if, as I believe, the mystic is wrong and rationality is a guide to truth, then having a fully developed worldview also requires some ability to make rational assessments. Moreover, widespread and egregious violations of rationality tell against having a fully developed worldview. I do not mean that one must be a well-oiled reasoning machine or that one must have no inconsistent or irrational attitudes or beliefs. But certainly having a fully developed worldview requires that one's attitudes, beliefs, and abilities evidence enough rationality to make everyday social interaction, participation in social life, possible.

These few remarks give, I trust, at least some rough idea of what a "personhood schedule" might look like. Of course, the *law* cannot employ anything this complex. The law simply sets a drinking age, a voting age, and so on. To some extent this gives arbitrary results: certainly some fifteen-year-olds are more responsible, and so more qualified to drive, than some forty-year-olds. However, the time, expense, invasion of privacy, and opportunities for abuse involved in a system that evaluated each citizen on his individual qualities would be prohibitive. So, for practical reasons, the law acts on the fiction that all eighteen-year-olds are alike in being enough of a person to merit the right to vote, and no seventeen-year-olds are.

Two last points should be noted. First, not everyone with a fully developed worldview could articulate the necessary concepts, either to others or to herself. Most people are quite inarticulate about the conceptual framework they routinely employ. Someone may conceive of friendship as a mutual-aid pact without having the slightest idea of how to answer the question "What is friendship?" To have an attitude, as we saw earlier, is simply for a certain kind of story to be applicable to one's behavior, circumstances, and inner occurrences.

Second, having a fully developed worldview does not require that one's adoption of beliefs and such be "free." Suppose that Jones is a perfect reasoner. If Jones is presented with a valid deductive argu-

ment in whose premises Jones has greater trust than in the negation
of the conclusion, Jones cannot but accept the conclusion. In an important sense, Jones's adoption of beliefs is not "free"; when presented with such an argument, she has no choice. Like it or not, she
must believe the conclusion. Surely she does not, on those grounds,
fail to have a fully developed worldview. What makes a worldview
fully developed is its connection to living a full, good human life.
And I have already suggested that free will is not, as such, an important element of *eudaimonia;* there is nothing valuable about free will
as such.

PROBLEMS OF PERSONAL IDENTITY

Now that we have a clearer idea of what it is to be a person, we can
address some of the traditional problems of personal identity. Although I will not give a detailed treatment of all the perplexities that
surround personal identity, I would like to say something about how
one might approach some of the most intractable difficulties.

There are two commonly held views about personal identity. The
bodily-continuity thesis seems to treat persons primarily as bodies. In
any case, it says that my continuing identity rests on the sameness of
my body; in general, stages A and B are the same person if they have
the same body. More precisely, A and B are stages of the same person if and only if the body of A is spatio-temporally continuous with
the body of B (or with a continuous series of intermediate stages).
The other major view, the memory thesis, suggests that memory is
the thread that binds selves over time. A and B are the same person,
according to the memory theory, if B remembers what happened to
A. More precisely, A is the same person as B when there is a chain of
stages linking A and B such that, for every two adjacent stages, the
later one includes at least one memory of an event remembered or
experienced by the earlier one.

My view of personhood differs from both. The crucial point is that
there are several distinct notions of "person," each serving a different
purpose. If one wants to know whether a later stage should be
blamed for the misdeeds of an earlier stage, the question is one about
the *moral status* of the later stage, and so the appropriate notion is
that of moral personhood. Questions about who inherits under a
will, however, concern not the moral status of a stage, but its legal
status under inheritance law. Since what gives something moral
standing and what gives it legal standing are not the same, there is no
special reason to expect that sameness of moral personhood and

sameness of legal personhood will never diverge. Thus the way to answer problems about personal identity is to (a) identify which type of personhood is relevant to the problem and (b) apply the criteria for *that type* of personhood. Finally, I suggest that moral personhood rests neither on bodily continuity nor on continuity of memory, but on continuity of worldview. I hope to show that my approach to personhood avoids many of the problems faced by the two standard accounts of personal identity.

Amnesia

Memory loss poses a problem for the memory theory. The so-called "brave officer" paradox, first articulated by Thomas Reid,[67] is one well-known example. Reid's problem considers three stages in the life of Riley: Riley as a small lad, as a young officer, and as an elderly general. As an elderly general, Riley remembers having done some brave deed in his first campaign, but remembers nothing of his childhood. During that first campaign, Riley the young officer remembered having been whipped for stealing apples when he was a small lad. Now if the memory account is correct, the general is the same person as the young officer, for he remembers having done the deeds of the young officer. And the young officer is identical to the small lad, for he remembers the whipping. But since the general does not remember anything that happened to the lad, it would seem that the general and the lad are not identical, at least if memory is the criterion for personal identity.[68]

Even more troublesome, however, are cases of total amnesia. Suppose that at time t the tuba player drops his instrument during a performance of a concerto for tuba and penny whistle. Ebeneezer, asleep in the first row, is hit on the head by the falling instrument and loses his memory. So Ebeneezer shares no memories at all with any stage prior to time t, when the tuba fell. Thus, according to the memory theory, he is not identical to anyone before time t. He was "born" at time t as a thirty-eight-year-old man. But this is absurd. Surely poor Ebeneezer should not be disinherited, for example, simply because he lost his memory. Only the bodily continuity criterion, it is argued, can avoid this untenable result.

The first point to be made is that most cases of amnesia are temporary. So there will be later stages who remember both what is now happening to A and what happened to some pre-t stage, B. And so, at least on Grice's version of the memory theory, A may be identified with B. But suppose that the memory loss *is* permanent.[69] Does Ebeneezer lose his bank account and his estate? Once again, the situation is not as bad as it might seem. Perhaps Ebeneezer can remember no specific events that occurred before t. But surely many "memories," in the broader sense, remain. He is not, presumably, unable to walk, talk, and do arithmetic, unable to ride a bicycle or plan for the future. Even a victim of amnesia has an adult personality, a system of goals, desires, expectations, dispositions, understandings, and so on (in short, a worldview). One can recognize young Ebeneezer's moral personality in Ebeneezer's current judgments, values, propensities, and the like. Ebeneezer retains much of what constitutes moral personhood. So there is still sufficient continuity of worldview to allow us to identify Ebeneezer now as the same moral agent as young Ebeneezer. (This suggests, though, that instead of the "memory" theory we should talk about the "worldview" theory. Propensities are as important as memories.)

Nonetheless, it is not impossible that someone should suffer absolutely total amnesia. Suppose, for example, that after the blow to his head, Ebeneezer is like a new-born child. He must be toilet trained, taught to walk, and so forth. Moreover, his experiences before t do not subtly affect his character development after t. None of his experiences before t are causally relevant to his subsequent character formation. The slate is, as it were, wiped entirely clean. Then it would follow from my view that Ebeneezer now is not the same moral agent as young Ebeneezer.

So it is a consequence of my view that absolutely total amnesia results in a new moral person. But this, I think, is exactly as it should be. It would be quite improper, for example, to punish Ebeneezer now for the crimes of young Ebeneezer. (Remember that all of young Ebeneezer's criminal tendencies are wiped away. Nothing whatsoever that led young Ebeneezer to crime remains in Ebeneezer now.) It would be quite unfair to require Ebeneezer now to keep young Ebeneezer's promises. (Remember that it will take years before Ebeneezer now is even able to understand what a promise is and that nothing that led young Ebeneezer to make the promise remains in Ebeneezer.)[70] Ebeneezer now and young Ebeneezer, in those circumstances, are distinct moral agents.

Of course, there are intermediate possibilities. Perhaps Ebeneezer after t, although not infantile, is markedly different in character from young Ebeneezer. In such a case we do not know what to say; it is much like the case of the fifty-year-old neurosurgeon who was a juvenile delinquent at sixteen. As I said earlier, we have only a rough grasp of the psychological theory upon which continuity of moral agency depends. So our intuitions about extensive but not total psy-

chological change are somewhat fuzzy. Should we blame Ebeneezer
now for young Ebeneezer's misdeeds if Ebeneezer now is quite different from young Ebeneezer? It depends on the nature of the change.
And here we have no clear answers. But the general idea is clear
enough: we blame Ebeneezer now to the extent that young Ebeneezer
is recognizable in the Ebeneezer now before us. And that is what my
theory suggests we should do.

Bernard Williams has raised an interesting counterargument to this
approach. Suppose, he begins, that the chief of police tells me that
tomorrow he will torture me. Naturally, I will be frightened and apprehensive. Now, Williams continues, suppose I were to learn that
before I am tortured I will come to "not remember any of the things I
am now in a position to remember." So the person who will be tortured shares none of my memories. Hence, according to the memory
theory, it is not *me* who will be tortured. And so I ought to rejoice
that *I* will not be tortured. In fact, however, I would not feel greatly
relieved. Learning that I will lose my memories before being tortured
would not do much to cheer me up. Williams reinforces his point by
reminding us of an actual case. It is quite possible that I might one
day revive after an automobile accident without memories and in
great pain. That is something that, right now, I very much do not
want to happen to me. Yet, were the memory theory correct, there
would be no reason to feel distress over this possibility. For it would
not be "me" who felt the pain.

My theory, of course, depends not just on memory but on the
whole of one's worldview. Williams, however, is prepared for me.
His next move modifies the argument to apply to "character" as well
as memories. After all, it would not make me feel much better to
learn that before I am tortured (or, in the accident case, before I
regain consciousness), changes will be made in my character, and I
will be given a new set of memories. Again, says Williams, I can
imagine going mad and thinking that I am George IV, and that too is
something I do not want to happen to me.[71]

The power of Williams's approach is that he links his thought experiment to circumstances (madness and traffic accidents) that might
in fact befall us. Thus the price of disagreeing with him seems quite
high. We should have to say that it would not concern us to go mad
or to wake up with amnesia and in great pain. And no one would
consider such possibilities with cheerful indifference.

There is, however, a way out. Williams's way of stating the argument conflates fear of death with fear of future discomfort. Certainly
I am apprehensive about going mad, just as I would be apprehensive

were alien organisms likely to kill me and take over my body. This does not show that it would still be *me* who is mad or possessed of an alien mind. Rather, madness means the end of life as I know it. And I do not want my life to end.

Moreover, Williams himself points out that there is a sense in which his description of the situation begs the question. Williams's description asserts that it is *I* who will be tortured, rather than some-one who *replaces* me. This is a crucial assumption. After all, if I fear being *replaced* by someone who will be tortured, what I fear is death, not the subsequent torture. (In fact, as Williams acknowledges, I would fear the loss of memory or personality even without the tor-ture.) Williams's response (on p. 187) is that, after all, when someone predicts that I will be given an operation that induces amnesia, after which radical changes will be made in my personality, after which I will be tortured, "I seem to be able to follow him successfully. And if I reflect on whether what he has said gives me grounds for fearing that I shall be tortured, I could consider that behind my fears lies some principle such as this: that my undergoing physical pain in the future is not excluded by any psychological state I may be in at the time. . . . This principle seems sound enough." Again, "if A is capa-ble of expecting pain, he is capable of expecting pain preceded by a change in his dispositions" (p. 191). This response seems inadequate. One wants to know how complete the change in my character is going to be. After all, my character can be altered, while retaining considerable continuity with my character before the "interference." If that is what Williams has in mind, then, given my criterion, I re-main the same moral person. Given my criterion, there is a change of moral personhood only if the "interference" results in a (near) total change of character, affecting (nearly) *all* of my dispositions, goals, attitudes, and beliefs. So if the change in character is not radical and sweeping, Williams's imagined case does not tell against my view. On the other hand, if there is a *total* change of character, then it is no longer clear that I have good grounds to fear the *torture*, although of course I do have good reason to fear the *"interference"* that will result in the termination of my moral personhood, since the inter-ference will mean the end of life as I know it.

Nonetheless, Williams's point has some force. I *do* understand what is meant by saying that *I* will be tortured after a total change in character; that statement is not a logical error, it is not incoherent. And that suggests that being the same person as A cannot simply *amount to* having the same character as A. If it did, Williams's state-ment would be incoherent. Moreover, there is an alternative way of putting Williams's argument that seems irrefutable. Let us call my body after the radical change of character "Rhadames." Now suppose that I have a choice about whether Gilbert, a complete stranger, will be tortured and Rhadames lead a happy life, or Rhadames will be tortured and Gilbert lead a happy life. Is it really *irrational* to have even the slightest preference? Yet this is precisely what the memory and character views of identity seem to require; since Rhadames is no more "me" than is Gilbert, it would be irrational to prefer that it be Gilbert rather than Rhadames who is tortured.

We must be careful here. Since I admire Ghandi and think little of Strom Thurmond, I would prefer that someone throw darts at a picture of Strom Thurmond instead of Ghandi. But surely this does not mean that I think the picture of Ghandi *is* Ghandi or that throwing darts at his picture hurts Ghandi. Perhaps my preference that Rhadames not be the victim of the torturer's peculiar skills is similar in nature. So my queasiness at Rhadames' distress does not mean that I think Rhadames is me or that torturing Rhadames hurts me.

I do not think this response will do, however. Why do I feel uncomfortable when I see someone throw darts at the image of Ghandi? Insofar as my discomfort is not wholly irrational, it is because throwing darts at a picture is a traditional form of disrespect, hostility, or contempt. It is a gesture with rhetorical import, and I do not approve of the rhetorical import of the act. But surely torturing Rhadames does not (or need not) express hostility or contempt for my pre-altered character. So I do not feel uneasy at the thought of Rhadames' being tortured because I think the torturer is expressing hostility or contempt for my present character. Hence my discomfort is not analogous to what I feel when I see someone throwing darts at Ghandi's picture.

But perhaps this shows merely that while it is not irrational to prefer that darts be thrown at Thurmond rather than Ghandi, it is irrational to care even a little about Rhadames. Of course, I might have other goals that would be set back by Rhadames' being tortured. For example, the sight of Rhadames' distress may cause discomfort to my less rational friends, whose well-being matters to me. If so, what I care about is not Rhadames as such, but my friends. Let us, therefore, rephrase our question. Is it rational to have even the slightest preference for Rhadames' well-being *as such* (noninstrumentally)? And here I want to say that it is. This result, it seems, cannot be reconciled with traditional memory and character views of personal identity.

Traditional memory or character views have further problems. For example, even though we do not blame A for B's misdeeds if A's character is sufficiently different from B's, we do not want to keep A from inheriting property willed to B, nor to declare A's wife a widow (though we may wish to grant her a divorce). Fortunately my account, unlike more traditional "psychological" accounts of personal identity (such as the memory view), can accommodate such objections. On my view, there is more than one conception of personhood; moral personhood is but one of several species of personhood.

When someone says "I did it," she may be referring to herself as a legal person, or as a moral person, as a biological person, or whatever. (There is a kind of hidden indexical here: strictly speaking, she means I$_{moral\ agent}$ or I$_{legal\ person}$ did it.) It is almost always safe to ignore this complication, since legal, moral, and biological personhood are generally coextensive (moral persons do not generally engage in body swapping.) Only in confusing contexts need we be clear. Suppose this body woke up with Ronald Reagan's memories, character, and so on. Out of this mouth come the words "I was born in Paterson, New Jersey." Whether this assertion is true depends upon whether it means "I$_{biological\ person}$ was born in Paterson, New Jersey" (in which case it is true) or "I$_{moral\ person}$ was born in Paterson, New Jersey" (in which case it is false). Thus, since some types of personhood do survive total change of worldview, the statement that I will be tortured after a complete change of worldview is fully coherent. It does not invoke moral personhood but biological personhood. And biological personhood is not affected by absolute loss of memory or by radical changes in character.

Moreover, it is not irrational to give preference to Rhadames, I suggest, because I do not view my body as a kind of slipcover for my soul. Because a moral agent is not a little man inside my body but a feature of the operations of this body over time, my conception of myself is tied to my body in an intimate way. My being generous just is these hands giving out alms. Eyes are not windows on the soul but realizations of the soul. So this face and these hands have a special role in my self-conception. True, the connection between this body and my moral agency might be severed under certain imagined conditions. But it is a connection nonetheless. So it is not irrational, other things being equal, to give some slight preference to these hands and this face. Biological identity counts for something, and, on my view (unlike conventional memory or character views), Rhadames and I are the same biological person. So, although Williams's argument tells against more-conventional memory or character views, it does not undermine mine.

Again, we should be very loath to refuse to permit A to inherit property willed to B, despite the total amnesia. When it comes to inheritance, we want to treat A and B as the same person. But although that is a powerful objection to traditional memory or character accounts of personal identity, it presents no problem for my approach. For even though A and B are not the same moral agent, they are the same legal-inheritance person. The reason for this is fairly clear. Inheritance, in our legal system, is largely a matter of familial ties. Other things being equal, our inheritance laws favor a forty-year-old biological son whom the deceased never met over a close friend of the deceased. If the deceased died intestate, the law would award the estate to the son and make no provision for the close friend. Yet the relation between the deceased and the son he never met is purely that of biological progenitor. It seems clear that our inheritance law places greater weight on biological personhood than it does on, for example, moral personhood. Now despite the change in personality, A and B exhibit continuity of biological function. So even if A's character is radically different from B's, A and B are the same biological person. So allowing A to inherit property willed to B presents no problem for my account. Similarly, A may be the same "marital person" as B, even though A and B are not the same moral agent.

Thus my approach is able to give a more satisfying account of amnesia and change of character than its competitors. My account explains why we would not hold A responsible for the misdeeds and promises of B, yet would allow A to inherit property willed to B. Neither the memory nor the bodily-continuity account can do this very readily.

Replication

The possibility of producing "copies" of persons raises difficulties for both the memory and bodily continuity theories of personal identity. Of course, at least at present, the possibility of replicating people seems at best remote. Some people dislike speculating about possibilities so far divorced from everyday experience. They can see no point to the exercise. So let me say why thinking about clones, duplicates, and the like, can be quite useful.

Science-fiction and bizarre examples help us see what is really central to our concepts and what is incidental. They help show us what is significant about the real cases we encounter. For example, how can we tell if what is crucial to our concept of personal identity is sameness of character or sameness of body? In "real life," after all, the two always go together; stages with the same memories and character always have the same body. So we cannot examine two stages with the same character but a different body. How, then, can we decide whether character is the basis of personal identity and bodily continuity incidental, or bodily continuity the important feature, which, as it happens, is accompanied by sameness of character? Well, since we cannot separate them in fact, we separate them in thought; we can imagine a situation in which the two do not coincide. We might, for example, imagine that my character is shifted to someone else's body. If we feel very strongly that the new body is still me, that suggests that character, not bodily continuity, is the key to our sense of self. It is strong evidence that what makes me think I am the same person as the Eugene Schlossberger of 1979 is not the fact that we share the same body. In other words, the "science-fiction" example helps clarify what is important to us about actual cases and what is not. But we must be very careful that we do not prejudice the outcome by the way we describe the case. We are accustomed, as readers, to accept the narrative presuppositions of the writer. So if I say "suppose I woke up one morning with a new personality," you are inclined to accept my presupposition that my body is me, just as you are inclined to accept my presupposition that I am my character if I say "suppose I wake up one morning with a new body."

Let us proceed, then, to our first case. Suppose that Smith, who is an archvillain, produces an exact duplicate of her body. Immediately after replication, the replicating machine destroys the original Smith body. Now Copy-Smith (the duplicate) and the original Smith are not bodily-continuous. So, according to the bodily-continuity criterion, Copy-Smith is not the same person as the original Smith. Yet the duplicate body (including its brain) is indistinguishable from the original body; the duplicate body has all of the same neural and biochemical patterns that the original body had. So the duplicate of Smith has all of the original Smith's memories, characteristics, dispositions, desires, goals, attitudes, and so forth; it thinks and behaves exactly as Smith did.[72] Surely it would be wrong to say that Smith has committed suicide, that Copy-Smith is a new person, who may not be punished for Smith's deeds or held accountable for Smith's debts and promises, and that Copy-Smith is not married to Smith's husband. One cannot escape justice or marriage so easily. Yet this is what the bodily-continuity criterion seems to be committed to.

We can put the problem another way. Suppose I am offered a choice. Either my body will be placed in suspended animation for two hundred years, or my body will be destroyed, and in two hun-

dred years an exact duplicate of me as I am at this moment will be
created. We must imagine that the possibility of something going
wrong is the same in both cases and that no changes will occur in my
body while it is in suspended animation. Now I will probably be
unhappy about either choice. But is there really any reason for me
to prefer one alternative to the other? Yet, according to the bodily-
continuity theory, one option amounts to death, while the other
does not.

The counterpart of this problem for the memory theory of personal identity is the "Guy Fawkes" objection raised by Bernard Williams.[73] Suppose that we encounter upon the streets of London two
individuals, each of whom possesses all the memories of Guy
Fawkes. Let us suppose further that each possesses Guy Fawkes's
worldview, acts exactly as Guy Fawkes would act, and so forth. Are
there now two Guy Fawkes, both of whom should be sent to prison
as punishment for Guy Fawkes's misdeeds? Williams thought the answer to be a resounding "no," and so, he concluded, bodily continuity must be the key to personal identity.

I will argue that my view is able to resolve both of these quandaries. Let us consider bodily replication first. Although it is clear
that, according to my criteria, Copy-Smith is not the same biological
organism as the original Smith (unless we modify our conceptions of
human biological functions), it is also clear that Copy-Smith is the
same moral person as the original Smith. For we can tell a convincing
psychological story that links, in the requisite way, the original
Smith's worldview to Copy-Smith's worldview. So, on my account,
Copy-Smith would be punishable for the original Smith's crimes, accountable for her promises, and so on.

Whether Copy-Smith can inherit property willed to the original
Smith depends upon the criteria for inheritance-personhood (a sub-
species of legal personhood). Our discussion of amnesia, in which it
was claimed that inheritance law places greater emphasis on bodily
continuity than on moral personhood, might suggest that Copy-
Smith cannot inherit. However, although it is clear that current law
places greater emphasis on bodily continuity than it does on moral
personhood, it does not follow that inheritance law rates bodily *dis*-
continuity above moral personhood. If moral personhood is more
important to inheritance-personhood than is bodily discontinuity,
then Copy-Smith may inherit property willed to the original Smith.
Of course, we can suppose that the original Smith body survives but
with the worldview (that is, the dispositions, attitudes, memories,
feelings, and so forth) of some other person, say Kublai Khan. Now

the original Smith body is continuous with "Kublai-Smith" (the Smith body with Kublai's worldview). Here we would be genuinely torn between awarding the estate of the original Smith's mother to Copy-Smith and awarding it to Kublai-Smith. If transformations of this sort became common, some revisions in our inheritance law might result. (That is, we would have to reconsider our notion of inheritance-personhood.) Similar comments might be made about whether Copy-Smith is married to the original Smith's husband; the answer depends upon the criteria for marital personhood.

Note that what allows us to avoid counterintuitive results in the case of Copy-Smith is the flexibility gained by distinguishing among rather different notions of personhood. Each notion of personhood is appropriate to a different question about Copy-Smith. That same flexibility is also quite useful in discussing the second of our two quandaries, the case of the duplicate Guy Fawkes.

I wish to bite the bullet on the Guy Fawkes case and claim that both current-day Londoners are the same moral agent as Guy Fawkes. But before I bite it, I intend to sugarcoat the bullet. Suppose that in 1606 someone were to speak to the historical Guy Fawkes as follows: "Nearly four hundred years in the future, two gentlemen will roam the streets of London. Each will possess all of your memories, your dispositions, your attitudes, values, and beliefs." Suppose also that Fawkes had good reason to believe this curious prediction. Would it not be rational for the historical Fawkes to provide for the future welfare of *both* gentlemen, in exactly the ways in which rational individuals provide for their own futures? Again, if Guy Fawkes were to say "I will be resurrected in the late 1900s," would he be mistaken? Finally, would it not be appropriate to punish both men for the crimes of Guy Fawkes? After all, both men remember having committed those crimes, feel about those events exactly as the Guy Fawkes of 1606 would, are precisely as likely to commit similar crimes in the future as was the Guy Fawkes of 1606, and so forth. Is that not reason enough to punish them for the crimes committed (and never punished) in the 1600s?

A proper answer to this last question, of course, requires a theory of punishment as well as a theory of personal identity. For whether one stage should be punished for the crimes of another depends upon the purpose and justification of punishment as much as it does upon identification of the two stages. For example, suppose the only purpose of punishment is deterrence, and no deterrence is effected by punishing the two latter-day Guy Fawkes. Then they should not be punished for the crimes committed in the 1600s, even if both Guy

Fawkes are the same moral person as the Guy Fawkes of the 1600s. Moreover, punishment is a legal as well as a moral concept, and so more than moral desert is involved. Consider someone who would have committed a crime, decided to do so, but before taking a definite step was prevented from realizing his intentions by unforeseeable circumstances. Perhaps he is morally deserving of punishment. Yet it would violate our canons of jurisprudence to send him to jail. So I am not going to argue that both Guy Fawkes should be jailed. Instead, I will simply suggest that both Guy Fawkes satisfy whatever purely retributive requirements there are for punishment. If one could read the minds, without reservation and without error, of the Guy Fawkes of 1606 and both Guy Fawkes of the 1980s, one would find no difference; *ex hypothesi,* every criminal instinct, desire, propensity and recollection of the one is duplicated in the others. What, then, could make one Guy Fawkes morally worthy of punishment and the others not? (Remember that one may be *morally worthy* of punishment without punishment's being appropriate.) I can see nothing relevant to the moral evaluation of individuals that one Guy Fawkes has and the others lack. (The matter becomes yet clearer if we adopt the account of responsibility proposed in the next chapter and the notion of abstract justice explained in Chapter V.)

These considerations support the claim that although neither gentleman is the same biological person as the Guy Fawkes of 1606, both are the same moral person as Guy Fawkes. They are also the same moral agent as each other. That sounds bizarre, no doubt. But remember that they act in exactly the same ways, think exactly the same thoughts, and so on. Therefore, since they perform exactly similar actions, if one commits a crime, so does the other. Hence one Guy Fawkes cannot be guilty of committing a crime the other did not commit. Of course, if their worldviews later diverge (and that is inevitable, since their experiences from now on will be somewhat different), they henceforth become distinct moral agents. For there is no story of the right sort connecting the one's beliefs with the other's actions. (This shows that, if such fissures can occur, sameness of moral agency is transitive only in the direction of the past.)[74]

Still, there are some nagging questions to be answered. Are the two latter-day Guy Fawkes entitled to claim the long-since-dispersed estate of the historical Guy Fawkes? The answer here depends upon the criteria for inheritance-personhood. And there is no necessity for inheritance-personhood to employ the same criteria as moral personhood.[75] Similarly, suppose that we meet someone named Sheila in the streets of present-day London. Sheila has the same worldview as the wife of the historical Guy Fawkes. My claim that each latter-day Guy Fawkes is the same moral agent as the historical Guy Fawkes does not commit me to saying that the latter day Fawkeses are married to Sheila (nor does it rule out that possibility).

In sum, the Guy Fawkes case turns out to be no different from any other case of fission. Suppose that my body were to divide into two qualitatively indistinguishable human bodies as a result of widespread mitosis, much as amoeba are wont to divide.[76] Which of the two is me?

Derek Parfit has an interesting response to this question.[77] He claims that I "survive" as both of the new bodies, even though I am not "identical" to either (and so survival does not imply identity). Moreover, says Parfit, most of the things that determine survival are matters of degree. In fact, Parfit thinks that what matters most is what he calls "psychological connectedness," which bears a certain resemblance to my notion of continuity of worldview. Bernard Williams criticizes Parfit's application of his view to moral personhood.[78] Many moral notions, Williams points out, require a strict determination of identity. For example, suppose I promise you that in ten years' time I will pay you ten dollars. Ten years later someone asks me for the ten dollars I promised to pay. If that person is not you, I owe him nothing. And what sense are we to make of the suggestion that he is *partially* you? Do I owe him only part of the ten dollars? Or is my obligation to repay the money less serious, less binding, than it would otherwise be? Surely the answer is "no," in both cases. Similar points could be made about criminal liability. If ten years ago a self who is "weakly connected" to you killed two teenagers, are you criminally liable for killing only one of them? Or are you only "weakly guilty" of murder?

I want to suggest that Williams and Parfit are both, to some extent, correct. Parfit is right that sameness of person is not, strictly speaking, identity; no two stages are identical, for they are *two* stages, not one stage. Moreover (and here I go a step further than Parfit), there are several types of sameness of person, appropriate to different areas of concern. And Parfit is right that most of the criteria for moral (as well as several other types of) personhood are matters of degree. But it does not follow that judgments of sameness are matters of degree, that sameness of person is not all or nothing. There may be a threshold of sameness, even if the *criteria* for sameness are all matters of degree. "Person," after all, is a status term. Now some statuses can be had by degrees; in some senses of "person," I have argued, one can be a "partial person." But other statuses are all or nothing; one is either eligible, ultimately, to vote in a particular election, or one is not. (There are no half votes in our electoral system.)

We are now in a position to address the problems of fission and fusion. There is not one answer to the question "which of the two new bodies is me," but several. Neither, presumably, is the same biological person as the presplit "me." They are both the same moral agent as the presplit "me," although they will diverge almost immediately (for worldviews change rapidly). Thus they are equally entitled (morally) to the ten dollars that A promised me. However, his liability is limited to ten dollars. Since greater stress is placed on the limit of his liability than on the entitlement of the promisee, the two "me"'s must split the ten dollars between us. (Were greater stress placed on the entitlement of the promisee, A should have to pay each "me" ten dollars.)

Thus there is a sense in which A is obliged to pay me less money (although, since both bodies are "me," there is a sense in which A still must pay me ten dollars). Both are fully punishable for the misdeeds of earlier stages (for there is no limit upon the total punishment exactable for a crime; if two people are equally guilty of a murder, they do not split the sentence between them). In short, my approach has all the advantages of Parfit's view, yet avoids some of its disadvantages. For example, I need not deny, as he must, that there *is* an important sense in which I do not survive mitosis, and in which Smith does not survive the creation of Copy-Smith. For neither Smith nor I survive as the same biological organism.

Thus my account, unlike more traditional accounts, is able to handle the problems caused by both mental and bodily duplication.

CONCLUDING REMARKS

In this chapter, I have tried to articulate a comprehensive picture of moral personhood. The primary "argument" for this picture is the light it sheds on the role that personhood plays in understanding ourselves and our practices. I have tried to show that my account helps illuminate the mind-body problem, the problem of personal identity, the reason that persons are morally evaluable, and the special consideration persons deserve (their "rights"). The following chapters will draw upon this picture of personhood in explaining moral responsibility, punishment, desert, and personal emotions.

As I noted earlier, my account has had to remain sketchy in certain key respects. In particular, one cannot specify in detail, without a normative picture of human nature, what "psychological continuity" consists in and what makes a worldview sufficiently developed. I would like to conclude by addressing this deficiency, as much as time permits, with an example of how a particular normative claim about human nature has specific consequences for my account. Suppose that Aristotle is right that we are by nature "social animals." More specifically, suppose, as I would argue, that community is an essential ingredient of the good life. By a "community" I mean a group of individuals who share a publicly understood set of practices, institutions, conventions, and paradigms that reflect a commitment to a common moral vision.

This needs a bit of explaining. A *practice* is a regulated activity with a point. For example, chess and ritual greetings are practices, because there are more or less strict rules for chess and ritual greetings, and these activities have a point. (Indeed, because the rules for chess and ritual greetings are quite strict, we may call them *"rule-governed* practices.") Scientific inquiry is also a practice. It is an activity with a point. And, although there are no strict rules for scientists to follow, there are canons of evidence and procedure (for example, double-blind testing of certain medications), features of a good or strong explanation (such as simplicity), accepted procedures for announcing results, and so on. (We may thus call scientific inquiry a *"rule-guided* practice.") Music composition in the twentieth century is also a practice, though a more diffuse one. There are some schools of music that have strict rules (such as serialism), others that have models of operation (such as what one might call the "let's-see-how-many-unusual-sounds-we-can-get-out-of-this-instrument" school), and others that use a set of accepted values (such as rhythmic and harmonic complexity and invention). Composing twentieth-century music is thus a regulated activity, though not necessarily a rule-oriented one. And it has a point, although there is considerable debate about what precisely the point of composing music is.

Institutions are more or less clearly defined bodies with more or less clear roles that fulfill a social role in a publicly understood way. Medicine is an institution, since it is relatively clear who is a health-care provider, there are relatively clear roles (physicians, nurses, and so on), and there are publicly understood ways in which health-care providers go about attending to health needs.

American suburban society shares a *paradigm* of "being a neighbor." For example, it is appropriate to ask one's neighbor, merely by virtue of being a neighbor, for a cup of sugar and for the loan of a lawnmower, but it is not appropriate to ask to borrow an amount of money considerably less than the worth of the lawnmower.

A group of people constitute a *community* when these paradigms, practices, and institutions are ways of working out a common life reflecting common values. The practices and institutions of the scientific community, for example, are dedicated to the search for human knowledge, a value at the core of science as an activity.

If we accept that community is a key ingredient of human flourishing, there are important consequences for the notion of personhood. The first consequence is that it is a precondition for full moral personhood that the agent have sufficiently rich socialization concepts to be able to understand social cooperation for a common goal and to grasp what practices, institutions, and paradigms are.[79] Because ducks cannot understand and respond appropriately to even rudimentary institutions, they are not full persons. One test for the full personhood of autistic individuals is to ask, "to what extent is this individual capable of understanding what it is to participate in a simple community?" (Notice that one can be a full person and *choose* to be a hermit. The question is not "is this individual part of a community," but "does this individual have the conceptual sophistication to be *able* to participate in a community?")

The second consequence is that the way I understand my relationships to the social world expresses my personhood: the practices, institutions, and paradigms I use in living my life are part of the person I am. Suppose, for example, that I am offered a better job in a new city. My wife offers to give up her job and follow me, knowing that this means her taking a worse job. How I respond to my mate's offer depends on my paradigm of marriage, my working concept of a marriage. If I see a marriage as a mutual-assistance partnership, I may take a utilitarian view of the matter, asking myself if the gain in my job status outweighs the loss in my wife's. If my conception of marriage centers on sharing an excitement about life, I will ask myself if life will be more exciting for us in the new city than it is here. If I view marriage as a contractual arrangement between mutually disinterested persons, I will drive the best bargain for myself that I can get and so take my wife up on her offer. If I view marriage as the working out of a rich life for each partner, in which the other participates centrally, the decision will be more complex. In any case, how I respond will reflect my concept of marriage, and that is a part of my personhood. Thus my response reflects my personhood. Again, if I feel that "doctor knows best" and take the medicine my physician prescribes without, for example, looking up the drug in the PDR, then my behavior reflects my concept of the institution of medicine, and that is an aspect of my personhood.

Third, my identity over time will reflect continuity of my social understandings. A single conversation with a persuasive medical ethicist may radically change my view of medicine as an institution. The class period I spend on friendship has greatly changed some of my students' model of friendship. These changes do not turn agents into new persons. But if I radically change *all* of my social concepts, that is strong evidence that I am a new moral agent, no longer chargeable with my former virtues and vices.[80]

I hope this brief discussion helps illustrate the way in which a detailed normative picture of human nature would fill in the missing details of my account of moral personhood.

III

A Theory of Responsibility

DEFINING RESPONSIBILITY

THERE ARE THREE elements of a theory of moral responsibility. First, we need a *definition* of moral responsibility, a clear statement of what it means to say that A is morally responsible for x.[1] Second, we need an *account* of when and why A is responsible, in that sense, for x. (The third element, an explanation of why that definition of the word "responsibility" is the one we should be concerned with, will be provided in Chapter V.) There are, after all, many different ways in which the word "responsibility" is used in English,[2] and each of these ways would call for a different sort of account. So I should like to pinpoint what it is my account is meant to capture. It is important to be clear about this, because in this book I will use the word "responsibility" in a rather particular way. This section defines a rather limited sense of the phrase "morally responsible." Whatever the phrase "A is responsible for x" may ordinarily mean in English, all *I* will mean by it is that A and x meet the conditions given below.

When I say that A is morally responsible for x, I will mean two things. First, x is the sort of thing that moral theories evaluate, the sort of thing that moral theories deem good, bad, or indifferent. In other words, x has some moral status. Second, any moral taint or luster x possesses applies as well to A. That is, the moral status of x helps determine the moral status of A. So there are two conditions for moral responsibility:

1. as the result of a moral calculation, x is deemed good, bad, or indifferent by T (the moral theory in question), and
2. any favor or disfavor that T accords to x accrues to A's moral account.

Explanation of Condition 1

The first condition states that it must be appropriate to ask whether x is morally offensive or desirable; x must be proper grist for the moral mill. I do not mean by this that x must be either a good thing or a bad thing; x might be morally neutral. One would expect, for example, a good moral theory to tell us that choosing skiing over reading detective fiction as a form of recreation is morally neutral. It is neither a good thing nor a bad thing. Nonetheless, choosing to ski is a proper subject for moral scrutiny. It is the sort of thing we expect moral theories to judge. For example, an act utilitarian would evaluate my choice by calculating the amount of happiness that would be produced were I to ski and the amount that would be produced were I to read an Agatha Christie novel. Let us assume that an equal amount of happiness would be produced in either case. Then she would say that, in opting for the slopes, I have done neither badly nor well. Here my decision to go skiing was found to be morally neutral as a result of a *moral calculation*. Similarly, a Kantian might ask whether the maxim (general principle of conduct) expressed by my decision is coherently universalizable, whether (roughly) I could reasonably say "I want everyone to treat my maxim as a moral law." So both act utilitarianism and Kant's view have criteria for moral evaluation that apply to my choice. By way of contrast, it makes no sense to ask whether the orbit of Jupiter expresses a universalizable maxim. The criteria for moral evaluation enshrined in Kant's moral theory cannot be applied to Jupiter's orbital movements.

The point here is that moral theories establish moral parameters; they indicate which aspects of the human condition have moral significance. A strict utilitarian, for example, holds that the only moral parameter is happiness. So only those things that lead to happiness or unhappiness are subject to moral evaluation. Alternatively, certain forms of Christianity hold that the only moral value is obedience to God. According to those views, x has moral weight if and only if x can meaningfully be evaluated in terms of cheerful conformity to God's will. (Does x express, result from, or constitute obedience to God?)

It follows that whether x is appropriate for moral scrutiny depends not only on x, but also on the moral theory involved. Consider a moral theory that regards size as the only moral value: the bigger the better, it says. Short is bad, tall is good. Thus it would regard my height as a characteristic that is subject to moral evaluation. Most moral theories, of course, would consider my height to be morally irrelevant. So one can only speak of a thing's meeting condition 1 with respect to a given moral theory.

For our purposes, however, things are a bit simpler. We are primarily concerned with praise and blame. And in praising or blaming someone, one generally has a moral theory (or at least the outlines of a moral theory) in mind; in order to decide that someone is blameworthy for x, one must first decide that x is bad. Let us call the

moral theory that is being used (explicitly or implicitly) to evaluate A
the "relevant" moral theory or "the theory in use." When I say that
x is appropriate for moral scrutiny, I will mean that the relevant
moral theory, the theory used to evaluate A, has criteria for moral
evaluation under which x falls. Of course, if one wants one's evaluation of A to be *correct,* the relevant moral theory should be the "correct" or "true" moral theory.

This last point requires some attention. Many doubt that there is a
"correct" moral theory. And if there is no objective moral truth,
moral views cannot properly be deemed correct or incorrect. But in
that case, human actions cannot properly be deemed good or bad,
and human beings cannot properly be praised or blamed. If amoral-
ism undermines my account of moral evaluation, it is because amor-
alism undermines moral evaluation itself. But amoralists are not the
only ones who deny that there is a correct moral theory. Moral relativists hold that moral judgments are true or false only relative to a
given moral theory T. For example, social relativists think my act is
good or bad only relative to the prevailing beliefs of my society. In
general, they hold, praise or blame is deserved only with respect to a
moral theory T. (For a social relativist, T will be the moral code of
my society.) But even if the moral relativists are right, A is blameworthy (according to T) to the extent that his moral outlook is flawed
(according to T). My comments about A's moral view being "correct" apply, *mutatis mutandis,* to his view's being correct *according
to T.*

Again, we must keep clearly in mind the difference between my
making a moral evaluation of A based on my positive morality plus
what I know of A, and the moral truth about A. Obviously, in judging you, I can use only the moral theory *I* think is correct. And I
must use my best guess about the psychological story to be told
about you. When you judge yourself, you will perhaps use a different
moral theory to determine which traits rate "moral demerits" and
which traits rate "moral brownie points." Which moral theory is
used to evaluate someone, then, depends upon who is doing the evaluating. But unless the relativists or amoralists are right, my evaluation of you will be correct to the extent that my moral theory is (or
approximates) the true one. I should use moral argument and rational scrutiny to make my moral theory as close as possible to the
correct one, but there is, of course, no guarantee. Thus my judgments
about you are always fallible; I may be mistaken in my beliefs about
how good or bad a trait is, and I may be mistaken about you, about
what your values and attitudes are. However, virtually all of our

judgments about anything are fallible. It is not irrational of me to plan for tomorrow, based on my belief that I will be alive then, even though it is possible that I will die in thirty seconds. As in all things, we do the best we can.

Restrictions on the Relevant Moral Theory

It is obvious that one cannot give a detailed and rigorous account of moral responsibility that will accommodate *every* moral theory, no matter how bizarre. Recall our strange moral theory according to which size is the only value. Given that theory, one would not be responsible for killing saints or raping nuns, although one would be responsible for being short. And, after all, to one who holds this peculiar view, the fact that I chose to kill a saint, did so, and bragged about it afterward would have no moral significance; those facts would be irrelevant to any moral evaluations of me he might make. Moreover, on such a moral theory there is no such thing as negligence; there is nothing one *ought to do* except, perhaps, be tall. So in order to discuss, in any detail, negligence, responsibility for emotions, and such, we will have to make certain assumptions about the relevant moral theory. Since I wish to give a detailed account, I will make several such assumptions. Not all of what I say depends upon the correctness of all of these assumptions; the reader who rejects one of them will still find many of my arguments applicable.[3]

The word "moral," as I use the term, is quite broad. In general, any evaluation of one's outlook, one's "mental set," is a morally good, bad, or neutral thing, a proper subject for moral scrutiny. The reasons for this construal of "morality" were touched upon in Chapter II. There is nothing valuable *per se* about the physical world of quarks and electron states. Morality has application only to world-views, to the ways we see the states of quarks and electron states as significant, as falling under a conceptual framework of goals, aesthetic canons, charientic standards, and so forth. Conversely, what makes human beings subject to moral evaluation is the fact that they, unlike stones, "make sense of" the world about them by bringing standards of evaluation to the optical irradiation patterns to which they are subject. Hence human beings are good or bad to the extent that their worldviews are good or bad.

In sum, I assume that the relevant moral theory has criteria for evaluating (as good, bad or indifferent) all judgments, as well as the dispositions, attitudes, beliefs, emotions, and the like that express or reflect such judgments. For the sake of convenience, I will make certain natural assumptions about these criteria; murder, I will assume, is a bad thing, while concern for the welfare of others is a good thing.[4]

Explanation of Condition 2

The second condition for moral responsibility is that whatever moral taint or luster x possesses attaches to A. That is, to the extent that x is morally offensive or illustrious, A is morally offensive or illustrious. For example, although Cain's killing of Abel is morally pernicious, my moral worth is not diminished by Abel's death. On the other hand, my choosing to ski rather than read detective stories does affect my moral status and so satisfies condition 2. True, my choice is (presumably) morally neutral. But *were* choosing to ski judged, in general, morally offensive, my having chosen to ski would mean that I am (to that extent) morally imperfect. Indeed, someone who holds that physical activity is morally preferable to mental activity would consider me to be morally flawed because I preferred reading to skiing. In short, I am morally accountable for my choice, must bear the moral cost, if any, of my choice, even though, as a matter of fact, I incur no moral credits or debits. Put another way, the moral value of my choice, whether positive or negative, is added to my "moral score," my moral account. Since the value of choosing to ski is zero (neither positive nor negative), my moral account is unaffected by adding to it the moral value, for better or worse, of my decision to ski. Condition 2 is satisfied, then, when the moral worth of x, whether negative, positive, or zero, is transferrable to the moral worth of A.

Concluding Remarks

When I claim, then, that A is morally responsible for x, all I am saying is that x is appropriate material for moral scrutiny (according to the moral theory in use) and that any moral undesirability or desirability that attaches to x attaches as well to A. Now I am quite willing to admit that there are other ways in which the word "responsibility" is often employed. And perhaps Ted Honderich is right that *ordinarily* when we say that someone is responsible for something, we presuppose that he could have done otherwise.[5] But that is not what I will mean when I say that A is responsible for x. In other words, whether the ability to have done otherwise is a prerequisite for responsibility is a substantial question about responsibility. It is not a question about the meaning or definition of the phrase "moral responsibility." This is a crucial point that must be kept firmly in mind. For much of what follows will depend on it.

AN ACCOUNT OF RESPONSIBILITY

The outlines of my conception of responsibility are now visible. As moral agents, we are each a worldview in operation, that is, the framework of attitudes, judgments, values, commitments, perceptions dispositions, and the like embodied in our circumstances, acts, thoughts, and feels. To the extent, then, that my attitudes and judgments are morally unsavory, I am morally unsavory. For my attitudes and judgments (partially) constitute what I am as a moral agent. So whatever is morally flawed or lustrous in my worldview is a flaw or virtue of mine. Thus I am responsible for, accountable for, and can be praised or blamed for, my worldview, for the way the attitudes, beliefs, dispositions, goals, values, judgments, and perceptions that constitute my unique outlook on the world are expressed in my behavior, thoughts, feelings, and circumstances.

We still lack, however, a rigorous account of responsibility and a clear way of applying this conception to the intricacies of human life. This section develops such an account. Before supplying that account, let me remind the reader that what I am calling "moral responsibility" amounts, roughly, to moral evaluability: to say that I am responsible for something means that I can be judged a better or worse person because of it. My view is thus roughly equivalent to saying that we should eliminate the "ordinary" notion of moral responsibility and replace it with the concept of moral evaluability, since, I will try to show, moral evaluability can do all the work for us that moral responsibility is supposed to do.

Criteria for Responsibility

The basic idea of my account is that people are responsible for instantiating properties that express their worldviews. Not all such properties count; they must include all the information required by the moral theory used to evaluate the agent, and the agent must be a full person at the time (that is, she must have a fully developed worldview that is properly expressed in her behavior). So I am responsible for the sufficiently specific traits I instantiate (while I am a full moral person) that express my worldview.

More precisely, a person, A, is responsible for instantiating a trait, P, if and only if

1. P is a contextually bound (that is, sufficiently specific) trait partially constitutive of personhood,
2. A (properly) evidences or instantiates P, and
3. A is a full moral agent while instantiating P.

Each of these conditions requires some explanation.

Condition 1 requires two things. First, P must be partially constitutive of personhood. It must be one of those traits whose possession, collectively, makes A the unique moral person he is. As we saw in Chapter II, a trait P is partially constitutive of A's personhood if it expresses or helps constitute A's worldview. So being selfish and liking spinach are partially constitutive of personhood, but being short and having blue eyes are not. Second, P must be "contextually bound." By this I mean that P must be sufficiently specific; vague traits are not proper grist for the moral mill. For example, showing disrespect for the law in Nazi Germany is relevantly different from showing a similar disrespect in a society with good laws. So *having shown disrespect for the law* is too vague a trait for which to hold A responsible (it is insufficiently contextualized). The trait must contain more information. (Perhaps *having shown disrespect for the law in a society that has evil and murderous laws* would suffice.)

How specific must a trait be in order to avoid being "too vague"? What information, in other words, must be provided in order for a trait to be sufficiently contextualized? The answer is provided by the relevant moral theory, that is, the theory we are using to evaluate A. As we saw earlier, each moral theory tells us which things count toward being good or bad. A trait is sufficiently specific (for that moral theory) when it includes all of the relevant factors that count toward being good or bad. Suppose, for example, that our moral theory says that sincerity is all that counts. Then P must include all the relevant information that would help us decide if A is sincere. For example, *having said "x"* is too vague. In deciding whether saying "x" expresses sincerity or insincerity on A's part, we need to know whether A thought "x" was true. So we cannot hold A responsible for the trait *having said "x"*. The relevant trait, the one for which we hold A responsible, might be something like *having said "x" while believing that "x" was false*. In other words, if some fact about A or A's circumstances would cast additional light on the extent and manner in which A's instantiating P reflects sincerity or insincerity, that fact must be contained in P. Otherwise P is not sufficiently specific. In general, a trait is sufficiently contextualized for a given moral theory T if and only if it contains all the information T requires in order to make a complete moral evaluation of the situation.

So even though there are many ways of describing any act or circumstance, there is, for each moral theory, a "correct" description. Each moral theory gives us a set of traits that are sufficiently specific:

for every moral theory there is a correct parsing of each case into contextually bound traits. If Harry slaps his landlord, the correct parsing of his slap into traits (according to theory T) is the parsing that provides a full data report for a moral evaluation (according to the criteria provided by T).

Of course, it is often convenient to speak somewhat loosely, to include some features that may not, ultimately, be relevant, or to exclude others that are. For many purposes, it is enough to give an *approximately* correct description of the trait for which someone is responsible. Precision is often cumbersome and unnecessary. (Remember Wittgenstein's remark that saying "stand roughly there" is usually more useful than telling someone to occupy a precise latitude and longitude). But when precision is required, it is available.

Condition 2 is rather straightforward. It simply states that one cannot be held responsible for a trait one does not instantiate. Of course, one can be held responsible for instantiating the trait of *not* having done x. And one may be held responsible for approving of what someone else did or for causing someone to do x. In such cases, one is responsible for the trait of having approved of or caused x. And those are traits one did instantiate.

Condition 3 requires A to have a certain moral status; he must be a full moral person. That is, he cannot be held responsible for instantiating P unless, at the time he instantiated P, he had an adult worldview that was properly reflected in his activities. Small children and catatonics do not meet this condition and so may escape responsibility for many of the traits they instantiate. The notion of full moral agency is discussed in more detail in Chapters II and V.

To summarize, then, traits partially constitutive of personhood are attributable features of one's states, activities, and attendant circumstances that express, embody, and/or constitute one's worldview. One's worldview, in turn, is the network of attitudes, dispositions, and such that express, embody, and/or constitute one's manner of seeing and responding to the world. One is morally responsible, I hold, for instantiating all and only those traits that (1) reflect, express, or embody one's worldview or the manner in which that worldview is reflected in one's behavior, (2) provide a full data report for the relevant moral theory, and (3) are instantiated by one while one has a fully developed worldview that is properly reflected in one's behavior.

It will prove helpful, I think, to show how this account of moral responsibility applies to some traditionally puzzling situations. In the next section, we will examine duress, negligence, and ignorance. The discussion should clarify both my position and its advantages over more traditional approaches to moral responsibility.

Duress, Negligence, and Ignorance

Suppose that Mickey is told he will be summarily shot unless he tells a small lie. Mickey, we will assume, has good reason to take this threat seriously. So he tells the lie. Traditional moral wisdom holds that Mickey is not responsible for telling a lie.[6] Mickey's choice, it is sometimes said, was not "free." So we cannot hold him responsible for lying. A few traditionalists regard Mickey's act as voluntary. Kenny, for example, says, "It is clear that the allowance of necessity and duress cannot be argued for on the grounds that actions done under these compulsions are not voluntary actions."[7] Still, most traditionalists think Mickey can't be held responsible. And, in any case, we do not blame Mickey for lying.

Cases like Mickey's produce a certain sense of uneasiness. After all, it was within Mickey's power not to lie. In fact, he would have told the truth had he been willing to risk the consequences. Moreover, whether we blame Mickey depends on the nature of the threat. In some cases, we might blame Mickey for buckling under. For example, suppose someone threatens to tickle Billie unless Billie shoots his brother. Here duress is no excuse. Being shot is considerably worse than being tickled. So Billie ought to have suffered being tickled rather than shoot his brother. It is unclear, then, how much duress is needed to free us from responsibility. In fact, there seem to be intermediate cases. As Kenny points out, neither duress nor necessity is an excuse for murder under English law.[8] But consider Dillon's plight. Dillon's brother is kidnapped by gangsters. Dillon is told that unless he shoots his landlord, the gangsters will murder his brother. If Dillon reluctantly kills his landlord, he may be blameworthy. But surely Dillon is not as blameworthy as someone who kills out of avarice.

Aristotle had rather mixed feelings about such cases. He calls such acts "in a sense voluntary, in a sense not," although they are "more like voluntary actions" (1110a10–20). And Aristotle's criterion, that the "moving power or principle" not be "external to the agent," is not very helpful. It would not be wholly incorrect to say that the cause of Mickey's lying was the threat of execution. But neither would it be entirely wrong to say that the causes of his lying were internal to Mickey. Insofar as intentions and desires ever cause acts, Mickey's lie was caused by his intention or decision to lie, his desire to avoid death, and so forth. In any case, his mouth and tongue were controlled by his central nervous system. Mickey's telling the lie is not like being blown by the wind. So the voluntarity of acts done under duress or necessity is notoriously difficult to assess. Thus duress is problematic for traditional accounts of responsibility. I am not saying that the problems posed by duress for traditional approaches are insoluble. But they are pressing and difficult, and any "solution" is likely to be quite controversial.

On my account, however, acts done under duress pose few difficulties. Duress, I suggest, does not diminish one's responsibility in the slightest. It does, however, modify *what* one is responsible for. And if what one is responsible for is less evil, then one is less blameworthy. Now my account helps us analyze Mickey's case in three ways. First, by analyzing traits instead of acts, we can be more specific and flexible about what Mickey is responsible for. We can distinguish, for example, between *having lied* and *having lied under threat of execution*. These are two distinct traits. By contrast, the traditional account cannot make this distinction easily. It analyzes acts. And having lied and having lied under threat of execution are not two different acts Mickey performs, but two ways of describing the same act.[9] Second, the requirement that traits be sufficiently specific and constitutive of personhood helps us find the right traits. Finally, my account helps explain why Mickey is not blameable and Billie is.

Let us look more closely at the case of Mickey, for it illustrates well the way in which my account of responsibility works. By telling his lie, Mickey instantiates numerous traits. A trait, after all, is simply an ascribable feature, and there are many features we can ascribe to Mickey as a result of his having lied. Mickey instantiates, for example, the trait of having told a lie. However he is not responsible for that trait, since it is insufficiently specific. (It leaves out data required for a full moral evaluation.) Presumably, the moral theory in use considers telling a lie under threat of death, if a bad thing at all, not as morally odious as telling a lie for the thrill of deception. So the fact that Mickey was threatened is morally relevant. Hence *having told a lie* is insufficiently specific. So Mickey is not responsible for instantiating the trait *having told a lie*.

Now the traditionalist may wish to insist that the reason we think telling a lie under threat of death less bad than telling one for the thrill of deception has to do with voluntarity. I disagree. After all, both Billie and Mickey were threatened. Yet the fact that Billie was threatened with tickling does not absolve him in the least. What distinguishes the two cases is not a difference in voluntarity. The reason lying under threat of execution is less heinous than lying for the thrill of it is not that it is less voluntary.[10] The reason lying under threat of execution is less heinous than lying for the thrill of it is not that it is less voluntary. Rather, lying for the thrill of it shows unconcern about the truth, while telling a lie in order to save one's life does not. Mickey's act shows only that Mickey values his life more than unswerving honesty. And one can value honesty highly even if one values one's life more. Indeed, Mickey's moral judgment, that one's life counts more than small dishonesties, is, presumably, the correct (or at least nearly correct) moral judgment. By contrast, Billie showed that he valued not being tickled over respecting the fundamental rights of others. And that is clearly an incorrect moral judgment. Billie's values are fundamentally flawed.

Mickey also instantiated the trait of having told a small lie in order to avoid being murdered. That trait is (presumably) sufficiently contextualized. It gives us the information our moral theory needs to approve of that trait. It is also partially constitutive of personhood. The fact that Mickey is willing to tell a lie rather than face execution tells us something about the sort of person he is; it reflects his worldview. (It shows he values life more than he values absolute honesty.) So, given that he is a full moral agent at the time, Mickey is responsible for instantiating the trait of having told a small lie under threat of immediate execution. The relevant moral theory, we are supposing, deems this trait to be morally neutral; it is neither a good thing nor a bad thing. Billie, on the other hand, is responsible for instantiating the trait of having shot his brother under threat of immediate tickling. That trait is blameworthy, since it is, presumably, wrong (incorrect) to value avoiding the small discomfort of being tickled more than the lives of others.

So duress, according to my account, does not diminish responsibility; rather, it modifies the traits for which one is responsible. And this seems to be the correct result. Whether one is blameworthy for yielding to duress is a matter for a moral theory to decide, not an account of moral responsibility. After all, according to most moral theories it is morally permissible to lie in certain circumstances. Which circumstances warrant lying depends upon the moral theory. Act utilitarianism, for example, holds that lying is permissible if the total resultant happiness (that is, the total happiness produced minus the total unhappiness produced) of lying is greater than the total resultant happiness of telling the truth. A strict Kantian, by contrast, might hold that one ought never to lie under any circumstances (in which case the trait evidenced by Mickey *is* morally pernicious). In other words, it is a direct consequence of act utilitarianism that Mickey ought to lie, and a direct consequence of strict Kantianism that Mickey ought to speak the truth. Thus whether or not Mickey is blameworthy is not a question about moral responsibility, but a question of normative ethics, a question about the moral permissibility of lying under threat of execution. The important question is not whether Mickey's lying and Billie's shooting are compelled, but whether it is wrong to lie when threatened with execution, and whether it is wrong to kill to avoid being tickled.

One may put the point as follows. Would Mickey say that his lie was *justified*, that he did the *right thing* in the circumstances, or would he say that there is nothing to justify, that he is simply not accountable for the words that came out of his mouth? Surely he would say the former. By way of contrast, one would not try to justify a muscle spasm. There is nothing to justify, for one is (normally) simply not accountable for muscle spasms. It seems clear, then, that Mickey is accountable for his choice. After all, Mickey was simply presented with a difficult choice. And surely we are accountable for our difficult choices; we can be asked to justify them, deserve blame for choosing wrongly, and sometimes deserve praise for choosing correctly. After all, a supererogatory resistance to duress is surely praiseworthy. But if one is accountable for resisting duress, why is one not also accountable (though perhaps not blameworthy) for not resisting it? In both cases one made a choice that can be morally evaluated, deemed a right choice or a wrong choice. Indeed, it is often the difficult choices that most reveal our moral characters. Thus the reason we do not blame Mickey is not because he is not accountable for his choice, but because he made the right (or at least an acceptable) choice.

In sum, then, Mickey is responsible for several of the traits he instantiates when telling the lie and not responsible for many others. Since the traits for which he is responsible are morally neutral, Mickey is not blameworthy. And they are morally neutral because they reflect acceptable moral values. By contrast, some of the traits for which Billie is responsible are blameworthy. Thus Billie and Mickey are equally *responsible* for the traits for which they bear responsibility. But the traits for which Billie is responsible are (morally) *bad* traits, while the traits for which Mickey bears responsibility are not. In other words, duress does not diminish responsibility in the slightest. It may well, however, affect the nature (and so the blameworthiness) of the traits one is responsible for evidencing.

Recklessness and negligence also illustrate the virtues of my account. The difference between recklessness and negligence can be simply stated. A person is reckless if she *knowingly* takes an improper risk, if she was *aware* of the risk, and she is negligent if she takes an improper risk she *should have* known about or been mindful of, whether she actually thought about it or not. Recklessness thus depends on what one *is* aware or conscious of, negligence on what one *ought to be* aware or conscious of.

Acts of negligence and acts performed in ignorance are problematic for traditional accounts. Suppose, for example, that Joel causes an automobile accident because he did not check local traffic laws before driving. He is, let us say, an American driving in England and does not know that in England one drives on the left side of the road. His English brother Buster causes a similar accident, not because he is ignorant of local driving laws, but because he is careless about obeying them. In an important sense, Buster and Joel perform the same (types of) actions. They may even, in some sense, have made the same choices (for Buster may not have chosen to drive on the wrong side of the road; he may simply not have paid proper attention). Yet their moral situations are markedly different.

Again, this is not a decisive rebuttal of the traditional view. But any traditional analysis of Joel's and Buster's cases will be difficult and controversial (it will raise, for example, controversial questions about the nature of voluntarity).

On my account, however, the matter is relatively simple. Joel is responsible for instantiating numerous traits. He is responsible for some but not all of them. He is not, for example, responsible for instantiating the trait of having caused a traffic accident; that trait is insufficiently contextualized. Relevant information is lacking. We need to know more about the circumstances of the accident before we can evaluate it morally. We do not know which values are involved. Nor is Joel responsible for evidencing the trait of having unintentionally caused an accident, for that trait is not partially constitutive of personhood. One cannot, after all, answer (even in part) the question "what sort of person is Joel?" by saying "the kind of person who unintentionally caused a traffic accident." That does not reveal anything about his worldview. Of course, we do characterize people as "accident-prone," and perhaps in this sense "the sort of person who unintentionally causes accidents" is a partial answer to the question "what sort of person is Joel?" But now the relevant trait is "being accident-prone." This trait, when properly analyzed, may reveal something about Joel's worldview (for example, he is careless). If so, he is responsible for being careless. But then one *ought* to be held

responsible for being careless. And if Joel's accident reveals carelessness on his part (whether or not the carelessness was an important
causal factor), then Joel is responsible for having been careless. In
any case, one can certainly answer the question "what kind of person
is Joel?" by saying "the kind of person who does not bother to check
local traffic laws before driving." This trait *does* reveal something
about Joel's worldview, about his attitudes toward the safety of
others, the inconvenience of having to look up the law, and so on.
So, other things being equal, Joel is responsible for instantiating the
trait of not having bothered to check local traffic laws before driving.

Of course, other things may not be equal; there may be relevant
circumstances not reported by the trait mentioned above. If Joel's
drive was occasioned by an emergency, that information is (presumably) relevant to a moral assessment. For now a different set of values
is involved (including the importance of saving a life). In that case,
Joel is not responsible for instantiating the trait *not having bothered
to check local traffic laws;* that trait is insufficiently specific. Again, if
there is no reason for Joel to consider seriously the possibility that
local traffic laws may differ from those to which he is accustomed,
the trait mentioned above may be insufficiently contextualized. If, for
example, the relevant moral theory adheres to the so-called "reasonable man" standard, then the trait in question is sufficiently specific
only if it contains all information needed to determine whether Joel
took the care that a reasonable person would have exercised in his
circumstances. (Note that Joel would still be responsible for evidencing the trait *having failed to check local traffic laws before driving
under circumstances in which reasonable care would not require
checking local traffic laws.* But that trait is morally neutral, so Joel
would not be blameworthy.)

The crucial lesson to be learned from Joel's ill fortune is that negligence always presupposes an unacceptable ranking of values on the
part of the negligent individual. In Joel's case, to say that his failure
to check local traffic laws is negligent is to assert, for example, that
Joel did not place a high enough value on the safety of other motorists. For had he placed more importance on their safety, he would
have thought that the risk to their safety, though, as far as he knew,
rather slight, outweighed the three extra minutes of sleep he gained
by not getting up earlier to look up the law, to make sure that no
curious but important feature of English traffic laws escaped his attention.

Cases of negligence are not always this straightforward. Sometimes
the "point of negligence" occurs higher up in the chain of events.

Suppose, for example, that I make a joking remark about having a heart attack to a friend whose father has just died of a heart attack. I did not mean to be cruel. I just "was not thinking." I am negligent, however, because if I placed a higher value on not hurting my friend, I *would* have been "thinking." We can imagine a different scenario; suppose that I did not know that my friend's father had just died. I may be negligent because, had I placed a higher value on attending to my friend's needs and feelings, I would have noticed that she was unhappy and asked about the cause of her unhappiness. I judged that my desire to tell her a humorous anecdote was of more value than attending to her emotional condition. And such a moral ranking is, presumably, incorrect.

The claim that I am negligent, in other words, is based on the claim that I made an incorrect moral judgment (even if not a conscious or deliberate one). One can be negligent in any of several different ways. But in each case there is a moral failing, an inappropriate ranking of competing values. What is culpable about negligence is not activity, per se, but a defect of worldview expressed by one's act(s) or failure(s) to act.

One consequence of this account of negligence is that one can be negligent even if no harm ensues. I am negligent if I light a match near an open can of gasoline, even if, by good fortune, no explosion occurs. I am negligent if I decided to light the match but discovered that I had no matches in my pocket. I am even negligent if I would have lit the match, but gave the matter no thought because I knew I had no matches. It may well be, of course, that no crime can be committed without an *actus reus,* an illegal act, and that no grounds for a civil suit exist unless some damage is suffered. But I am still *morally* responsible for instantiating blameworthy traits.[11] And this seems to be the right result; I am, on those grounds, a worse person than someone otherwise like me who would not have lit the match even had she had one, and even had she wanted to smoke her pipe. Traditional accounts, which evaluate actions or choices, have no mechanism for expressing this sort of negligence.

Recklessness can be given a similar treatment. A person is reckless if he knowingly assumes a morally culpable risk. Such a risk is morally culpable if it reflects a morally flawed cost-benefit analysis. It is immoral, for example, to hold that the benefit won by driving quickly to the shore (that is, an extra hour on the beach) is worth the risk of killing another motorist. It is immoral to hold this, of course, because it is an incorrect moral judgment. It is simply incorrect that an extra hour on the beach is of more value than the absence of the risk that my speeding poses to others. Again, Buster is responsible for instantiating the trait of failing to pay sufficient heed to which side of the road his car occupied. This does express his worldview, for it shows that he made an incorrect moral judgment about the value of not endangering other motorists. Note that this is a different trait from the trait for which Joel is responsible. Which trait is more blameworthy, of course, is a matter for the relevant moral theory to decide.

Wrong Acts Done from Good Motives

Very often a bad act shows *something* good about the actor. Conversely, many of our acts, even some of our good acts, fall short of moral perfection. A single action, after all, involves numerous traits. Usually, some of these traits are praiseworthy and others blameworthy. As one might expect, my account of responsibility is particularly helpful in analyzing such "mixed" acts. Suppose, for example, that Abner believes that all non-Christians will suffer eternal torment unless killed with a silver knife, and so, after his best attempts at suasion have failed, kills Abgorrah with an argent blade. Abner is responsible for instantiating several traits. Some of these are praiseworthy. It is hard to deny, after all, that showing concern for another is a good thing and equally hard to deny that Abner showed concern for Abgorrah's welfare. So Abner deserves praise for his concern (he is praiseworthy for instantiating the property of having shown concern for another's well-being) and for his courage and commitment in pursuing his moral vision. On the other hand, he may be blamed for his fanaticism and for having violated another's rights. We may hold him responsible for having acted irrationally and for having this curious religious belief.[12] If, in Abner's circumstances, it is reasonable to believe as he does, then perhaps having his curious belief is morally neutral. The analysis of Abner's plight can be as complex and multifarious as one's moral theory permits. Clearly, the blame Abner incurs far outweighs the praise he is due. Overall, he acted wrongly and should not have killed Abgorrah. But the fact remains that he is due some praise. My view, by evaluating each trait singly, gives a precise account of the moral credits and debits Abner has accrued. By contrast, the traditional view permits only a single question: "Was Abner responsible for killing Abgorrah?"

Before going on, it may be helpful to summarize briefly the main points illustrated by our discussion of duress, negligence, recklessness, and "mixed" acts. First, when one performs an action, one instantiates more than one trait. Some of those traits do not meet the criteria for moral responsibility. They are too vague or do not reflect one's worldview. (How specific a trait must be depends on the moral theory in use. It must provide all the information the moral theory requires.) Some of the traits for which we are responsible carry blame, some carry praise, and others are morally neutral. Duress and mitigating circumstances do not diminish responsibility. Rather, they alter the traits for which we are responsible. Finally, my account makes it relatively easy to give a satisfactory analysis of some cases that have seemed puzzling or difficult for more traditional accounts of responsibility.

Responsibility for Emotions

One rather striking result of my account is that we are responsible for our emotions. Most traditionalists have disagreed. We cannot be blamed for our emotions, they have claimed, because our emotions are not within our control. A minority of traditionalists have tried to argue that we can control our emotions. I am going to suggest that we are responsible for our emotions *whether or not we can control them*. This has two noteworthy consequences. First, the extent to which we can "control" our emotions has always been a thorny tangle of problems. My view avoids that thicket altogether. But the crucial point is that, since my argument that we are responsible for our emotions does not make or depend upon the assumption that we can control our emotions, it follows that we can, at least in principle, be held responsible for things we cannot control. For we would be responsible for our emotions whether or not we could control them. Thus responsibility for emotions is a kind of test case. If my argument is convincing, the traditional view is wrong. For if we are responsible for our emotions whether or not we can control them, then control cannot be a central prerequisite for moral responsibility.[13]

WHY WE ARE RESPONSIBLE FOR OUR EMOTIONS. At first blush, it may seem that we never blame people for their emotions. I suggest, however, that we often judge people adversely because of their emotions.[14] Consider the case of Charlie. Charlie derives great pleasure from the sight of animals in pain. Mind you, he never *causes* animals to suffer. But when he comes upon a wounded animal, the sight affords him much delight.

Now recall that all it means to say that Charlie is responsible for relishing the sight of animals in pain is (1) that enjoying the sight of animals in pain is the sort of thing moral theories evaluate, and (2) that to the extent that such enjoyment is a good or bad thing, Charlie is morally illustrious or flawed. Both of these conditions, I will argue, are met.

It seems hard to deny that the first condition is met. Delighting in the pain of animals seems to me, at least, to reflect values that are simply unacceptable. It bespeaks a lack of concern and compassion. (Ordinarily, at least, if one is truly committed to concern and compassion for other beings, one cannot feel delight when they suffer.) And this is a bad thing; it is opposed to the correct moral stance. If concern for others is morally valuable, then feelings that reflect indifference to the sufferings of others are morally undesirable. Surely it would be preferable, from a moral standpoint, were such enjoyment not to occur. (Even a utilitarian, who values happiness, might hold that valuing happiness in others is preferable, morally speaking, to not valuing happiness in others.) But even if we suppose that enjoying the pain of animals is morally neutral, condition 1 is met. This is just the sort of question to which we turn to a moral theory for guidance. It is appropriate to inquire about the moral desirability of such feelings. Delight in the suffering of others is the sort of thing to which a moral calculus can be applied; one's moral theory ought to take a stand on Charlie's feeling. And that is all that is required for condition 1 to be met.

It seems equally odd to deny that the second condition is met. To the extent that taking pleasure in the pain of animals is morally unsavory, Charlie is morally unsavory. After all, if concern for the well-being of others is morally valuable, it seems impossible to deny that Charlie would be morally improved were he to stop enjoying the sight of animals in pain. Again, surely someone who is otherwise just like Charlie but does not enjoy the torments of animals is morally preferable to Charlie. So Charlie would be a morally better person were he to stop taking such sadistic pleasure. And hence it seems absurd to claim that although Charlie's feeling is morally odious, and that although Charlie would be a better person were he to stop having that feeling, Charlie himself is in no way morally flawed.

So Charlie is responsible for enjoying the sufferings of beasts even though his conduct is faultless and even if he cannot help feeling the way he does. Nothing in the above argument requires that Charlie be able to control his emotion. So even if he can, in fact, control his emotion, his responsibility for that emotion does not *rest upon* his ability to control it.

At this point the reader may be tempted to say any of several things. First, she might say this result is counterintuitive; it seems wrong to hold someone responsible for his emotions. How can we blame Charlie, particularly if he never acts badly, if he never tries to cause animals to suffer? Second, she might object that we can control our emotions; she may say, with Sartre, that we can choose our emotions, or she might say that we can do various things to bring about a change in our emotional responses. Third, she might agree that we are responsible for our emotions in my restricted sense of "responsibility." But it is not that restricted sense with which we ought to be concerned. I will answer each of these in turn. (Several further reasons for thinking that we cannot be responsible for what we cannot control are considered in the section entitled "Objections.")

COUNTERINTUITIVENESS. Three things about my claim seem "counterintuitive." First, we seem to have a prephilosophical conviction that people are not responsible for emotions they cannot help feeling. Second, more generally, my view seems to make us responsible for almost everything, and so it seems as if it is not humanly possible to avoid moral condemnation. Finally, my view seems to have several counterintuitive consequences. None of these charges, I will argue, provides a good reason for rejecting my view.

No doubt it does seem odd to say that Charlie is responsible for his emotions even if he cannot help having them. But a bit of reflection may help to soften our prejudice.

The first point to remember is that there are several legitimate uses of the term "responsible." I am only claiming that Charlie is responsible for his emotions in one of these senses. There may be other senses in which he is not responsible. My claim is just that Charlie may be judged adversely, deemed morally defective, because of his emotion. And it is not so odd to say that Charlie's emotion makes him a morally worse person. For the fact that Charlie enjoys the sight of an afflicted animal does, after all, reveal something about him as a moral being. Whether or not they are chosen, our emotions express and partially embody our values, our moral outlook. As we saw in Chapter II, the pleasure Rolfe feels when an attractive stranger smiles at him depends upon a variety of values Rolfe holds; he feels pleasure because, for example, the smile reinforces Rolfe's belief that he, Rolfe, is a handsome fellow, and because Rolfe has certain attitudes about the value of physical attractiveness or about the value of things one can expect to obtain because one is attractive. Thus Rolfe's emotion, like Charlie's, draws upon, expresses, is shaped by, and embodies a complex network of attitudes, values, aspirations, expectations, and the like.

Here some readers may doubt the link between values and emotions. Emotions, some might say, are irrational urges that have a life of their own, as it were. Perhaps Charlie's emotions violate, rather than reflect, his values. Poor Charlie is the victim, as it were, of runaway emotions. But if the discussion in Chapter II is correct, this is nonsense. Neither emotions nor values are little pieces of us. Emotions are not mere sensations. Much less are they peculiar forces, pushing us about willy-nilly. Rather, our emotions and our values are elements of the story we tell about ourselves, part of the way we make sense of our behavior and experience. We attribute values and emotions to someone by telling a coherent story about her. So there is a sense in which, at least by and large, our emotions *have* to fit our values.

Now what Charlie's emotion reveals is that there is something morally offensive about the values and attitudes Charlie holds. And surely someone who has morally invidious values is a morally flawed person. Since salubrious values are morally better than invidious values, I cannot see how one can deny that Charlie would be morally better were he to exchange his invidious values for salubrious ones. Thus to the extent that Charlie's emotions are morally invidious, Charlie is morally invidious. And that is all I mean by saying that he is "responsible" for his emotions.

Indeed, it seems bizarre to say that although Charlie's feelings are morally unsavory, Charlie is in no way morally unsavory. To say this is, it would seem, to deny that Charlie's emotions are part of what he is, to make Charlie's emotions external to him. Just as an ugly hat can be worn by a beautiful person, the traditional view seems to be saying, so a good person can have evil emotions. But this view of Charlie is surely mistaken. His feelings, after all, are not external appendages with which he finds himself burdened; they are not, as it were, lint clinging to his moral agency. Charlie is not some mythical "pure chooser," devoid of emotions, who is reduced, as it were, to choosing between the buttons on some "inner console," a moral ghost whose choices are limited by the emotions, aptitudes, and attitudes his console includes. Charlie is not a homunculus inhabiting the nether regions of Charlie's skull, who cannot be faulted because the console at his disposal does not contain the button "do not feel this emotion." Rather, Charlie's emotions are part of the person he is, part of his moral being. And so if Charlie's emotions are invidious, then to that extent Charlie is invidious. (We will meet the pure chooser again later in this chapter.)

Does this not, the reader might be tempted to ask, make us responsible for *too much*? Does not my view consign us all to lives of unremitting blame? In a sense it does: to err is human, and moral perfection is not humanly attainable. However, it does not follow that we must spend our lives in self-castigation. First, although almost every time we feel an emotion we are thereby responsible for *something*, what we are responsible for need not be very bad. After all, my view insists upon a fine-grained analysis in terms of traits: the traits must be specific, and we must be judged on the basis of all the appropriate traits involved, good and ill. This has two important consequences. First, Jones's failure to feel grief at the death of her mother may turn out, when the psychological story to be told about her is fully articulated, not to be as bad as it may seem. What Jones's lack of feeling shows about her need not be the same as what Meursault's in Camus's *The Stranger* shows about him. It might show, for example, only that she is in shock. Although she is responsible for going into shock at the news of her mother's death, that does not seem to be a very bad trait. Second, we should be evaluated on the *balance* between our moral "brownie points" and our moral "demerits," not simply castigated for our imperfections. Indeed, a theory of moral responsibility according to which it was plausible that a human being might never be responsible for any failing is not true to the character of human life. Even the best of us is flawed in many ways. This does not, however, mean that human beings are by nature evil, or bad, or sinful. A good person who is not morally perfect is nonetheless a good person and should be praised and valued. She has reason to take pride in the moral luster of her life. Morality, I insist, is not an insatiable parent who ignores our successes and virtues and scolds us for every minor imperfection. Good is good enough for anyone short of the angels.

PRAISE AND BLAME. "Maybe you are right that Charlie is a worse person because he enjoys the suffering of animals," the traditionalist might say. "But unless he can help his feeling, it is improper to blame him for being a bad person or to praise him for being a good person." To answer this worry, we have to look a little more closely at the notions of praise and blame.[15]

We might praise an athlete for her strength, a rose for its sheen, or a hen for the number of eggs it lays. In this sense, praise is merely recognition that someone or something has a quality or property thought to be desirable. But what is of interest to moral responsibility, the traditionalist will say, is moral praise. Now I am tempted to say that moral praise is merely recognition that someone has a quality or property thought to be morally lustrous. And so if Charlie has a morally lustrous trait, however he came to have it, it is certainly appropriate to recognize that fact. So moral praise is due Charlie, whether or not he could help being good.

But the traditionalist will not be content with this answer. She will say that something's being "morally lustrous" cannot just mean that morality requires us to see it as a good thing. For surely morality obliges us to welcome as desirable the end of a famine. And so a drought that relieves a famine would be morally praiseworthy. And this is absurd. So "morally lustrous" must mean something like "intrinsically moral." And, if she has Kantian inclinations, she might say that nothing is intrinsically moral except a good will; only acts freely chosen with regard for the right are intrinsically morally worthy.

But of course it is this last assertion I wish to deny. What is good, ultimately, is a certain sort of life: a life of reflection, commitment, care and concern for the value of others, and so forth. In another sense, what is good is having the correct moral views and commitments. The good life and the good worldview are inseparable. As I suggested, to have a belief or view is for a certain kind of story about the whole of one's life to meet certain criteria of explanation. Conversely, we cannot describe a good life, in a way that captures what is good about it, without explicitly or implicitly adverting to moral views and commitment. A good person's life, when described purely in neutral behavioral terms, is no longer recognizable as good. (Imagine what such a description would look like: "now she moves her arm two centimeters," and so forth.) The good life is good because it reflects and realizes the correct moral views. And one has the correct moral views insofar as one leads a certain kind of life. One who says "reflection is an important moral good," but who never reflects, either does not have the belief she says she has, or, by sacrificing reflection to other things she values, such as gaining power, shows that she believes that reflection is less fundamentally good than power.

So I want to say that a trait is intrinsically good if it reflects commitment to and belief in correct moral values, and hence, ipso facto, reflects or embodies what is morally significant in human lives. This answer seems to be a plausible one. In any case, it certainly eliminates drought-ending rainfalls and physical strength from the realm of the morally lustrous.

My answer, then, is that moral praise is recognition of commitment to and belief in correct moral values, and so a recognition that a person's life, in some way, realizes what is valuable in human life. Now nothing in this definition demands that the acts that express what is valuable in human life be freely chosen, nor that commitment to correct moral beliefs be within one's control. So if I am right, praise does not require control or free choice.

The only response left to the traditionalist, it seems to be me, is to insist that it is precisely free choice that is valuable in human life. Kant, for example, seems to talk this way, though I think most people misread Kant. In any case, if it is free choice as such that makes human life valuable, then only freely chosen acts are properly morally praised (even if my definition of moral praise is correct). Fortunately, the traditionalist is simply mistaken about the intrinsic value of free choice. The case of the Wanter, I think, shows that there is nothing particularly valuable about free choice as such.

Similar remarks might be made about blame, except that we use the word "blame" in a wider variety of ways. Suppose a more productive coworker is appointed to the position I had hoped to obtain. I may blame her for my not getting a promotion, though I do not think her productivity is a bad thing. So there is a wider variety of nonmoral blame than there is nonmoral praise. In any case, I think moral blame may be characterized as recognition that someone has views hostile to the morally correct views, and so leads a life, in some respect, at odds with what is valuable in human life. (Here "at odds with what is valuable in human life" must mean something more than "not consistent with something of value in human life." After all, one cannot do everything. It is absurd to blame Mother Theresa for not being a great musician, even though, let us assume, music is one of the things that is of value in human life. It would be absurd even if the life of service to immediate human needs, though very good, is less good than the life of service to art. Traits need not be perfect to avoid being bad.)

At this point the traditionalist might respond that my definitions of moral praise and blame capture a legitimate use of the words. But they do not capture the use she has in mind. She might even say that it is part of the very meaning of the word "blame," as she uses it, that the evil trait or act was not inevitable.

Here I would say that it is my use of the words "praise" and "blame" that is important for our moral practices, such as punishment, contract law, moral evaluation, and so forth; we need no extra sense of "praise" and "blame" to explain and justify those practices and concepts. The way to show this, of course, is to produce accounts of punishment, contract law, and such. This task is partially accomplished in Chapter V, which discusses gratitude, resentment, and retribution, and will be completed in future works.

RESISTING EMOTIONS. Nonetheless, one might charge, my view has some counterintuitive consequences. Consider the case of Robert, who not only enjoys the sight of animals in pain, but also tortures them in order to see them suffer. Surely Robert is worse than Charlie. Yet both equally enjoy the sight of animals in pain. Indeed, one might even want to praise Charlie for resisting the temptation to torture animals. Charlie cannot help feeling what he does (let us suppose), but he can control what he does about it. And it is that, the objection runs, for which he should be held responsible.

My response is that, according to my view, Charlie is indeed better than Robert. For Charlie is responsible for instantiating two traits, the trait of having felt enjoyment in the suffering of animals and the trait of refraining from indulging in torturing animals. The former is blameworthy and the latter praiseworthy. Perhaps the praise due him for the latter trait outweighs the blame due him for the former. If our moral theory values overcoming temptation more than never feeling temptation, Charlie is even more praiseworthy than Ellie, who does not torture animals and never felt any pleasure in their suffering. In any case, Charlie is less blameworthy than Robert, who instantiates the particularly evil trait of having tortured animals. Thus my view can account for the difference between Robert and Charlie; it is even consistent with (though it does not entail) Charlie's being a better person than he would be if he never felt the urge to torture animals. So this objection does not tell against my view.

CONTROLLING EMOTIONS. Some philosophers have argued that we are responsible for our emotions because they are within our control.[16] Thus, they might argue, the fact that Charlie is a worse person because of his unsavory emotion does not show that we are responsible for things beyond our control.

This objection misconstrues the nature of my argument. For my argument in this section does not purport to show that we are responsible for things that are, in fact, beyond our control (although several such examples are to be found elsewhere in this work). Rather, it is meant to show that responsibility does not *depend upon* control. That is, I am not arguing that

1. we are responsible for our emotions,
2. we cannot control our emotions, and
3. therefore we are responsible for things beyond our control.

Rather, I am arguing that

1. we are responsible for our emotions *even if* we cannot control them,
2. therefore controlling our emotions is not a precondition for being responsible for them, and
3. therefore control is not a precondition for responsibility.

That is, my argument that we are responsible for our emotions does not depend in any way upon our being able to control our emotions. Hence control is not, *per se,* a requirement for moral responsibility. So my claim here is consistent with the claims (1) that everything we are responsible for is something that we can *in fact* control (though I dispute this elsewhere), and (2) that control is a sufficient condition for moral responsibility. But since the traditional view holds that moral responsibility depends essentially upon control, my claim is enough to show that the traditional view is mistaken.

In any case, the question of control is notoriously vexing.[17] It has proven difficult to define "control" in any satisfying way. Moreover, it seems clear that although I am not "helpless" with respect to my emotions, I do not have any reliable and straightforward method of controlling them. I cannot choose them the way I choose from a dinner menu. ("I think I will feel grief now. No, on second thought, make that amusement.") And although I can do various things that might cause my emotional responses (and the beliefs upon which they are based) to change, our present command of psychological principles is sketchy at best, and so the results of any program of emotional change are rather chancy.

TRIVIALITY. At this point one may tempted to respond as follows. Perhaps it is true that in my special sense of "responsible" Charlie is responsible for his emotions. But my special sense is not what we intend when we make the ordinary-language claim that Charlie is not responsible for his emotions. Thus my claim, although true, is of little interest.

However, if Charlie is morally responsible (in my special sense) for his emotions, there are some important consequences. Condition 2 of my definition of moral responsibility guarantees that Charlie is morally evaluable on the basis of his emotions. In addition, I argue in Chapter V, we may properly resent or feel grateful to him because of his emotions, and, if his emotions are evil, the "desert" requirement for punishing Charlie for his emotions are met. So it is a matter of no small moment that Charlie is responsible, in my sense, for his emotions.

HUME AND MOTIVES

My view has its roots in the Humean insight that character is the font of responsibility. The theory Hume builds on this insight has been criticized in a variety of ways. A few comments regarding the differences between Hume's view and my own might help clarify both what my position is and how it addresses some of the objections raised against Hume's view.[18] Hume asserts that virtue and vice are just the causes of pleasurable and unpleasurable moral sentiments. These sentiments arise in us when we contemplate the motives that caused an agent to act. Hume concludes that agents are responsible, ultimately, for acts committed at liberty, and caused not by passing or casual states of the agent, but by motives that are not themselves considerations of morality, and whose contemplation excites moral pleasure or displeasure.[19] I should like to point out what I take to be six errors in Hume's view.

First, Hume's claim that liberty, suitably defined, is a precondition for moral responsibility opens the door to a variety of objections. If determinism is true, if all our acts are caused in accordance with universal laws of nature, it may be argued, Hume's view violates the Principle of Alternate Possibilities and the dictum that ought implies can. Moreover, some have charged that upbringing and heredity constitute "external violence."[20] That is, although we can will not to be a miser, whether we do or not is a result of our heredity and environment (we cannot will to desire to will not to be one).

Whether or not such arguments succeed is a rather complicated question. I argue that it is preferable to deny that liberty is a precondition for moral responsibility. There are better answers to these objections than arguing, as most compatibilists have done, that even if determinism is true, people still "could have done otherwise" and are "free" in the appropriate sense. Compatibilists' attempts to define "free" and "could have done" have met with much controversy. My view, which does not make liberty a precondition, avoids that particular thicket altogether. Hume, however, cannot adopt this suggestion. For his claim that responsibility depends ultimately upon *causes* of actions does not enable him to say, as I can, that how an act was caused is irrelevant to moral responsibility.[21]

Here, then, is a second error; Hume is quite wrong that persons are only blameable for x if they had a bad motive that *caused* x. For one may be culpable for having blameable motives or attitudes even if those motives caused no relevant actions. As I suggested in Chapter

I, William, who would have abused public trust had he held office, is blameable. But his evil propensity did not cause any actions. Indeed, to take another example from Chapter I, Harry's slapping of his landlord suggests that one can be responsible for something one did not cause at all. Harry's hand struck the face of his landlord without any assistance from Harry himself. Bill's machine caused the slap, not Harry. True, what made Harry blameworthy was his intention to slap the poor landlord. But what is significant is not the causal relation of Harry's intention to the slap (there was none), but what Harry's intention shows about his worldview.

Moreover, because I take the ground of responsibility to be what our actions (among other things) show about us, rather than what causes us to act, when I claim that one may be blamed for x, I am not committed to any particular story about how x was caused. For example, I claim that we are responsible for our emotions. This does not commit me to any particular claims about how emotions are caused. I need assert only that having certain emotions *reveals* something about one's attitudes that may be of moral significance. By way of contrast, Hume seems committed to the rather controversial claim that morally evaluable attitudes *cause* the relevant emotions.

The third error concerns the bearers of responsibility, what it is we are responsible *for*. Hume is never quite clear about this point. He generally speaks as if we were responsible for acts (although he does say that in judging acts we "regard only" motives). For reasons given earlier, I suggest that we are responsible not for acts as such, but for properties we instantiate.

Fourth, Hume seems to think that one is not responsible for one's passing fancies, nor for acts caused by passing fancies; only acts that are caused by enduring motives reflect upon us morally. If he thinks this, he is mistaken, for our passing fancies and momentary passions do not occur randomly; they indicate something about us as moral agents. That Jones has passing fancies for women may show that Jones sometimes regards women not as persons but as pleasant objects. But that attitude is not, in any ordinary sense, the *cause* of his giving Jane a carnation. Of course, if Hume means only that we should not *now* be blamed for acts that show *nothing at all* about what we are *now* like, he is quite right. But what is revealed by actions such as Jones's whimsical floral gift is, often, not properly described as a *cause* of those actions. And so to say that we may be held accountable for what such acts reveal about us is to deny that causes of actions are what ground responsibility.

Fifth, Hume insists that the relevant motive must not itself be or include a moral judgment. And Hume is quite right that if an act's being virtuous is nothing other than its cause exciting moral pleasure, then to say that an act's cause was the agent's regard for that act's virtue would be "to reason in a circle." So much the worse, then, for Hume's account of virtue. For it seems evident that the fact that Jones places great importance upon the morality of his acts while Smith does not is relevant to a moral assessment of Jones and Smith. Surely it is a morally salubrious quality of Jones that he is deeply concerned with the moral character of his acts and a morally unsavory quality of Smith that he is not.

Sixth and finally, Hume begins his argument by assuming that a virtue is merely whatever causes a pleasurable moral sentiment. Thus for Hume the question "under what conditions is A responsible" becomes "when does A excite in us a feeling of moral pleasure or uneasiness of which he is the object?" As a result, Hume's argument is unconvincing to those who do not accept his "moral sentiment" view of ethics. My arguments make no such assumption.

OBJECTIONS

The central conflict between my account and its more traditional rivals concerns the role of autonomy and control. I contend that one can be responsible for what is beyond one's control, provided that the traits involved reflect one's personhood, and that one can be responsible for traits even if one could not do otherwise than instantiate them. More traditional views deny these claims. As Ted Honderich puts it, "In general, ascriptions of responsibility depend on the assumption, which is very nearly universal, that the actions which evoke them are not the only possibilities."[22]

So far we have seen a number of reasons for thinking the traditional view wrong. But a view so widely held cannot be dismissed without examining the reasons behind its nearly universal acceptance. So it is time to consider the arguments that a traditionalist must give to support his position. They do not, I suggest, stand up under close examination.

Self-evidence

Some writers have claimed that it is simply "self-evident" that one cannot be held responsible for things beyond one's control; only the ignorant or the violently angry ever deny it. C. A. Campbell, for example, in the oft-quoted paper "Is Free Will a Pseudo-problem?" claims that those who have attained "a tolerably advanced level of reflection" would not hold an agent responsible for doing x unless the agent "could have chosen otherwise than he actually did."[23] Again, Paul Edwards seems to think it evident that "from the fact that human beings do not ultimately shape their own character . . . it follows that they are never morally responsible." His argument seems to be that people only blame others when they (a) are not aware of a deterministic chain of causes, or (b) do not reflect seriously and in an "educated" manner on this topic, or (c) are "dominated by violent emotions like anger, indignation or hate."[24]

Now as empirical claims, such assertions are simply false (as Richard Brandt points out).[25] Daniel Dennett, Robert Merrihew Adams, and this writer have, presumably, reached a "tolerably advanced level of reflection," and were, when writing, reflecting both seriously and in an "educated" manner, and were not dominated by hatred or anger. Moreover, the preceding discussion has given at least *some* reason for thinking that this purportedly "self-evident" claim is false. So claims of "self-evidence" will not suffice; an argument is needed.

Inanimate Objects

One consideration that might appear to support the traditional view concerns inanimate objects such as cobblestones, corkscrews, and computers. As Ted Honderich writes, "I cannot hold it against the corkscrew that it did what it did, because that was all it could have done. There was, from the point of view of its contribution, no other possibility."[26] The argument seems to go as follows. We do not blame inanimate objects for the harm they cause. The only reason we do not blame inanimate objects is that inanimate objects cannot act otherwise than they do. So were the Principle of Alternate Possibilities not true, it would be rational to excoriate computers and stones for the harm they do. But since it is clearly irrational to blame computers and corkscrews, the Principle of Alternate Possibilities must be correct.

At first glance this argument might seem convincing. In fact, however, there *is* an alternative explanation of our failure to blame computers for their shortcomings and falling stones for the havoc they wreak. For computers and stones lack worldviews (as far as we know). They do not make evaluative judgments, nor do they assent to or dissent from states of affairs. Thus the damage done by a falling stone does not express the stone's worldview; there is no worldview to be expressed.

Conversely, a computer that had bona fide beliefs and feelings, that cared about what happened to it, and so on, *would* be subject to moral praise and blame. If there are computers with bona fide moral views, then there are (morally) good computers and bad computers. The fact that they came to be good or bad as a result of programming does not make them any less good or bad. A truly sadistic computer (as opposed to a "sadist simulator") is no less vicious than an equally sadistic adult; it takes no less enjoyment in the suffering of sentient beings, experiences equal relish at the sight of pain, and so on.[27]

Thus the fact that we do not blame computers or stones does not demonstrate that autonomy or the ability to do otherwise is a prerequisite for responsibility. Rather, it shows that we do not attribute worldviews to computers and stones.

Punishment

Others have argued that it is wrong to punish someone for something she could not help doing, and so a malefactor is not morally responsible for her misdeed unless she could have done otherwise. This argument, however, is faulty. Contrary to Schlick and Bradley, "A is blameworthy" does not entail "A should be punished."[28] There are numerous theories of punishment, each with different preconditions for punishment. On some of these theories, punishment may be inappropriate even when (morally) deserved. For example, if what justifies punishment is deterrence, then it is at least arguable that punishment is not appropriate unless it is *effective*. Assume, then, that punishment is improper unless cost-effective as well as deserved and that punishing people for what they cannot help doing is not cost-effective as a deterrent. Then we should not punish people for what they cannot help doing, even when they *deserve* punishment. (In other words, punishment may be disutile even when the retributive demands for punishment are met.) Whether one thinks a given act should be punished, in other words, depends as much on one's theory of punishment as it does on one's theory of responsibility. Thus even if people should never be punished for something they cannot help,[29] it does not follow that people are never *responsible* for something they cannot help.

Ought Implies Can

It is often said that "ought" implies "can"; it is illicit, senseless, or improper to say that A ought to do x unless A can do x. If A cannot do x, it cannot be said that he ought to do x. And so A cannot be held responsible for not doing x if he cannot do x. Because the feeling that "ought" implies "can" is both deep and widespread, this point deserves some discussion.

The first point I want to make is that this objection conflates exhortation with evaluation. It is indeed pointless to exhort someone to do what he cannot do, senseless to direct someone to perform an impossible deed. Since the word "ought" is often used to direct behavior, there is indeed a sense in which "ought" implies "can." But it does not follow that one cannot be evaluated on the basis of things one cannot help. For to insist that moral goals and values are exhausted by what one can sensibly be exhorted to do or be is to beg the question.[30] Even if "A can sensibly be exhorted to do x" entails "A can do x," it does not follow that "A would be a better person were he x" entails "A can be x." (Indeed, to conflate duty with moral value is to deny meaning to the concept of supererogatory acts.)

An analogy might prove helpful. A physically underdeveloped person, let us suppose, can never be a good football player. It is bootless to exhort her to play well; she cannot. It does not follow, however, that it is improper to evaluate her play. She engages in playing football and is a bad football player, whether or not she can help being so. Similarly, although it may be pointless to exhort one not to feel a given emotion, one who feels a morally offensive emotion can be deemed morally offensive.[31]

Nonetheless, many feel that, if Jones cannot do something, it is too harsh to condemn Jones for not doing what he ought to have done. So I want to show that denying that "ought" implies "can" is not as harsh or unfair as it may seem. Two distinctions will help.

The first distinction is between what I call "hard" and "soft" oughts. Hard oughts are obligations, rigid limits of conduct that we must strive to stay within. Soft oughts exert a moral pull that any morally sensitive person should feel. For example, because wisdom is a key virtue, people ought to pursue wisdom. Moreover, to the extent that I achieve wisdom, I am a morally better person. However, human beings have finite resources, and so I am not a bad person if, while respecting wisdom, I decide instead to pursue a life of service. On the other hand, I am a bad person to the extent that I fail to value wisdom, that I fail to perceive pursuing wisdom as something I ought to do. It follows that if Jones is incapable of pursuing wisdom, he fails to do something he ought to do, though he need not be a bad person. Indeed, Jones may be a good person even if he is capable only of lesser virtues. The kind shoemaker may not be as good a person as the brilliant and kind ethicist, but that does not make her a bad person. Good is good enough.[32]

So it does not seem unduly harsh to say that soft oughts do not imply "can." In addition, I would suggest that some hard oughts do not imply "can." Consider the fact that one hard ought may be overridden by another. I ought to keep my promises, but I ought to save a child from drowing if I can do so easily and without risk. Since the latter has priority, I should save a drowning child even if that means breaking my promise to my adult son to be home for lunch. Some writers try to handle this by claiming that the obligation to keep a promise is only a prima facie obligation. However, as A. John Simmons points out, it is more accurate to say that the obligation to keep my promise to my son is overridden by the obligation to save a life.[33] After all, the obligation to my son does not go away: I still owe him something, such as an explanation and, perhaps, a "rain date." Thus violating a hard ought is sometimes required by morality itself. This does not make me a bad person, since the moral demerits earned by failing to keep my promise to my son are outweighed by the moral brownie points earned by saving the child. In other words, earning moral demerits is a fact of human life. A good person is someone whose balance sheet is positive, not someone who has no demerits. Thus earning demerits for violating a hard ought one cannot help but violate does not condemn one to being a bad person. It simply means that one has to work harder in other areas to be a good person.

The second distinction is between inabilities that reveal attitudes and inabilities that do not. If I cannot give to charity because I have no money, my not giving reveals nothing at all about my attitude toward charity. For this kind of inability one is not responsible, even on my view. But if my harsh childhood has made me unable to give to charity, my inability does reveal a morally flawed attitude toward charity, and for this I am responsible. After all, I would be a morally better person were my attitude toward charity to change. (I will discuss this point at more length later.) Much of our sense that it is unfair to insist that ought does not imply can comes from looking at examples of the first sort. Most of the time, when I cannot do what I ought, my not doing what I ought shows no moral failing, no moral flaws in my worldview. It would indeed be unfair to blame me for this kind of failing. But it is not this kind of failing that is at issue.

The final source of our feeling that "ought" implies "can" comes from the sense that life should be absolutely just *ab initio*. I will discuss this point in the following section.

Moral Luck

It seems patently unfair as well as unkind to blame someone for a piece of bad luck. In games, for example, we distinguish between losses that result from poor play and those that are a matter of "bad luck." To say of a bridge game that it is "bad luck" that the spades broke unevenly is precisely to say that the player cannot be blamed for it (nor his opponent praised). Yet it would seem that much of what we praise or blame people for is a matter of good or bad "moral luck."

John Hospers and Thomas Nagel have argued that if determinism is correct, if my character is merely a matter of environment and inheritance, then whether I am good or bad is merely a matter of luck. Hume is quite right, grants Hospers, that if I perform good deeds it is because I am a good person. And it is also true, Hospers admits, that with strenuous effort one can often overcome the effects of a bad upbringing. But, insists Hospers, that too is "all a matter of luck." For "whether or not you are the kind of person who has it in him to exert the efforts is a matter of luck."[34] And surely, he continues, it is unfair to praise or blame someone for being lucky or unlucky. Thus unless one can choose one's character, unless, in other words, one's acts are (ultimately) within one's control, one cannot be held responsible for what one does, chooses, or feels. As Thomas Nagel puts it, "It seems irrational to take or dispense credit or blame for matters over which a person has no control, or for their influence on results over which he has partial control. Such things may create the conditions for action, but action can be judged only to the extent that it goes beyond those conditions and does not just result from them."[35] Let us examine the matter of moral luck in some detail.[36]

It is undeniable that neither praise nor blame is due one who wins or loses a lottery. Of course, one might be held responsible for having bought (or failed to buy) a lottery ticket. But one cannot be blamed because the ticket one bought happened not to be the *winning* ticket. It is also true, to use another of Nagel's examples, that one is no better a person because no one happened to be standing on the sidewalk when one's car swerved out of control. These are matters of luck. And perhaps it is a matter of luck whether or not one has had a good upbringing. But there are several ways in which something may be "a matter of luck." Not all of those ways undermine responsibility.

Suppose, for example, that Hilbert tortures Clarence. Clarence is not, in fact, a masochist. Now it is not Hilbert's fault that Clarence is not a masochist. Yet it would be absurd to claim that an act utilitarian cannot blame Hilbert because, were Clarence a masochist, Hilbert would have done a good rather than a bad deed. Similarly, it would be fatuous to claim that a Kantian cannot blame Herbert for telling a deliberate falsehood, S, simply because, had circumstances been different, S would have been true (and so Herbert would not have told a falsehood). It is merely a piece of bad luck for Herbert that the statement he uttered was in fact not true; it is not Herbert's fault that the state of affairs described by the sentence "S" does not obtain. Such arguments from luck are clearly absurd. That some event in a chain of events is a matter of luck does not make the whole chain "merely a matter of luck."

Thus one must be fairly circumspect in speaking of "mere matters of luck." Why is it that people are not praised for winning the Irish Sweepstakes, nor blamed for losing it? The answer, I suggest, is that holding a winning ticket does not characterize one as a moral agent, does not express one's personhood. It shows nothing about one's worldview, about one's beliefs, attitudes, values, and so forth. It is not, in other words, the fact that external circumstances play a causal role that obviates praise or blame. For Hospers is quite right that even if the *proximate* cause of an act is "internal," that is, even if the act is caused by desires and beliefs, those desires and beliefs are themselves effects of external circumstances (that is, the genetic makeup of one's parents and the circumstances of one's environment). In some sense, the causes of our acts are always, at least in part, external. But moral responsibility, according to my account, does not depend upon the *cause* of an act or trait. It depends, rather, upon whether the act or trait *expresses* or *reflects* one's worldview. One could, after all, have the very same worldview and yet not have won the lottery in which I bought a ticket. That is, there is nothing in the worldview itself, in the agent's goals, values, and the like, that tells for or against the ticket she bought being a winning ticket. So winning the lottery is not partially constitutive of personhood. It is because winning is a matter of luck *in this sense* that we do not praise winners of lotteries. By way of contrast, Midas the miser could not have had the very same worldview and yet fail to be a miser. His miserliness is part and parcel of his attitude toward money, the value he places on helping others, and so on. Thus Midas's miserliness is not a matter of luck in the appropriate sense.

Of course, criteria based on counterfactuals are always somewhat suspect. Perhaps one could argue that I could not have lost the lottery and still have the same worldview. For, if determinism is correct, in order for me to have lost the lottery at time t, some circumstance before t would have had to have been different. And that difference in circumstances would have causally influenced my worldview in some way. Thus my worldview at t would have to have been at least minimally different than it in fact was. Because of such problems, my point is best put as follows. When one refers to Midas as a miser, one has (partially) described his personhood. But when one refers to me as "the winner of the lottery," one has presented no information at all about my personhood. Of course, if you know that I won the lottery, you might be able to make some predictions about what my worldview *will* be like. Perhaps I will be cheerful. But it is my cheerfulness, not its cause, that reflects or embodies my worldview. And my cheerfulness is something I am responsible for, whether caused by winning a lottery or not.

So being a good person, feeling the right emotions, and so on, are not "matters of luck" in quite the same sense as is winning a lottery, even if my goodness and my emotions are caused by circumstances beyond my control. There is a relevant disanalogy between Midas the miser and a lottery winner. Hence the argument from luck does not succeed.

Perhaps, however, I have been too hasty in dismissing Nagel's arguments. Nagel, after all, distinguishes between four kinds of moral luck. I have addressed but one. Consider the case of the drunk driver, Al, who swerves up on the sidewalk. He is lucky that no one is there; had someone been walking on the sidewalk, he would have hit and killed her, and thus be guilty of negligent homicide. As it is, however, he is guilty only of reckless driving, a much less serious offense. Is not this a matter of moral luck? Or consider the case of Beckmann, who, for nonpolitical reasons, emigrated to Argentina in 1932. (For example, his firm transferred him to its Argentina office.) Had Beckmann stayed in Germany, he would have become a Nazi. Fortunately for him, he did not, and so led a quiet, blameless life. Two possibilities are of interest. In case 1, Beckmann is gentle and good, but cannot resist social pressure. He is, like most people, a conformist and will not stand up against the prevailing views of his society. Hence his life as an Argentine was full of kindness. But he would have been very different in Nazi Germany.[37] (I will call this fellow Beckmann1.) In case 2, Beckmann is a vicious sadist, who found no outlet for his sadism in Argentina. (I will call the sadist Beckmann2.) Either way, one might ask, is not Beckmann the beneficiary of moral luck?

Two things need to be said about these cases. First, one must distinguish between morally evaluating someone and assessing other things, such as legal liability. It is true that Al did less harm than he would have done were someone strolling on the pavement. And how much harm he caused affects his legal position. Harm is also an important component of personal feelings. Personally, I regard Al differently from the way I would regard a driver who maimed me. Harm also influences how one regards oneself. (One wants not only to *be* good, but to *do* good.) So Al and Beckmann may be lucky in escaping legal liability, personal resentment and long-lasting feelings of remorse, chagrin, and loss of self-esteem. But the amount of actual harm done is not important to a purely moral evaluation of him. From the strictly moral point of view, Al and Beckmann2 are no better as *persons* because they caused less harm. Their moral flaws, moral failings, are the same in either case.

So Al is no less morally responsible for his reckless disregard of others' safety. And Beckmann, in both cases, is morally responsible for the traits he evidences. Beckmann1 is responsible for his weakness in the face of social pressure. This is no minor failing: part of what makes Beckmann1's weakness so reprehensible is that such weakness endorses evil when evil is prevalent. Thus Beckmann1's move to Argentina does not rescue him from moral turpitude. But it goes without saying that the inability to resist social pressure is not as bad as genocide. Beckmann2, of course, is straightforwardly responsible for his sadism, his evil values. Nonetheless, the case of Beckmann1 raises an interesting question. There is an important moral difference between being a weak, gentle person and being a weak, sadistic racist. Because his firm chose to transfer him, Beckmann1 never developed racist beliefs, never took delight in the extermination of Jews, and so on. So although Beckmann1 is still a bad person, his emigration did improve his moral lot. So there is a real sense in which Beckmann1 is the beneficiary of moral luck.

I am not sure why this sort of moral luck, for good or ill, presents a problem. We must not picture Beckmann1 as a hapless victim of circumstance, like a man tossed by the ocean waves. The worldview of the hapless sailor is frustrated, prevented from being expressed by the powerful waves. Beckmann1's worldview, however, is not violated by circumstances; he does not find his body doing things he desperately wants it not to do.

One can imagine cases that are somewhere in between the case of Beckmann1 and the case of the man tossed by waves. Suppose I am unfairly placed in jail. As a prisoner, I notice that prison life affects me in ways that I find horrifying; the constant fear, degradation, and such lead to behavior patterns I can neither avoid nor accept. I desperately wish to get out of prison so as to avoid turning into the person I am becoming.[38]

It is not clear to me, however, why we should expect to be insulated from this sort of luck.[39] We try to seek circumstances that will bring out the best in us. We try to find an environment in which we can grow. Whether we succeed or not is generally not entirely within our control; it involves a degree of luck. This is a fact of life we must simply accept. If one has a conception of life as a court of justice, in which everything that happens to one is based on prior merit, then this sort of fortuitousness is disturbing. Moral luck of this sort violates a conception of life as absolutely just *ab initio*, in which everyone, from birth to death, has an equal chance to be good. Perhaps the fact that whether we grow or wither as persons depends, to some extent, upon external circumstances is incompatible with belief in a certain sort of God, a God who is a dispenser of perfect justice. Interestingly, however, there is Biblical warrant for a rather different conception of God. As the writers of Ecclesiastes and Job perceived, the world is not just. God, in those two books, arbitrarily apportions good and ill. She is not a dispenser of Divine Justice. The human task is to make the most of life in an unjust world. In the world of Job and Ecclesiastes, life is not absolutely just *ab initio*.

The absence of absolute justice *ab initio* does not undermine moral assessment. It simply does not follow that because the world is not absolutely just *ab initio,* individuals cannot be praised or blamed.[40] Indeed, it seems odd to insist that because whether we turn out to be good or ill is to some extent a matter of circumstances, we cannot be praised or blamed. Can we not praise an artist for his skill when it is a matter of luck that he did not begin with a defective piece of marble? Of course, the impressiveness of the sculpture does not depend *only* on whether the marble is defective. It depends as well on the hands, eyes, and brain of the sculptor. But then whether I am good or ill does not depend only on whether I am born in Argentina or Germany. It depends upon my physiological and psychological makeup as well.

Now it is true enough that I did not *make* my psychological and physiological makeup. But this does not mean one cannot praise me for being good. What is it, after all, one praises when one praises me? Put another way, I *am* that psychological and physiological makeup. To praise me *is* to praise that psychological and physiological makeup; that is what I am. To say that I cannot be praised for my makeup because I did not create it is to view me as a strange sort of homunculus, independent of all my thoughts, dispositions, aspirations, and the like, just as the sculptor is independent of his clay or marble. It is to rest one's faith upon what I call "the myth of the pure chooser." But the "pure chooser" is a mythical beast; it presents an unacceptable picture of the self. Alas, the myth of the pure chooser is a powerful myth. It seems to underlie much of our moral discourse. So it worth looking at in more detail.

The Myth of the Pure Chooser

Our discussion has revealed a major flaw in the traditional conception of responsibility. The traditional view as well as the arguments from moral luck and the Principle of Alternate Possibilities seem committed to viewing the self as a kind of "pure chooser," to whom all emotions, attitudes, and such are external. And this is not a tenable view of the self as a moral agent. If I am right about this, then I have uncovered a powerful reason to reject the traditional view, the Principle of Alternate Possibilities, and the argument from moral luck.

After all, if a morally pernicious trait is part of the person one is, then one is, to that extent, a morally flawed person. In order to deny that I am morally responsible for my heinous emotions, I must deny that my emotions are part of me. For example, one cannot fault me for being short. For were I to list all the features that characterize me as a moral being (rather than as a body), my height would not be among them. *Qua* moral agent, my height is external to me, part of the circumstances in which I, as a moral agent, find myself. Indeed, it is not incoherent to suggest that there might be another organism on some parallel world who is, *qua* moral agent, indistinguishable from me (has the same worldview, and so on), yet is tall. So my height is not a feature of my moral personhood, although it is a feature of my biological personhood. But can one make the same claim about one's emotions? Could there be an organism that is indistinguishable from me *qua* moral agent, yet who felt gratitude under the same circumstances in which I did not? Are my emotions external to me as a moral agent in the same way that my fingernails are external?

Indeed, as our discussion of moral luck revealed, the problem goes yet deeper. Suppose someone says, "I cannot be blamed for my psychological makeup unless I made or created it." Who is the second "I" in that sentence? That second "I" is mysterious indeed. Since that "I" is supposed to choose or create my psychological makeup, it must be independent of that psychological makeup. So it cannot, at least originally, include any psychological characteristics. That second "I" is, *ex hypothesi,* some curious entity independent of all psychological and physiological characteristics. It must be a kind of "bare" chooser, who does not herself have any characteristics, but comes to acquire them as the result of her choices.

In other words, it is plausible to deny that I am responsible for my emotions, attitudes, and such only if I am a sort of "pure chooser," a homunculus inhabiting the nether regions of my skull. The homunculus makes choices, as it were, by pressing buttons on a console. Our homunculus does not have emotions, capacities, attitudes, and so on. Rather, these are features of the console that limit her choices, not features of the pure chooser who operates the console. If my neighbor Mary is ungrateful, that is the fault of the console that Mary the pure chooser has at her disposal. One cannot blame Mary the pure chooser for not pressing the button that says "feel gratitude"; there is no such button on the console. And it is unfair to blame Mary the pure chooser for the limitations of the console she operates. If the self as moral agent is really a pure chooser of this sort, then Mary is not responsible for her emotions and attitudes. And she is not responsible for the acts brought about by those emotions and attitudes. Those acts and emotions are not features of Mary, but of the mechanism at her disposal.

Similarly, it seems plausible to insist that moral responsibility depends on the ability to do otherwise only if I am a pure chooser. In that case, all I can be blamed or praised for is my pure choices, and, since attitudes or actions I cannot avoid having are external to me, *I* cannot be blamed for them. If, by contrast, they are truly *part* of me (*qua* moral agent), then to the extent that they are bad, *I* (*qua* moral agent) am bad. So the Principle of Alternate Possibilities also seems committed to the self as a pure chooser.

It is also this view of the self that underlies arguments from moral luck. Only if Mary the moral agent is a pure chooser can one regard her having felt gratitude as akin to winning a lottery. To have a morally acceptable feeling is to be fortunate in the console one has been given, much like winning the lottery is being blessed with a winning ticket. By contrast, if Mary is the instantiation of her feelings, attitudes, and the like in a body acting in the world, as I claim, then her having morally flawed feelings means that *she* is morally flawed. Given that characters are good or bad at all, it makes sense to say that *I* cannot be praised or blamed for my character only if I am something apart from, external to, my character.

So the traditional view is forced to view Mary as a pure chooser of this sort. But this myth of the pure chooser is clearly an unacceptable picture of the self as a moral agent.[41] I am not a stripped-down homunculus without emotions and attitudes who must do the best I can with the limited number of "buttons" at my disposal. Such a homunculus would be bereft of all that I recognize as myself. It would be a Lockean "I-know-not-what," a notorious "bare particular." This is a high enough price to pay for the traditional view.

But worse is yet to come. For it is not clear how something without any predispositions, beliefs, attitudes, emotions, and so on could make a significant choice. A pure chooser could not choose at all, in any morally important sense. It is not just that nothing would *cause* our pure chooser to choose, though this is a serious difficulty. The worst problem is that there would be no *basis* for choice, nothing to render one option better or more appealing than another. The pure chooser, for example, could not press a button because it was the morally right thing to do. That would require the chooser to have a moral attitude. And she could only acquire that attitude by pressing a button saying "have moral attitudes." But why choose that button? Not because she has an antecedent commitment to morality; such a commitment must, *ex hypothesi,* have been chosen.[42] So the behavior of the pure chooser could not reflect any moral values. Were we pure choosers, we would not be moral beings. We would not be persons.

Moreover, moral agents are worthy of special respect. Now if the self as moral agent is a pure chooser, then it must be free will alone that is the basis of the special respect due moral agents. (After all, everything else that could underlie rights has been stripped away from the self.) Thus the traditional view is committed to saying that it is only because free will is so morally lustrous and valuable a property that I must endure poverty rather than kill Mary, give special consideration to her goals even at the cost of achieving my own, and so forth. But this, as the argument concerning the Wanter showed, is just false.

Thus it seems clear that we are not pure choosers. There is no nonmiserly Midas who is, to his chagrin, limited by the miserly dispositions that environment and heredity force upon him, no nonmiserly Midas frustrated by the lack of nonmiserly buttons on his console. For better or worse, miserly Midas is the only Midas there is.

Other Counterexamples

There are a variety of apparent counterexamples to the claim that we can be responsible for things beyond our control. It is argued that people are not responsible for acts resulting from duress, hypnosis, brain tampering, inability, insanity, and the like. The reason for this lack of responsibility, it is urged, is lack of control. Thus control is a necessary condition for moral responsibility. We have already discussed some of these cases. Chapter IV contains an extended discussion of them: each such case is treated as an argument by analogy for the claim that determinism undermines responsibility. In general, my response to such cases is that either (a) the person involved is, in fact, morally responsible, though perhaps not blameworthy, or (b) my account gives an alternate explanation of why the person involved is not responsible. That is, sometimes the inability, duress, and so on changes the meaning of the act, so that, although the agent remains responsible, she is not displaying the values or attitudes her act would otherwise indicate. In other cases, the agent is not responsible, not because the act was beyond her control, but because, for example, the agent did not have a coherent worldview. The reader is directed to Chapter IV for a fuller discussion.

Concluding and Summary Remarks

To be morally responsible for something is, roughly, for that thing to count in my moral ledger: I am morally responsible for an act or thought or feeling when I am a better or worse person, I get moral brownie points or demerits, to the extent that the thought, act, or feeling is morally good or bad. (That is, since all we need from moral responsibility is moral evaluability, either we should construe moral responsibility *as* moral evaluability, as I do, or, what is roughly equivalent, *mutatis mutandis,* we should *replace* moral responsibility with moral evaluability.) A trait that a full person evidences counts in his moral ledger when it is specific enough to include all morally relevant information and also expresses his worldview.

There are several reasons for thinking that neither control nor causal history are directly relevant to moral responsibility. The first argument is that there are counterexamples not only to the thesis that one is responsible only for acts and choices, but also to the claim that one is not responsible for what is beyond one's control. Harry from Chapter I is responsible for slapping his landlord, although the slap was not within his control and was brought about by Bill's machine, not by Charlie's will. Similarly, Charlie is responsible for the pleasure he takes in the suffering of animals, even though the pleasure is not an act and not within his control. We will encounter another powerful counterexample in Chapter IV: Suppose an alien tampers with Brian's brain by "erasing" all of Brian's beliefs, values, desires, memories, and the like and giving Brian a new set. By coincidence, the alien gives Brian back exactly the brain-states he had before the tampering. Brian now acts exactly as he would have without the alien's intervention. The intervention thus has no effect on Brian's responsibility. This shows that causal history is not, per se, relevant to moral responsibility.

The second argument has two steps. Step one consists of establishing that what is of moral significance about us is our worldviews, that is, the moral stance we take in leading our lives, and that we are better or worse persons insofar as that worldview is (roughly) correct or incorrect.[43] Thus, I argued, what we are properly responsible for is traits that constitute and/or reflect that worldview. Step two consists of showing that some traits that are beyond our control, such as certain emotions, can partly constitute and reflect our worldviews, and that (as the case of Harry shows) "reflecting" is not a causal notion. Therefore, we can be responsible for things beyond our control, and causal history is irrelevant to moral responsibility.

Conversely, the arguments that one is not responsible for things beyond one's control do not withstand scrutiny. Our intuitions seem to be shaped by two misleading metaphors, that of the falling stone and that of the lottery. True, we do not blame a falling stone for the damage it does. But then a stone cannot be immoral, though it can do harm. We judge people to be immoral because people, unlike stones, have (in the broadest sense) moral perspectives; they are capable of viewing their lives and the world around them in terms of a network of values. It is this moral perspective, not "free will," that grounds our perceptions of people as good or bad (and not merely harmful or useful). There are, of course, cases in which we seem to think someone is excused from responsibility for something because it was not within his control. Such cases seem to be counterexamples to my account, because they are cases in which loss of control or inappropriate causal history seems to mean that the person involved is not morally responsible. We have examined some of these cases already and will look in detail at some further examples in Chapter IV, such as hypnosis and brain tampering. Such cases fit one of two patterns. In some cases the person is, in fact, responsible. However, the lack of control changes what the person is responsible for, because it changes the meaning of the act. Thus I am responsible for telling a lie under duress, but telling a lie under threat of execution reveals something different about my values than does telling a lie for the fun of it. The threat does not remove my responsibility, but it may remove the blame, because the choice I am responsible for (namely preferring to lie rather than die) may not be a wrong choice. In other cases the person is not responsible, but for some reason other than lack of control. For example, suppose I knock over a vase as a result of a muscle spasm. I could not foresee that I might have a muscle spasm, as I have never had one before and know of no medical condition that might lead to a muscle spasm. I am not responsible for knocking over the vase. This is because, I would suggest, the spasm reveals nothing whatsoever about my attitudes and values. By contrast, when something beyond my control does reveal something about my attitudes and values, I remain responsible.

More generally, there are several reasons for preferring my account of responsibility to more traditional accounts. One reason is pragmatic: my account permits detailed analyses of such troublesome cases as acts of omission, acts performed from ignorance, and so on. Another is that my account gives a better explanation of the basis of moral evaluation and rests upon a more acceptable conception of the self as moral agent. One's character is not external to one in the same way that lottery tickets are. Who and what I am is independent of whether my ticket is the winning ticket or the losing ticket. But who and what I am is not independent of my character. Of course I did not "make" my character; the very concept of an "I" who stands behind my character is incoherent. To judge my character adversely *is* to judge *me* adversely. In short, not everything that may be called "a matter of luck" undermines responsibility (as the cases of Hilbert and Herbert demonstrate). X's being a matter of luck means that I am not responsible for x only when x reveals nothing about my worldview. In general, the traditional view, and in particular the arguments discussed above, rest on an untenable view of the self as a moral agent; they seem committed to and derive their plausibility from the myth of the pure chooser.

Finally, as we have seen, the apparent reasons for holding the traditional view turn out to be illusory. Indeed, the "counterintuitiveness" of my view is diminished when one (a) disentangles the relevant sense of "responsible" from other senses of the term, (b) recognizes that one can be responsible for morally neutral traits, (c) realizes that being blameworthy does not necessarily mean that punishment is appropriate, (d) recalls that one can be responsible for several traits instantiated by performing a single act, (e) distinguishes between soft and hard oughts, and (f) realizes that being a good person does not mean being free of moral demerits, but rather having a good moral balance sheet. There is no shame in being less than perfect; good is good enough.

One final argument remains to be made. My account has important consequences for the problem of determinism. I intend to show that, given my account of moral responsibility, determinism poses no threat to moral responsibility. Once this is established, two important points emerge. First, the fact that my account leads to this result provides a further reason for adopting my account. (I presume that the compatibility of determinism and responsibility is at least desirable, even if, as some hold, it is unattainable.) Second, if my account is correct, the spectre of determinism can be laid to rest. Even if determinism is true, it is appropriate to hold persons morally responsible for their acts and traits.

Thus it is to a consideration of the problem of determinism and moral responsibility that I now turn.

IV

Determinism

ONE OF THE HOARIEST of ethical debates pits responsibility against determinism: if everything I do is governed by universal laws of nature, can I be held responsible for my actions?[1] If my account of responsibility is correct, most discussions of responsibility and determinism have concentrated on the wrong questions. This chapter, it is hoped, will redress that wrong.

Why have so many worried that if determinism is true, people are not responsible for what they do?[2] Most writers who think determinism and moral responsibility are not compatible (the "incompatibilists") begin by assuming that freedom or the ability to have done otherwise are preconditions for moral responsibility. They argue that if determinism is true, then no one could ever have done otherwise than she did, and none of our acts are free or autonomous. So no one is ever morally responsible for her acts.

In response, those who think determinism and moral responsibility are compatible have done one of two things. Some have tried to reconcile determinism and freedom. They have sought a definition of "freedom" that allows our acts to be both free and determined. Spinoza, for example, claimed that an act is "free" if its cause stemmed from the actor's nature. (Hume and Schlick also tried to reconcile freedom and determinism.) Others have worried about the meaning of "could have done otherwise." They have argued that even though laws of nature governed my act, I could have done otherwise than I did. There are numerous and oft-discussed difficulties with both of these approaches.

If my account of responsibility is correct, however, moral responsibility requires neither freedom nor the ability to have done otherwise. So even if determinism means we lack autonomy or alternate possibilities, that does not threaten responsibility. Thus much of the literature is irrelevant. The incompatibilist arguments from freedom and alternate possibilities depend on false assumptions. Similarly, so what if determinism means that our acts are beyond our control, or have external causes? Neither control nor having "internal" causes is necessary for moral responsibility.

Still, the incompatibilist is not beaten. True, most incompatibilists have talked exclusively about autonomy, control, and alternate possibilities. But there are other arguments for incompatibilism.[3] In particular, there are a number of interesting arguments by analogy. These arguments suggest that if determinism is true, all of our actions are like acts for which we do not hold people responsible. I will mention seven of these arguments by analogy. If determinism is correct, one might argue, all our acts are like those (a) done by the mentally deranged, (b) occurring under mitigating circumstances, (c) done under duress, (d) resulting from physical inability, (e) performed as a result of some form of "brain tampering" (for example, hypnosis or "brainwashing"), (f) performed by computers or stones, or (g) that are mere matters of luck (such as winning a lottery). The arguments in question have the following form:

1. No one is responsible for acts that result from derangement/ mitigating circumstances/ duress/ physical inability/ brain tampering/ computers or stones/ luck.

2. If determinism is true, all our acts are similar (in all relevant respects) to acts that result from derangement/ mitigating circumstances/ duress/ physical inability/ brain tampering/ computers or stones/ luck.

3. Therefore, if determinism is true, we are not responsible for any of our acts.

Now it is clear that if the premises are true, the conclusion follows. But it is not clear that, given my account of responsibility, the premises are true. It has already been argued that, whether or not determinism is true, there are relevant differences between human acts and the acts of stones and computers (argument f), and between telling a lie and winning a lottery (argument g). The other five arguments, however, require closer examination.

Let me begin by telling a story. Midas, we will suppose, has had an unhappy childhood. Now the laws of nature dictate that anyone with a childhood and genetic makeup like Midas's will become a miser. Sure enough, Midas becomes a miser and performs various and sundry acts of parsimony. He never gives to charity, he refuses to help defray the costs of his deserving niece's medical education, and he gives paper clips as birthday presents. The incompatibilist wants to say that Midas is not responsible for his miserly acts, because his acts are just like those of the mentally deranged, or just like those who act under duress, and so on. Let us see how these arguments fare.

MENTAL DERANGEMENT

The incompatibilist might argue that Midas's miserly deeds are like acts of the mentally deranged. Imagine, for example, that Jeremy gets a wild look in his eyes, shouts cryptic messages, rushes out into the street, and shoots seven passers-by in sight of six police officers. When apprehended, he lapses into a catatonic state, emerging from his lethargy only on rare and brief occasions, during which he babbles incoherently. Clearly, Jeremy is not morally responsible for the shootings. Jeremy, the incompatibilist will say, acted from causally determined impulses; he was not a free and rational agent, but the victim of a disease. Jeremy could not help pulling the trigger, any more than a cancer patient can decide not to have a tumor. But, the argument goes, Midas is in the very same moral position. Just as Jeremy is the victim of his illness, so Midas is the victim of his childhood. Both merely respond to causally determined impulses. And so Midas is no more responsible for his acts than Jeremy is for his.

Will this argument hold water? I suggest not. For it is not the fact that Jeremy's acts were caused, or even beyond his control, that exculpates him. Rather, Jeremy is not responsible because he is not a full moral agent, a full person. But Midas has no such excuse.

On this point Strawson's "Freedom and Resentment" is helpful.[4] To treat Midas as one treats Jeremy is to refuse to treat Midas as a person. And, Strawson points out, we are unwilling to stop treating others as people. So we do not treat Midas as we treat Jeremy. "We cannot, as we are, seriously envisage ourselves adopting a thoroughgoing objectivity of attitude toward others," that is, treating them as nonpersons. (p. 198). For our present attitudes "have common roots in our human nature and our membership of human communities" (p. 201). "The changes in our social world" that such a change in attitude would entail are hard "for us to envisage as a real possibility" (pp. 203–204).

Strawson's answer, though illuminating, is inadequate.[5] However unwilling to do so we might be, the incompatibilist will say we *ought* to stop treating Midas as a person if he is, in fact, no more blameworthy than Jeremy. If our way of life is not rationally defensible, we should change it. Strawson, of course, is not unmindful of this objection. He gives two responses. First, he says, "such a question could seem real only to one who had utterly failed to grasp the purport of the preceding answer" (p. 198). Second, says Strawson, "we could choose rationally [between the personal and objective perspectives] only in the light of an assessment of the gains and losses to human life, its enrichment or impoverishment" (p. 199). These responses proved unconvincing to most incompatibilists. Some incompatibilists (for example, B. F. Skinner) *do* envisage a radically different form of life than we now lead. That answers Strawson's first argument. Second, Strawson seems to confuse the rationality of a belief itself with the usefulness of adopting it.[6] Suppose, for example, that it would make me happier to believe that my sister is innocent of the crime of which she is accused, despite the overwhelming evidence of her guilt. Belief in her innocence would be irrational. True, it might best serve my interests to adopt that irrational belief, and in this sense it might be "rational" for me to believe it. My interests may best be served by believing something false. But the question before us is not whether it is useful to believe that people are responsible for their acts (among other things), but whether it is *true*.[7]

Fortunately, my characterization of personhood suggests a stronger response. There are rational grounds for denying Jeremy (full) personhood while granting it to Midas. To be a (full) person, I have suggested, is to have a coherent network of goals, attitudes, emotions, and such that are properly reflected in one's interactions with the world. Anyone who fits this description counts as a person and can (legitimately) be held accountable. Now Jeremy does not meet this description. Either he lacks a coherent adult worldview, or his worldview is not properly reflected in his behavior (for example, he believes himself to be frying fish while he is in fact pulling the trigger).

Of course, not everyone we might call "deranged" lacks a coherent worldview (or a proper expression of that worldview in his acts). There are sick worldviews. But then, I suggest, not everyone we might call "deranged" lacks responsibility. If someone has a coherent but "sick" worldview, then he is an evil person. The sadist who is unable to form close bonds with others and enjoys only seeing others suffer, has a coherent set of attitudes and values, a way of viewing the world in evaluative terms, that make it appropriate to view him as a moral agent. He has the feelings appropriate to those attitudes, lives in a way that actualizes and shows commitment to those attitudes, and so forth. He has, in other words, a moral life. His attitudes may be immoral, and I doubt if he writes treatises on ethics or thinks much about right and wrong. Indeed, that is part of what makes him evil. The point is that his attitudes and actions do express a stand on matters of value, on what matters in life, on how one ought to live. Thus the perspective on moral matters his life constitutes can be judged incorrect. In this key sense, his life is that of a moral agent.

On the other hand, there are rational grounds for denying full personhood to at least *some* of the mentally deranged. Let us call this subgroup of the deranged the "insane." The insane are not responsible, I suggest, because we cannot tell a coherent story about them as moral evaluators that makes sense of their lives. We cannot attribute to them stable attitudes, coherent goals, values to which they are committed, and so forth. We cannot really regard their acts as expressing a moral framework, whether good or ill. Jeremy's failure to respect the rights of others, for example, is not an example of evil values. We cannot really say he incorrectly valued his comfort more than another's life, as we might say of someone who murders for gain. Jeremy does not really value *anything*. This is not because his acts are caused, but because we cannot tell the right kind of story about him. Jeremy's acts do not "make sense" as reflections of values. In general, the insane may have motivations, but not values. For example, we might say that Jeremy was lashing out at his mother. Unlike trees, the insane do have some sort of mental life. But the stories we can tell about why they act and about the sort of mental life they have do not attribute coherent moral attitudes. The insane may seek things, just as the tree seeks the sun, and we can tell stories about what they seek. These stories may be psychological stories. But they are not moral stories, stories about standards and values. Put another way, the world of the insane is not the sort of thing to which moral predicates apply. The very notion of compassion, for instance, makes sense only in a world in which other people are *people*, subjects of experience with some semblance of aims and values and feelings appropriate to those life goals. One cannot be compassionate toward the real number system, nor does it make sense to speak of honor among chairs. The insane, however, lack that conception of others (at least as a stable part of the world as it appears to them). And so it is inappropriate to charge them with lack of compassion, since the very concept of compassion has no application to their world. Notice that this is very different from the way in which a selfish person might not, in the way she leads her life, treat others as people. Selfish Verna understands what suffering is. She knows that certain things hurt her, and she has the ability to generalize from her own case to that of others. She gives a certain value to her own feelings, and the demands she makes for herself are true *demands*, things she thinks others *ought* to give her, not just wishes or desires or vented feelings. In short, Verna's concepts are developed enough that the idea of a person would make sense to her. That is why it is a moral failing of Verna's that she does not regard others as people. We might say that the logical space of her conceptual system makes room for others as a subject of experience, in the way that the logical space of Jeremy's conceptual system does not. Thus the selfish person's failure to view others this way may sensibly be regarded as taking a moral stance, while Jeremy's cannot.

In short, the insane cannot be bad or evil evaluators, because they are not, properly speaking, evaluators at all. There are no such grounds for denying personhood to Midas. Midas does exhibit a coherent (though flawed) adult worldview, and his worldview is appropriately reflected in his behavior.

Thus there is a relevant difference between the cases of Midas and Jeremy; the former is a full person while the latter is not. Hence it does not follow that Midas is not responsible for his miserliness.

It is worth pointing out a practical application of these reflections. Criteria for the insanity defense have been the source of much controversy. The M'Naghten Rules[8] (cognitive test) specify that a defendant is not guilty by reason of insanity if he (a) is incapable of distinguishing between right and wrong, or (b) does not know what he is doing. The control test suggests that defendants are not guilty by reason of insanity if the criminal conduct was beyond their control to prevent. The "substantial capacity" test combines the control and cognitive tests: "A person is not responsible for criminal conduct if at the time of such conduct as a result of mental disease or defect he lacks substantial capacity either to appreciate the criminality of his conduct or to conform his conduct to the requirements of law."[9] The product or Durham test insists that, in the words of Judge Bazelon, "an accused is not criminally responsible if his unlawful act was the product of mental disease or mental defect."[10] The presence test is yet broader: it is not necessary, on this view, to show that the unlawful conduct was caused by a mental defect. It is enough that substantial mental defect is present.

My view suggests a variant of the M'Naghten Rules: a person is not criminally responsible for an unlawful act if, at the time of commission, she lacked a sufficiently coherent worldview, or if her acts failed to reflect that worldview.

MITIGATING CIRCUMSTANCES AND DURESS

Criminals are less responsible for their misdeeds, it is sometime said, if there are mitigating circumstances. We distinguish provoked from unprovoked attacks, "cold-blooded" killing from killing done in the heat of passion, acts motivated by poverty or fear from acts of greed, and so on. And if the circumstances are sufficiently mitigatory, it is claimed, the doer escapes responsibility entirely. Now if determinism is true, it can be argued, then every deed is sufficiently mitigated by circumstances; the ineluctable compulsion of heredity and environment should be treated as mitigating circumstances that wash away all guilt.

The argument from duress is a special case of the argument from mitigating circumstances. Recall the case of Mickey, who told a small lie when threatened with imminent death. Mickey, the argument goes, is not responsible for his lie, since he acted under the compulsion of a threat upon his life. But Midas also acted under compulsion, namely the compulsion of causal law. Thus neither Mickey nor Midas is responsible.

This argument will not do, however. For as we have seen, although mitigating circumstances may diminish *blame*, they do not diminish *responsibility*. Mitigating circumstances serve to modify the *trait* for which one is held responsible. (For example, Mickey is responsible for the trait *having told a lie under threat of execution*, rather than for the trait *having told a lie*.) In other words, mitigating circumstances are relevant only insofar as they cast more light on the agent's worldview, on what his attitudes and values really are. We get a truer picture of the value Mickey places on honesty when we learn that his lie was prompted by the threat of execution. He values life more than he values avoiding small dishonesties. This does not mean that he values honesty lightly, as we might think were he to lie on a whim.

By contrast, the environment and genetic makeup of a criminal merely indicate how she *came* to have the set of dispositions, emotions, attitudes, and beliefs that constitute her worldview. They do not further characterize, make more explicit, the nature of the worldview with which a felon confronts the world. Thus they are not "mitigating circumstances" in the relevant sense, and do not obviate blame. And they certainly do not obviate responsibility.

The argument that determined acts are like acts done under duress fares no better. Mickey *is* responsible for telling a lie under threat of execution. But he is not blameworthy, simply because it is (*pace* Kant) morally permissible to tell a lie in order to save one's life. (If Kant is right, of course, then Mickey *is* blameworthy.) In other words, the lie must be weighed against the moral good of saving a life. But there is no similar countervailing moral consideration in Midas's case; Midas's miserly deeds are not done in order to secure some greater moral good. Thus the "duress" of causal law does not mitigate Midas's blameworthiness, much less his moral responsibility, for his miserly actions.

INABILITY AND CHOICE

More promising is the argument from inability. Suppose that Werther pushes Adalbert off a cliff. As a result, Adalbert falls upon an elderly woman and kills her. Adalbert did not act freely. He had no choice but to fall upon the woman, like it or not. So he is not morally responsible for her death. But is not the same true of Midas the miser, whose miserliness results from his unfortunate childhood? Just as Werther's shove caused Adalbert to fall upon the woman, so a bad childhood caused Midas to be a miser. Both are victims of the inexorable laws of nature. Thus Midas is no more responsible than is Adalbert.

Many compatibilists (for example, Hume) would reply that the cause of Adalbert's act is external, while the cause of Midas's is not. But this response will not do, for two reasons. First, we can change the example a bit and make the cause of Adalbert's fall internal. After all, Adalbert would not have been responsible had he fallen because of a sudden and unanticipatable muscle spasm. Yet the muscle spasm is not "external" to Adalbert. So what excuses Adalbert is not the fact that the cause of his fall is external to him. Second, suppose Midas's acts are caused by his attitudes and beliefs (though I have suggested that this is a misleading way of speaking). So it may be true that the immediate or proximate cause of Midas's churlish behavior is internal to him. But those attitudes and beliefs were caused by something external, namely the environment and genetic composition of Midas's parents. The cause of the proximate cause, in other words, is external. Ultimately, then, Midas's acts are due to external causes. Thus, it may be argued, Midas's miserliness is, ultimately, just like Adalbert's fall.

The compatibilist could try to solve these problems by redefining "internal cause." His new definition of "internal" must make Midas's bad childhood internal and make muscle spasms external. But the compatibilist must also explain the relevance of his sense of "internal cause" to moral responsibility. Why, we need to know, is it reasonable to hold people responsible for actions that are "internally caused" (according to his definition)? We have already seen ample reason to think this approach unpromising.

I would like to pursue a more promising path. Given my account of responsibility, the analogy fails. Adalbert cannot be held responsible for the trait *having killed an elderly woman;* that trait is insufficiently specific. And the trait *having fallen upon an elderly woman after being pushed off a cliff* is not partially constitutive of personhood; it tells us nothing about Adalbert's worldview. By contrast, Midas's miserliness does express his worldview. Hence Midas is responsible and Adalbert is not.

In a sense, I am simply applying Hume's dictum that we can be blamed for that which "stems from" our character. But unlike Hume's, my account is not a causal one. Indeed, the fact that Adalbert could not help but fall upon an old woman is not, *per se,* relevant; it is important only as *evidence* of something else. (If we know he could not help falling on her, we will not assume, as we otherwise might, that he does not value her life.)

Although this response to the argument from inability is sufficient to show that the analogy is faulty, it is worth spending a few moments on the concept of choice. There are several senses in which one may be said to make a "choice." The psychological notion of making a choice, of assenting or dissenting, is quite different from the causal notions of uncaused choice and uncoerced choice (two different senses of "free" choice). I want to discuss two sorts of psychological choices one can make.

Let me begin with a "weak" sense of choice, which I will call "$choice_1$." I weakly choose something when I go along with it, deem it acceptable, whether I have anything to do with it or not. To make a $choice_1$ is simply to approve of, accept, assent to, give one's imprimatur to, an action, condition, or state of affairs that circumstances present to one for assent or dissent. Now to deem something acceptable is to judge it (at least minimally) good. And moral agents are committed to what they perceive as good; part of what it means to value something is to be committed to bringing it about, to the extent one feasibly can. For example, if I $chose_1$ Walter Mondale for president in 1984, then I felt his election would be a good thing (all things considered), and I committed myself to do everything feasible to bring about his re-election. I say "feasible" because when I $choose_1$ something, I do not commit myself to performing physically impossible acts, nor to do things that interfere with other, more important commitments. So though I $chose_1$ Mondale, I am not committed to falsifying election returns. But within those limits, $choosing_1$ Mondale commits me to doing whatever brings about his election. This may just mean voting; given my other commitments (including those that stem from my other $choices_1$), nothing else might count as feasible. Obviously, the strength of my approval is important in determining what is "feasible": it may not be feasible to give up a month of my time for something of which I approve mildly, but it is certainly feasible to give up a month of my time in order to eliminate world hunger. So what counts as "feasible" may vary greatly from choice$_1$ to choice$_1$. Nonetheless, to choose$_1$ x, however tepidly, is *eo ipso* (a) to make an evaluation of x, to deem it good (at least relative to its alternatives), and (b) to commit oneself to doing whatever one feasibly can to bring about x. (I am ignoring here certain interesting complications occasioned by weakness of the will.)

So our choices$_1$ do have moral significance. For our moral evaluations and commitments reveal and constitute our moral characters. Surely A's judging something to be morally valuable and her commitment to help bring it about (whenever feasible) tell us about her character as a moral agent. It is relevant to a moral assessment of A; if she chooses$_1$ morally odious things, she is (to that extent) morally flawed. Someone who approves of Hitler's program of extermination, judges it a good thing, is an evil person, even if she never has the opportunity to lift a finger. So having chosen something, even in this weak sense, is something for which one can be held responsible.

Now Midas did make a choice in this weak sense, whatever caused his choice$_1$. He found himself in circumstances that called for assenting to or dissenting from giving money to charity, and he dissented. He gave his imprimatur to not giving. Perhaps it is true that in some sense he *had* to choose to be miserly. But choose he did. Of course, in this weak sense, Adalbert could have chosen not to fall upon the woman, though nature did not honor his choice. He may well have dissented from falling on the woman and committed himself to pursuing every possible means of missing her. None arose. Thus his choice made no practical difference. It did, however, make a moral difference; Adalbert would have been blameworthy had he chosen otherwise. For surely it would speak ill of Adalbert that he did not care whether or not he fell on the woman, or did not care enough to commit himself to doing whatever he could to avoid killing her. Surely someone with those attitudes is morally flawed.

Nonetheless, there is a sense in which Adalbert "had no choice," while Midas did. Adalbert's choice$_1$ made no difference in the course of events. As Adalbert was well aware, his choice$_1$ was causally irrelevant to what actually transpired. By contrast, Midas's choice$_1$ did affect whether he gave. Similarly, there is a sense in which I cannot choose to leap to the top of Mont Blanc without mechanical assistance (though I can choose$_1$ to do so). I know that my approving or disapproving will not affect whether I wind up on top of Mont Blanc. Let us call this stronger sense "choice$_2$." Someone chooses$_2$ when he believes that his choice$_1$ makes some causal difference. More precisely, A chooses$_2$ x if and only if (a) circumstances present x or A's assent for dissent, (b) A assents to x, and (c) A does not believe that his assenting to or dissenting from x is causally irrelevant to x's occurrence or nonoccurrence. A need not believe that his choice is enough to bring x about. And he need not think x will not happen without him. It is enough that A thinks his choice$_1$ will probably play *some* role in the causal story to be told about x's occurrence or nonoccurrence. After all, I can choose to move my arm even if I am not sure whether my arm will move. But I cannot choose$_2$ to move my arm if I feel certain that it will not move.

An agent, in other words, has, in any given situation, a "choice repertoire." I perceive a number of alternatives and think my assenting to one will have some effect on what actually happens. (My choice repertoire, in other words, is the set of perceived alternatives such that my assent to any one of them would be, to the best of my knowledge, a likely causal factor in that alternative's coming about.) When I dine in a restaurant, for example, my choice repertoire is (usually) limited to the items on the menu. If spinach is not on the menu, I am not being asked to assent to or dissent from the presence of spinach on my plate. (That need not prevent me from choosing$_1$ to order spinach. I may regret the absence of spinach. But if I do not choose$_1$ spinach, that need not be a choice$_2$ to *not* order it. We normally do not and need not consider what is out of the question.) Suppose, though, it is on the menu. The question of ordering spinach arises. I dissent from ordering it. And I believe that my dissent will probably mean that no spinach appears on my plate. So, in not ordering spinach, I have chosen$_2$ not to order spinach, even if my strong dislike for that leafy green made me *unable* to order it.

Thus Midas and Adalbert each made a choice$_1$, and each is responsible for his choice$_1$. Midas alone, however, made a choice$_2$.

A final point should be made. Suppose Midas's background was such that the very *idea* of giving to charity never occurred to him. He has never seen or heard tell of the practice of giving to charity. He literally does not know what charity is. In that case, giving to charity is not in his choice repertoire, and he did not choose (in either sense) not to give. He can still, however, be faulted because giving to charity is not in his choice repertoire. That lack is a morally undesirable feature of his worldview.

This point deserves some close attention, for it will seem troubling to many readers. How can we blame Jones for his evil views if he has never been exposed to anything but evil views? Is it sensible, for example, to blame an Eskimo for sending his parents out to die on the ice, if, in his society, that is the morally mandated practice and indeed the only way of dealing with aged parents that the Eskimo has ever encountered?

The answer is that if Jones has evil views, then Jones is evil. Let us say he is a male chauvinist, but grew up in a society in which male chauvinist attitudes have never been challenged and no alternative view ever presented. Now Jones would be a better person were he not a male chauvinist, and so he is morally evaluable on the basis of his male chauvinism. However, it should be said that Jones's brand of male chauvinism *must* be different from that of a male chauvinist in our society, and so his attitude may well be less *evil*. My point is that we learn something about Jones when we see what happens to his attitudes when he is exposed to a new way of thinking. Once he is confronted with an alternative, his worldview cannot be the same. This is part of the reason why traditionalist societies cannot survive exposure to modernity. The traditionalist mind-set depends essentially upon there being no alternatives. The Hindu in the small Indian village does not regard his way of life as one choice among many—it is just life. The act of seeing village life as a possibility among others irrevocably changes the way of life itself. True, even after being exposed to nonchauvinist ways, Jones may remain a male chauvinist. But he is a different (and worse) sort of chauvinist. Before, he simply thought "women are not hunters." Now, living in a society in which women do hunt, he sees that women can hunt. So he must either change his view or take a further step. For example, he can ignore the evidence and insist that women are more careless hunters than men. Now he is not only a chauvinist, but intellectually dishonest as well. There are many other possibilities. But the one thing he cannot do is maintain his prior assumption that it is just a given of life that women do not hunt, as it is a given of life that people do not reproduce by mitosis. Thus the mind-set of what we might call the "aware" chauvinist is both different from and worse than the mind-set of the unchallenged chauvinist. Thus it is indeed worse to be a male chauvinist who knows what he is doing, is aware of the alternatives, not because the aware chauvinist has more freedom, but because his attitude toward women is not the same as that of the unchallenged chauvinist.

The case of the Eskimo is also of interest. The story behind the Eskimo's sending his parents off to die is different from any story to be told about my sending my parents off to die. Given my view, we need to give a finer-grained analysis in terms of traits before we can evaluate the Eskimo. For example, the Eskimo is not guilty of either ingratitude or filial disrespect, as I would be. He is doing what he believes is the right thing by (his duty toward) his parents. It is thus not disrespect he shows, but respect (perhaps misplaced). Nor is he failing in his action to take note of the kindnesses his parents have done him, but is rather reciprocating, repaying his debt to them. His parents have done their duty toward him, and, reciprocating, he does his duty toward them. So he cannot be blamed for ingratitude, since he does not evidence it. Still, even when all of this is taken into account, there may be some moral demerits left. Suppose, for example, that the correct moral theory says that life is a supreme value, and it is thus incorrect to value anything over life.[11] Then there is a moral demerit attached to treating the dignity of one's parents as more important than their lives. If this is what morality in fact says, then the Eskimo is indeed bad in this way. Doing what the Eskimo does earns a demerit, and it is *his* demerit.

In sum, lack of exposure to morally sound views does not diminish responsibility, though such lack may modify or eliminate blame, because the lack is evidence that the attitudes we would otherwise attribute to the agent are not the ones he in fact has.

Yet another sort of inability, the inability to choose, is illustrated by a case given by Keith Lehrer.[12] Due to a traumatic childhood incident, Pasqual develops a pathological aversion to snakes. Pasqual is unable to choose to pick up a snake, though he would pick up the snake were he to choose to do so. This example is cited by several writers as evidence that one is not responsible for doing x unless one is able to choose to do otherwise. In any case, it may be argued, if determinism is true, all our choices are causally constrained in the same way that Pasqual's is. Thus determinism obviates responsibility.

On my account, Pasqual *is* responsible for his aversion to snakes, since the aversion is an aspect of his worldview. But what, exactly, does this responsibility amount to? Suppose Joey's pet garter snake slinks past Pasqual's legs through the open doorway, while Pasqual watches in horror. What does this show about Pasqual? Ordinarily, the failure to pick up the snake would mean a lack of concern about Joey's feelings: it would mean that Pasqual placed so little value on Joey's feelings that he could not be bothered to bend down and pick up the snake to prevent its escape. But Pasqual's aversion changes the value-interpretation we place on his action. For most people, the cost of picking up the snake is simply minor inconvenience. So if I fail to pick up the snake, it follows that I give greater weight to a minor inconvenience to myself than I do to Joey's heartbreak, and this is a morally culpable weighing of values. For Pasqual, the cost of picking up the snake is not merely minor inconvenience. Suppose that Pasqual can overcome his aversion, though at great personal cost. Then Pasqual's failure means that he gives greater weight to great personal cost to himself than he does to Joey's heartbreak, and this is a rather different conflict of values from the one I faced. (Note also that, since there is nothing morally objectionable, per se, about Pasqual's aversion to picking up the snake, Pasqual earns no moral demerits for the fact that the cost of picking up the snake is greater for him than it is for me.) In short, Pasqual's aversion does not eliminate or even diminish responsibility, but it changes dramatically what he is responsible *for*, since it changes the meaning of his act (or, in this case, his omission).

By contrast, Midas's aversion to giving to charity is of a different sort. Either the cost of giving to charity is no greater for Midas than it is for me, or the greater cost reflects uncharitable values. Either way, Midas is blameworthy in a way that Pasqual is not.

A final type of inability to choose is illustrated by the kleptomaniac and dipsomaniac, who "cannot keep from" stealing and drinking. Isaiah Berlin asks "what reasons," given determinism, "can you, in principle, adduce for attributing responsibility" that do not also "apply in the case of compulsive choosers—kleptomaniacs, dipsomaniacs, and the like?"[13] My response will depend upon the psychological story to be told about the kleptomaniac or dipsomaniac. One possibility is that the "compulsion" may be said to "distort the perspective" of the patient, so that stealing and drinking do not seem so bad to him. In this case, the patient is responsible, provided that the "distortion" is not of a sort that undermines the personhood of the patient. Another possibility is that although the patient disapproves of drinking/stealing, he feels a great urge to drink/steal, an urge to which, after a struggle, he yields. Here the patient is praiseworthy for both the disapproval and the struggle against the urge (both of which reflect a real commitment to honesty/sobriety) and is also responsible for the extent of self-mastery involved (which may be considerably more than average, even though the struggle was ultimately lost). This case is different from the case of Midas, who neither disapproves of nor struggles against his "urge" to refrain from giving to charity. A final possibility is that the patient disapproves, but finds his hand moving "against his will." In this (unlikely) story, drinking/stealing do not reflect, but rather violate, the patient's worldview, and so the patient is not responsible for drinking/stealing. Again, this is not true of Midas. In sum, in the only case in which the analogy holds, the kleptomaniac/dipsomaniac *is* responsible.

MIND TAMPERING

The most powerful of the arguments by analogy concern cases in which an agent's mind is tampered with in some fashion. For example, it seems peculiar to hold someone responsible for acts done under posthypnotic compulsion. And it seems wrong to blame someone for acts performed as a result of electrochemical "brainwashing," provided she had no way of resisting. But if determinism is true, Midas's mind is similarly "tampered with" by his environment. Does it matter, after all, whether the brain is altered by a surgeon's hand or by environment and heredity following the ineluctable laws of nature? True, brainwashing is *deliberately* induced by someone else, while Midas's miserliness was not. But what difference does this make? Midas's thoughts are still the product of outside forces.

It is usually helpful to have a story to talk about. So let me introduce Sheila and Brian. Sheila, we will suppose, has been hypnotized and told to carry out the first command she is given after hearing the phrase "categorical imperative." She is then awakened from her hypnotic trance. Unaware of the posthypnotic command, Sheila attends a lecture on Kant's moral theory, in the course of which the fateful words are uttered. As Sheila leaves the lecture hall, she accidentally collides with a rude and unfriendly soul, who mutters "go jump in the lake." Sheila, in the grip of posthypnotic compulsion, follows this advice. Since Sheila cannot swim, she drowns.[14] Is she responsible for killing herself?

Of course, as a matter of fact, posthypnotic suggestion rarely, if ever, overpowers a person's firm convictions. For present purposes, however, we may imagine Sheila to be the victim of a superhypnotist. Or we may picture a neurophysicist equipped with a device that enables her to control Sheila's neural impulses. The important point is that Sheila is compelled to drown herself, whatever her feelings about suicide might be.

The plight of Brian is yet sadder. One night, while reading *Tristram Shandy*, Brian is abducted from his bedroom by four deranged scientists. They alter Brian's brain so that he comes to believe that brown-eyed persons should be shot on sight. Before Brian is apprehended, he kills four brown-eyed taxidermists and a brown-eyed salesman from Liverpool.

The argument is that Brian and Sheila cannot be blamed because their acts were induced by external forces. It is worth noting that Brian *chose* to kill his five victims, in the strong sense of "choice" discussed earlier (that is, Brian chose$_2$ to kill five people). But neither Brian nor Sheila *freely* chose to do what they did. We should not blame Brian and Sheila, the argument goes, for the fault lies not in them but in their conditioning. Now, Midas too does what he does as a result of conditioning; his brain was "molded" by his unfortunate childhood, much as Sheila's was by posthypnotic suggestion and Brian's was by electrochemical manipulation. So Midas is no more blameworthy than are Sheila and Brian.

Needless to say, I do not think the argument succeeds. Let us begin with Sheila, since her case is the less problematic one. Why is it that we do not hold Sheila responsible for committing suicide? We absolve her, I suggest, not because her act was caused, but because the Sheila we know, who is happy and loves life, did not assent to and would not assent to suicide. Her act of suicide simply does not reflect her worldview, her attitudes, beliefs, feelings, and the like. The drowning tells us no more about Sheila's values than does the wart on her index finger. Of course, if the posthypnotic suggestion does accord with Sheila's worldview, if she had planned to commit suicide tonight even before meeting the hypnotist, would be pleased to find herself drowned if she could look back from heaven, and so forth, then I would say that she is responsible for the relevant traits, even though the cause of her action was posthypnotic suggestion. Recall the case of Harry the landlord-slapper; Harry is responsible for instantiating the trait of having slapped his landlord, even though the slap was caused by Bill's machine. Similarly, if one can regard Midas's miserly deeds, however caused, as expressions of his worldview, then Midas is responsible for them. (That is, he is responsible for the relevant traits instantiated by performing those deeds.)

But given that Sheila would not otherwise have committed suicide, her act reveals nothing about the attitudes, emotions, judgments, and the like with which she ordinarily confronts the world. Thus one could say of Sheila that her act of suicide did not reflect her worldview. In a very real sense, Sheila "was not herself" when she jumped in the lake. Sheila's body did the jumping. But none of the traits related to the suicide reveal anything about Sheila the moral person. Midas can make no such claim.

One must be very careful here. The man who strikes his son in anger might say, "I was not myself." He may deny that striking his son reflects his character, since when he is not angry he is gentle and considerate. Nonetheless, as we have seen, his act expresses his worldview and does reveal something about the way he understands and interacts with the world even when he is not angry. By contrast, there is nothing in Sheila's attitudes, emotions, and so on from which one can "read off" the act of suicide. *Ex hypothesi,* Sheila would jump in the lake *whatever* her attitudes, beliefs, and feelings might be. It is, of course, true of Sheila (as it is of everyone else) that when hypnotized in this fashion and told to jump in the lake she will jump in the lake. But this reveals nothing about the moral or psychological framework in terms of which Sheila, when not acting under posthypnotic suggestion, interacts with the world.

The case of Brian is more problematic. For Brian's deeds do reflect his attitudes at the time of the killings. So Brian's acts are partially constitutive of personhood. In fact, Brain could have done otherwise had he so chosen, at least to the extent that anyone can ever do otherwise if determinism is true. He chose to kill. And he made this choice because of his convictions. Brain is caused to kill only insofar as he has certain beliefs about brown-eyed people, just as I am caused to give to charity only insofar as I have certain beliefs about charity. It appears, then, that if Brian is not responsible for the killings, it must be because his beliefs were caused by external forces.

Let us look at Brian's case a bit more closely. There are several different stories that might be told about Brian, and each must be treated differently. A lot depends on the character of Brian's brainwashed mind. If Brian's belief is insusceptible to rational scrutiny no matter how much Brian values consistency and rationality, if he is hysterical, if he walks about with a perennially glazed expression, and so forth, then Brian is not responsible for the same reason that Jeremy is not. Even if Brian does not appear deranged or dazed, we are tempted to think Brian must be like the chess-playing computer, an affectless automaton. We are tempted to think that although Brian might say "all brown-eyed people should be shot," and act accordingly, he does not really *mean* it, any more than the computer *wants* to win. If this is the case, then Brian does not have a worldview and is not a moral person, according to my definition, and so is not responsible for anything.

Suppose instead that Brian does have feelings and so forth, but that his belief that all brown-eyed people should be shot is wildly and disturbingly inconsistent with his other beliefs, and that he is incapable of reasoning about his new belief, that it is not susceptible to change in the way his other beliefs are. For example, Brian believes in the value of human life, believes in a universal right to life, thinks that brown-eyed people are full persons, is considerate and helpful to others, and so on. But he also believes that all brown-eyed persons should be shot and is willing to act on this belief. Suppose also that his belief is implanted irrevocably, so that it is proof against all means of suasion. No matter how much Brian values reason and consistency, and no matter how powerful one's arguments, Brian's belief cannot change. Here Brian's act did express his belief, but surely Brian is not morally responsible for killing the taxidermist.

My response is to deny that it is possible for Brian, if he is a full moral agent, to have an isolated belief about brown-eyed people. We are assuming that Brian believes brown-eyed people are as trustworthy and decent as anyone else, that he values human life, and so on. How could he not notice that his belief about shooting the brown-eyed is radically inconsistent with his other values and attitudes? People do have an unfortunate tendency to "compartmentalize" their beliefs, refusing to notice gross inconsistencies. But the degree of inconsistency here is so great and the ramifications so important and far-reaching, that it is hard to see how Brian could be blithely untroubled by it, unless he is not a moral agent at all. The belief about brown-eyed people would *force* other changes in Brian's worldview, so that he would come to have a more or less coherent, integrated worldview. He might, for example, continue to respect the value of human life, but deny that brown-eyed people are human. But notice that this belief entails a radical change in Brian's view of life. After all, if what is of moral importance about humanity is having goals, and if brown-eyed people have goals, then brown-eyed people have the same moral status as the blue-eyed people Brian calls "human." So, in order to rule out brown-eyed people as human (in the relevant respect), Brian must change the way he views what is of importance about human life. As a result, the way he views all important human relationships will change. Of course, we are not perfect moral reasoners. We often have conflicting attitudes. And we may assert all sorts of incompatible things. But if Brian is a full moral agent, if he has the kind of feelings and commitments and ability to think that the rest of us do, then his attitudes are linked in a complicated web. This does not guarantee complete consistency, but it does mean that attitudes and values affect one another and change together. You cannot come to believe that brown-eyed people are not human without altering, in perhaps complex and subtle ways, your way of regarding what humanity consists in. (Remember, after all, that an attitude is not a piece of the brain, but a feature of the operation of the whole person). This is part of what it means to have a real worldview, to be a moral agent, to have a moral picture of life, to have bona fide attitudes. So I would suggest that unless Brian's inculcated belief about brown-eyed people becomes integrated into a more or less coherent worldview, he is not a full moral agent (and hence not responsible for killing the taxidermist).

This point has important consequences, for it means that there cannot be a kind, thoughtful racist. The slaveholder in the antebellum South either had to be intellectually dishonest or have widespread immoral beliefs. Perhaps he was willing to ignore the obvious evidence and insist that his slaves were either happy or subhuman. Perhaps he thought that it was natural and right that members of other races be enslaved. In that case, there are two possibilities. One possibility is that he had a radically different view of what is morally significant about human beings. In this case, his conception of all human relationships, such as friendship, must be importantly different from our own. The second possibility is that he was intellectually dishonest, cheerfully ignoring the gross conflict between his view about race and his view about what is morally significant about human beings. In short, his belief in slavery is not an isolated immoral belief, but a reflection of either deep intellectual dishonesty or widespread differences in moral perspective.

Suppose, however, that I am wrong about this. Still, Brian is not like ordinary moral persons. He is peculiar in a way we do not quite understand. After all, if Brian's belief bears no relation to his other attitudes, then in an important sense the belief is not his. So we might regard his belief about shooting brown-eyed persons as not really a part of his worldview, but as a foreign "graft," as it were, a stray belief as foreign to Brian as a tapeworm is to its host. There are two distinct pieces of Brian, we might say. One piece is the rest of his views that form a coherent worldview. The other piece is the "weed," the belief that brown-eyed people should be shot. Then we might identify Brian himself with the coherent worldview that excludes the belief about brown-eyed people and say that the killings did not express Brian's personhood, but only the "weed." It would be as if an alien had taken over his body, allowing Brain to function normally except in this one respect. So Brian is not responsible for the killings. In any case, if we are puzzled about Brian's status, it is precisely because his state of mind is so odd.

Midas's miserliness is not like this at all. His miserliness is not an anomalous attitude that conflicts with everything Midas believes, yet cannot be eradicated. Or if it is an ineradicable anomaly, Midas's inability to rid himself of miserliness shows something about Midas's attitudes towards consistency or rationality. Thus, if Brian's worldview is not fully coherent, the analogy fails; Brian has an excuse not available to Midas. The case of Brian is like that of Jeremy, not like that of Midas.

Let us therefore suppose that Brian's new worldview, although sick, is fairly coherent. His belief that brown-eyed people should be shot fits in with his other beliefs in the appropriate way. He is able to discuss his views and so forth. So the new Brian is a full moral person. The crucial question then becomes whether or not Brian's "conditioning" is reversible. If Brian's new worldview is permanent, then I think we must hold him responsible. However he came to have his repugnant views, he has them. Whatever he was in the past, he is now the sort of person who believes in killing brown-eyed persons on sight. If having that belief is morally pernicious, so is Brian.[15]

The mere fact that Brian's new worldview was caused in no way diminishes his responsibility. It is easy enough to show this. Suppose that, as chance would have it, our scientists give Brian exactly the attitudes and beliefs he had before. Thus there is no perceptible change in Brian. Neither Brian himself, nor anyone else, can tell preconditioned from postconditioned Brian. Brian does exactly what he would have done without being conditioned, feels exactly what he would have felt, thinks exactly what he would have thought, and so on. It seems absurd to insist that henceforth Brian is not responsible for his actions, cannot be punished or praised, and so forth. Brian would be quite right in protesting if we denied him the status of a moral agent. Yet the cause of Brian's actions is the scientist's conditioning; it is a mere accident that the personality they gave Brian happened to match precisely the one Brian already had.

So Brian is fully responsible, despite the fact that his beliefs resulted from brain tampering. This result may seem counterintuitive at first blush. But the air of counterintuitivity, I suggest, arises from two confusions.

First, it is hard not to think of someone in Brian's condition as deranged. We picture him crazed or robot-like, a zombie or a wild man. And we think of Brian's objectionable belief as a foreign element plunked down in the middle of what was a harmonious pattern. But ex hypothesi neither is true. Brian may have come to his belief in an unusual way, but he is capable of discussing his belief calmly and rationally, considering objections to it, providing justification for his odd tenet, and so forth. His belief is well integrated with his other attitudes. He feels the same sorts of chagrins, passions, angers, delights, and perplexities that others with similar views experience. Why is he any less responsible? Brian is a full evaluator, and an evil one.[16]

Second, we are tempted to think of the preconditioned Brian as still lurking about somewhere, waiting to be released. And we do not wish to blame *that* Brian for what the gang of four did to his body. But, *ex hypothesi,* postconditioned Brian is the only Brian there is or will be. The preconditioned Brian, whose best friends have brown eyes, is gone forever.

In short, the Brian who stands before us now is a full person, who acts, thinks, feels, reasons, and doubts just like anyone else. Indeed, in principle there could be someone on some other planet whose mental and physical features are now and will continue to be indistinguishable from those of Brian, but who acquired those features in the ordinary way. It would be odd indeed to say that although the two are indistinguishable in every other respect, both mentally and physically, one is responsible and one not, simply because they came to their present states by different causal routes.

The situation changes considerably, however, if Brian is "reconditioned," that is, returned to his preabduction state. It seems quite unfair to punish the reconditioned Brian, who, like the preconditioned Brian, is firmly opposed to shooting brown-eyed persons. Indeed, he might well be willing to sacrifice his own life rather than shoot another person, regardless of eye color. Brian can reasonably feel about the shootings much as one would feel about killing five people because the brakes on one's automobile, although recently checked, suddenly failed. The occurrence was certainly regrettable. But remorse would be inappropriate. For the sad event does not indicate a moral shortcoming of the perpetrator. After all, Brian's belief while under the influence of brain tampering reveals nothing at all about Brian's moral character *before* his abduction and *after* his reconditioning. Unlike the man who strikes in anger, Brian's shootings are quite independent of what he is otherwise like. He would have had the same beliefs while conditioned no matter what he was like before. (We are assuming that there is no way to resist the scientist's tampering.) By contrast, it is surely false that the man would have struck his son when called a liar no matter what he was like before. Similarly, *ex hypothesi* Brian's reconditioning removes all traces of his conditioned beliefs. Thus Brian as he stands before us now is unblemished; the killings reveal no moral flaw or shortcoming in the only extant Brian.

It is worth noting that because preconditioned and postconditioned Brian show continuity of biological function, they constitute a single *biological* person over time. But there are two *moral* persons here. The first, Brian$_1$, exists from birth until the moment of conditioning. Brian$_1$ is replaced temporarily by a *different* moral person,

Brian$_2$ (conditioned Brian), who in turn is replaced by the continuation of Brian$_1$ at the moment the conditioning is reversed. Brian$_1$ is not morally responsible for the traits instantiated by someone else, Brian$_2$. In other words, we can absolve reconditioned Brian because there is a recognizable person present whose worldview is in no wise expressed by the killings. Brian retains no vestige of the trait he once evidenced.

The case of Brian bears some resemblance to cases of genuine and radical repentance. If, as Hume says, "repentance wipes off every crime, if attended with a reformation of life and manners," then Brian's crimes are thoroughly scrubbed and disinfected. We absolve the true penitent of blame because the person now before us is, in an important sense, a different person. The mass murderer who truly reforms is simply not the sort of person who would commit mass murder. Of course, to the extent that one can see traces of the prior murderous personality in the penitent, one still holds him blameworthy. But if one knows that such traces are *entirely* absent, it is irrational to blame him.

Consider, for example, a former Nazi. His last act of atrocity was performed more than forty years ago. Is he still blameworthy? That depends, I suggest, upon what he is like now. If his beliefs have not changed, he is fully as culpable as he was forty years ago. Now suppose he is still the kind of person who would readily kill others if he thought them inferior. Fortunately, his beliefs have changed, and he no longer thinks of any group as inferior. So he would no longer kill anyone. Nonetheless, he is not free of guilt. The killings done forty years ago still express an evil aspect of his character, even though he would not perform those same acts now. And there are many other stories one might tell about our former Nazi. There are many ways in which the Nazi's evil deeds might still express aspects of his character, even though he has changed, and would not kill Jews today. To the extent that those evil deeds still express evil aspects of his character, he remains evil and remains blameworthy. But if he has changed so completely that we cannot see his past deeds as an expression of his current worldview in any way at all, if there is no psychological contact at all between his prior deeds and his current worldview, then he is truly not the sort of person characterized by those deeds. He is no more blameworthy than a repaired bridge is unsafe.

So the criterion for absolution is clear, even if it is often difficult to apply. To the extent that someone's former deeds express her present personhood, she is blameworthy. If her former deeds do not express her present personhood at all, she is fully absolved. This is quite a stringent requirement for absolution. I doubt that *any* former Nazis meet it.[17] But reconditioned Brian does.

Brian's fate is thus unlike that of Midas. Midas has not repented; he was and remains a miser. There is no generous Midas lurking in the background who can say, "Those miserly acts do not express my personhood." Miserly Midas is the only Midas there is.[18]

SUMMARY

None of the arguments commonly given for the claim that determinism obviates moral responsibility succeeds. Autonomy, freedom, and the ability to do otherwise are not prerequisites for moral responsibility. So even if determinism undermines autonomy, freedom, or alternate possibilities, it does not follow that determinism and moral responsibility are incompatible. Acts caused by environment and heredity, we have seen, are relevantly unlike deranged acts, acts done under duress, mitigating circumstances, or hypnosis; acts that result from physical inability or brain tampering, and the acts of stones or computers. They are also relevantly unlike winning a lottery.

Moreover, there are arguments for thinking that we are responsible for determined acts. Brian is not excused from responsibility if scientists give him the very same beliefs and feelings he had before they tampered with his brain. More importantly, there is an account of responsibility and moral evaluation that applies equally well to determined acts. Indeed, once we divorce moral responsibility from how an act or state is caused and realize that persons can be responsible for things beyond their control (as long as those things reflect their worldviews), it no longer seems plausible that determinism and responsibility are incompatible.

V

Punishment and Personal Emotions

THE PICTURE I have been drawing of moral responsibility is fully satisfying only if it can explain those facets of human life, such as punishment and personal emotions, whose justification depends, in some important way, upon moral responsibility. If, instead, we must invoke the traditional view to explain punishment and personal emotions, the conclusions of the last four chapters are less significant than they seem.

This is an important objection. It concedes that my account does give an adequate picture of moral *evaluability:* if someone is, on my account, morally responsible for a bad trait x, then she is a worse person because of x. Let us call what my view explains "Evaluation Responsibility" and the more traditional notion of responsibility "Traditional Responsibility." The objection is that it is Traditional Responsibility, not Evaluation Responsibility, that justifies and explains punishment, as well as such personal emotions as gratitude and resentment. Thus it does no good to show that Evaluation Responsibility is consistent with determinism if Traditional Responsibility is not. For it would still be wrong to punish criminals, still wrong to resent or be grateful to anyone. Again, even though we are Evaluation Responsible for our emotions, it would still be improper to resent us for our emotions, to punish us for our emotions, and so on.

The best way to answer this objection, of course, is to prove that it is Evaluation Responsibility, not Traditional Responsibility, that justifies punishment, personal emotions, responsibility in tort and contract law, and so forth. I will have much to say about these issues in a future work. Here, space permits only a more limited endeavor. If there is a plausible line of thought explaining, in terms of Evaluation Responsibility, those aspects of punishment and personal emotions that depend on moral responsibility, then the burden is on the traditional theorist to show why Traditional Responsibility *must* be reintroduced.

The purpose of this chapter, thus, is to show how my account of moral responsibility may be used to make intelligible the appropriateness of punishment, gratitude, and resentment.

PUNISHMENT AND RETRIBUTION

Punishment is where the sharp edge of moral theory meets the belly of reality. Often enough our moral convictions require us to harm someone, reluctantly, while pursuing some other aim. But only when punishing do any acceptable moral theories mandate that we inflict harm on someone precisely in order to harm her.[1] Not surprisingly, it is punishment that makes moral theorists most squeamish and moral judgments most troubling to make. It is one thing to judge another person adversely. After all, it is *my* judgment, and who else but I should make it? To translate that judgment into punishment, to override ordinary beneficence by deliberately inflicting an otherwise avoidable harm simply because we judge someone adversely, is to take a much more radical step, a step that disquiets all but the most arrogant of us. And so it is the practice of punishment that puts the most pressure on theories of moral responsibility, of blame and praise, of just desert.

This is particularly true of my theory of responsibility, which divorces responsibility from control. Perhaps, the reader might say, it is justifiable to regard someone less highly because he has unsavory emotions. But how can it be justifiable to punish someone for something he could not help? While I may justly think less of someone because of the ineluctable result of his heredity and environment, is it not barbaric to punish him for that?

A complete and adequate answer to these questions would consist of a detailed justification of the practice of punishment, using only Evaluation Responsibility.[2] Instead, we will concentrate on the one aspect of punishment in which moral responsibility plays a key role.

Legal punishment is a complex social practice. It must balance justice and utility, the interests of defendants and the interests of the society at large. Moreover, there is disagreement about the purpose and justification of punishment. Some see punishment as a method of behavioral control (general deterrence and rehabilitative accounts of punishment are examples). Others see punishment as an institution of meting out just deserts, that is, as a purely retributive institution, or as a rhetorical device for asserting publicly the wrongness of certain acts, or as a logically necessary response to the violation of rules, or as erasing an unfair advantage that a felon gains by criminal behavior. Some writers have tried to combine these ideas, for example, by insisting that the purpose of punishment is deterrence, but that it is morally permissible to use the defendant to bring about deterrence only if the defendant is morally responsible for her offense.

Since what concerns us here is moral responsibility, we can simplify matters somewhat. Insofar as moral responsibility is important to justifying punishment, it helps explain what I will call the *retributive aspect* of punishment, namely, the notion that a felon might *merit* or deserve harsh treatment because of his moral failings. The retributive aspect of punishment assumes a greater importance in some theories of punishment than in others. For example, to an extreme utilitarian, for whom punishment is justifiable just because, as a practice, it does more good than harm (the good achieved by deterring many is greater than the harm caused by incarcerating a few), blameworthiness may well be quite irrelevant to punishment.[3] By contrast, an extreme retributivist might hold that the retributive aspect is *all* that is relevant to punishment. We do not need to decide these issues here. Either the justification of punishment does not require a retributive principle, or it does. In the former case, the justification of punishment has nothing to do with moral responsibility, and so it is consistent with every theory of moral responsibility, including mine. Hence the objection to my theory of moral responsibility disappears. For the purpose of argument, therefore, I will assume that the justification of punishment does require some sort of retributive principle. If I can give a plausible version of that retributive principle, based solely on my account of responsibility, then the traditional view is not needed to justify punishment. Thus addressing our worry does not require a full theory of punishment, but only an explanation of retribution, that is, of why someone who has certain traits merits a worse fate than others who lack those traits.

My argument that my account of responsibility is sufficient to explain the retributive demands of punishment can be summarized briefly. First, moral evaluability is enough to generate a principle I will call "abstract justice." Next, a plausible (justifiable) retributive principle can be based on abstract justice. (There is also some reason to think that retribution is *not* based on absolute justice *ab initio*, as the traditional view would insist.) So, since abstract justice relies only on moral evaluability, it follows that moral evaluability is enough to generate a justifiable retributive principle. Since, the objection that concerns us concedes that my view of responsibility gives an adequate account of moral evaluability, it follows that my view of responsibility is enough to generate a justifiable retributive principle.

Hence the justification of punishment does not require the traditional theory of responsibility—my account is enough.

In sum:

1. Either (a) moral responsibility is not relevant to the justification for punishment, or (b) it is relevant only to the retributive aspect of punishment.
2. If 1a is true, then no theory of moral responsibility is needed to justify punishment.
3. Therefore, if 1a is true, the traditional view of moral responsibility is not needed to justify punishment: any view, including mine, will serve.
4. Retribution can be understood in terms of abstract justice.
5. Abstract justice need invoke only moral evaluability.
6. My account of moral responsibility gives an adequate account of moral evaluability.
7. Therefore, my account of moral responsibility gives an adequate account of retribution (from 4, 5, and 6).
8. Therefore, if 1b is true, my account of moral responsibility is enough for the justification of punishment: the traditional account of moral responsibility is not needed.
9. Therefore, the traditional account of responsibility is not needed to justify punishment: my account of responsibility is enough (from 1, 3, and 8).

The Retributive Aspect of Punishment

A short stint of conceptual housekeeping will make our task easier.

First, *moral responsibility* should not be confused with *criminal liability*, even in a perfect legal system. One can be morally blameworthy without being criminally liable. For example, suppose Judy decides to punch Punch when next they meet, but fails to do so because she happens to be tied to a chair during their next encounter. Judy is morally responsible for her malign intention. Provided that Judy never wavered in her commitment to punch Punch and really would have hit him were she not tied to the chair, she is morally no more lustrous than she would have been had the rope failed, enabling her to land a knockout blow. The strength of the rope tells us nothing about Judy's moral character. It reveals nothing about Judy as a moral agent, for it does not reflect, in any way, her moral values, attitudes, beliefs, perceptions, and so forth. So the rope's holding does not change Judy's moral position. But it completely alters her legal position. Judy is not legally liable for anything. She is not guilty of assault, since no one was assaulted. She is not guilty of attempted assault, since she took no step, preliminary or otherwise, toward bringing about the assault. Nor is she guilty of conspiracy, since no others are involved. Her malign intention leaves her morally tainted but legally impeccable.

Conversely, someone might be criminally liable but not morally lax. It is a crime to sell adulterated milk, no matter how scrupulous one was in trying to protect the purity of the milk one sells. What counts is the purity of one's milk, not the purity of one's soul. (Generally, though, the courts have countenanced strict liability only when the penalty is slight.)

Second, one should not conflate the *permissibility* of punishment with the *appropriateness* of punishment. Punishing felons is a social policy, and, like all social policies, is subject to two sorts of evaluations: (a) Is the policy wise, that is, does it cost-effectively serve valid social goals, and (b) is it morally permissible? The latter is a question about the legitimacy of the policy, the former about its advisability. For example, one may wear a heavy coat in July while visiting Baton Rouge. Morality, presumably, does not condemn one. But it is hardly a good idea. When visiting Baton Rouge, one is well advised to leave one's heavy coats in the closet. The converse, whether any impermissible things are advisable, is a matter of some controversy.[4] Generally, questions of permissibility take priority; they set the limits within which social policies may operate. But unless one is a strict Kantian, one must admit that the permissibility of a practice depends somewhat on its usefulness and its cost. For example, it is at least arguably permissible to maim one citizen in order to save the life of every other human being on the planet, but it is clearly not permissible to kill twenty innocent citizens in order to save one dog. So the cost, necessity, and usefulness of the act influence its permissibility. The converse is even clearer; the impermissibility of an act is, obviously, a good reason for not doing it. Thus "may we punish felons" and "should we punish felons," are two distinct questions. They are not, however, unrelated. Ideally, both questions should be answered by an adequate account of the aim of punishment.

Questions about the permissibility of punishment generally involve two questions: is the felon *subject* to punishment, and are we *entitled to mete it out?*

Let us suppose that Hans has broken the law. Is Hans subject to punishment? Two sorts of considerations are relevant. Hans may be punishable because of the needs and claims of others. That is, he may be *extrinsically* subject to punishment. Or Hans may "deserve" or "merit" punishment because of something morally dubious about him: he may be *intrinsically* subject to punishment. Intrinsic subjection, on my account, is explained in terms of abstract justice: my life situation (how well I do in life, how good or bad things are for me) should match or fit my moral situation (how good or bad a person I am). So Hans is intrinsically subject to a worse life if his moral situation is worse than his current life situation. More traditional views construe intrinsic subjection in terms of absolute justice *ab initio;* I am intrinsically subject to punishment if something within my control (in the relevant sense) is bad or evil, if I bring about (in the appropriate way) something morally unacceptable. Thus, for example, Hans is intrinsically subject to punishment (deserves a worse fate) if he freely and knowingly chose to do wrong. In either case, the idea is that, in some sense, people's lives should suit their moral situation, that there should be some sort of correlation between one's moral merits, what one deserves, and what one gets in life, how good or bad one's life is. We may call intrinsic subjection to punishment the "retributive requirement" for punishment. So Hans may be subject to punishment either because he himself merits it, meets the retributive requirement for punishment (intrinsic subjection), or because (a) others have entitlements that can only be satisfied by punishing Hans, and (b) those entitlements are stronger than any entitlement of Hans's *not* to be punished (extrinsic subjection).

Now even if abstract justice (or absolute justice *ab initio*) demands that Hans's life be made worse, it does not follow that *we* are entitled to mete out abstract justice (or absolute justice *ab initio*). It may be, for example, that although a good person is more entitled to live than a bad person, human judgment is fallible, and so no human being is entitled to kill on the basis of her judgments of relative merit. If so, a bad person is subject to being killed in order to save a good person, but no one is entitled to do the killing. Similarly, it might be that, in some sense, a perennially drunk or reckless driver "deserves" to be killed or injured in an accident, but not that anyone has the right to arrange for such an accident to occur.

Finally, even if a system of punishment is permissible, it does not follow that it is a good thing to punish felons. And a bad thing that causes suffering is clearly condemnable. Thus in order to punish Hans, we need to show that (1) either Hans's moral situation merits a worse life, or someone else has an entitlement requiring Hans's punishment that overrides Hans's claims not to be punished, and (2) we are entitled to be the instrument through which Hans obtains his just deserts, or we are entitled to be the instrument by which the extrinsic (other person's) entitlement is met, and (3) punishing Hans serves some legitimate, cost-effective social purpose, either *per se,* or because (a) there is a social policy mandating Hans's punishment that is *generally* cost-effective, and (b) making an exception to that policy is not cost-effective. (It is important to note here that social purposes need not be narrowly utilitarian. For example, one might argue that insuring abstract justice is a valid social purpose.)[5]

These distinctions are crucial for understanding the relationship of moral responsibility to punishment. For example, I will suggest that if Hans is responsible for x in my restricted sense of responsibility, that is sufficient to satisfy condition 1. On the other hand, though punishing people for their emotions may satisfy condition 1, it does *not* (generally) satisfy condition 3. Generally, punishing people for their emotions does not serve a legitimate social purpose.[6] Thus punishing people for their emotions is not (usually) a justifiable practice, despite the fact that (on my view) we are morally responsible for our emotions. Put another way, if I feel morally heinous emotions, then the retributive demands for punishment are satisfied: I am intrinsically subject to punishment for my evil emotions. Still, it would be wrong to punish me for those emotions, since more than intrinsic subjection is required for punishment to be justifiable.

Retributive Views of Punishment

To some readers, it may not be clear how a principle of retribution may be important to the justification of punishment. For their benefit, I will summarize briefly some views of punishment according to which retribution is central to the justification of punishment.

Whereas behavioral-control theories of punishment are concerned with affecting attitudes and behavior, retributive punishment is concerned with moral deserts. Just as some deeds merit both praise and reward, so, it is said, others merit both blame and punishment. Retributive punishment is "earned" by the evildoer; it is due her as an appropriate effect of her act. After all, we are unhappy when a felon escapes punishment not only because she will not be rehabilitated or because she and others like her will not be deterred from committing crimes, but also because justice has not been done. Notice that we do not feel this way about a dog who escapes punishment for digging in the garden. Herbert Morris argues that retributive punishment is mandated by the respect for persons a society should show.[7] To deny punishment to a felon is to treat her as a child or a dog, not as a responsible agent entitled to the moral fruits, for good or ill, of her actions. Thus Morris calls punishment a "right."

Kant so far divorces punishment from training that he insists that were a society to disband, it would first have a moral duty to execute its murderers. It is not only permissible to punish a felon who will pose no further danger to society (*ex hypothesi*, there will be no society to be endangered), but a positive duty to do so. "If legal justice were to perish," insists Kant in the *Metaphysical Elements of Justice,* "life in such a world would not be worthwhile."[8] Kant sees punishment as a duty of justice, and it is only by being just, Kant holds, that we deserve to be happy.

Retributivists differ about what principle of justice requires or even permits punishment. Kant, as usual, has several formulations of his view. For example, he seems to think that the autonomy of the felon is preserved only if we apply to the felon the maxim she herself has chosen to follow. A murderer, for example, has chosen to follow the maxim "do not respect human life." So in executing the murderer, we apply to her the maxim she herself has chosen. Thus we respect her autonomy, her choice of maxims, by executing her. (Does this entail that rapists should be raped? See the discussion of the social contract theory of punishment below.) He also asserts that punishment is necessary "so that everyone may come to realize the merit or desert of his acts, and that blood-guilt not remain on the people. For if it does, they will each be seen as an accomplice to the murder, a participant in the public violation of justice." Needless to say, Kant scholars disagree about how to construe these somewhat vague remarks.

James P. Sterba and David Richards attempt to give Rawlsian accounts of retribution. Sterba seems to combine deterrence arguments for having punishment at all with retributive demands upon the institution of punishment. He argues that it is rational for those in the original position to choose a system of punishment based on moral guilt (a system that recognizes *mens rea* conditions and excuses). Such a system, he suggests, provides citizens the best balance between safeguarding their interests against felons (via the deterrent effect of punishment for culpable offenses), while protecting themselves against punishment (since they will not be punished unless they deliberately or negligently do wrong). Thus a retributive system minimizes the risks of incarceration, while its deterrence value minimizes the risk of being a victim of crime.[9] Richards argues that "rules are thought or spoken of as imposing obligations when the rules justify the imposition of coercive sanctions to make people obey the rules."[10] Rules against killing, stealing, and such impose obligations because they "secure basic human interests without sacrificing the basic interests of agents required to act on them." Hence "in order to better secure obedience to these moral principles, forms of coercion would be found justifiable [in the original position], in that they better secure obedience to moral principles without imposing an undue burden on those coerced" (p. 239). Thus punishment "is a natural expression of our moral attitudes, constituting one of the ways in which we uphold and vindicate principles of treating persons as persons, principles which are the crucial foundation of humane and decent human relationships" (p. 241).

Robert Nozick gives us yet another view of retributivism.[11] "The wrongdoer," says Nozick, "has become disconnected from correct values, and the purpose of punishment is to (re)connect him. . . . The act of retributive punishment itself effects this connection" (p. 374). That is, "correct values are themselves without causal power, and the wrongdoer chooses not to give them effect in his life. So others must give them some effect in his life, in a secondary way. When he undergoes punishment these correct values are not totally without effect in his life (even though he does not follow them), because we hit him over the head with them. Through punishment we give the correct values, *qua* correct values, some significant effect in his life, willynilly linking him up to them" (p. 375). Thus although "punishment does not wipe out the wrong . . . the disconnection with value is repaired . . . nonlinkage is eradicated. Also, the penalty wipes out or attenuates the wrongdoer's link with incorrect values, so that he now regrets having followed them or at least is less pleased that he did" (p. 379).

Another variant is the "expiative" theory of punishment. As Wasserstrom points out, the expiative theory is hard to classify.[12] Like deterrence, it is concerned with future consequences, but like retribution, it fastens on what is owed to past moral guilt. Punishment, according to this view, aims at giving felons a way to expiate their crimes. It allows a criminal to put his crime behind him, and so, as Hyman Gross puts it, "restore himself to the ranks of the respectable citizens of the community."[13] Wasserstrom points out that this is at most an argument for making punishment *available* to felons who want to expiate their crimes. "It is not an adequate justification for punishing those who [do not] desire expiation" (p. 136).

One interesting consequence of retributive views of punishment should be noted. Since punishment, according to retributivism, may be meted out only to the blameworthy, it is wrong to punish a felon who, though she did wrong, is no longer morally tainted. Thus if, as Hume suggested, sincere repentance washes out all moral stain, it would be wrong to punish the sincerely repentant. Again, the repentant murderer has given up the maxim that human life should be sacrificed for personal goods. To execute her is thus not to apply her own maxim to her, since she now rejects that maxim. The maxim to which she now adheres is "never kill." To execute her now would be to deny her autonomy, her free choice of a maxim.

These arguments about repentance do not apply to what I will call "Hegelian" retributivism.[14] If one holds that the murderer, in killing, has brought an evil into the world, and that the balance of good and evil can be restored only by punishing the felon, then it is reasonable to punish the repentant felon. Despite the felon's repentance, the evil in the world ledger remains, and must be eliminated by punishment. Few philosophers have held this view, however, if only because it is far from clear how punishing the felon removes the original evil from the world ledger (while sincere repentance does not).

In sum, if the retributive view of punishment is correct, punishment is appropriate only if (1) the person being punished is morally responsible for her offense, (2) (thus?) the felon is not sincerely repentant (in the right way), and (3) the offense warrants the punishment (the moral turpitude of the offense is commensurate with the severity of the punishment).

Now it is important to note that all of these theories, as described above, are equally consistent with my account of moral responsibility and the traditional account. (Even Kant's suggestion that punishment is applying the felon's own maxim to herself is consistent with my account, if we construe "maxim" widely enough and do not insist that maxims must be "freely chosen." Rather, a felon may be treated as adopting a maxim insofar as that maxim reflects her worldview.) These theories explain the connection between punishment and desert. They do not give us an account of desert. In particular, they do not indicate whether desert is based on abstract justice, as I claim, or absolute justice *ab initio,* as the traditionalists insist. It is to this question we now turn.

Abstract Justice

Absolute justice *ab initio* insists that everyone have exactly the same chance, that no one is favored by circumstance. In particular, it requires that everyone have the same chance to be good or bad. It demands absolute moral equality between persons from the moment of conception. So absolute justice *ab initio* requires that everyone start in the same circumstances: at birth, each person has an equal opportunity and proclivity to act morally. And the only thing that may differentiate our moral circumstances, at any given time, is prior moral merit. No person may have a moral advantage others lack, unless that advantage was gained by moral merit. I have already suggested (in Chapter III) that life is not absolutely just *ab initio,* and that there is no defensible reason to demand that it be so.

Instead, I will base retribution on abstract justice. David Lyons refers to what I call "abstract justice" as "a theory of cosmic desert: good people deserve to fare well and bad people deserve to fare badly."[15] Broadly speaking, "abstract justice is served" means that what happens to people matches or fits their moral positions. So if little Billie, despite his parents' warnings, recklessly hops up and down on his bed as if it were a trampoline, and, as a result, bruises his toe, we might say that Billie's injury is "just." He deserved it, we might say. By contrast, we might bemoan the injustice of Hermione's serious injury, incurred despite her stringent and reasonable precautions. Similarly, we say that it is unjust that a good person is continually ill while a wicked person enjoys uninterrupted good health. Finally, when we say that it is unjust for one felon to receive a five year sentence and another to receive a suspended sentence, we mean (or might mean) that since the two felons' moral positions are the same, their life situations should be the same. What all these cases have in common is the insistence that the circumstances of people's lives concord with their moral merits. This is the conception of justice I call "abstract justice."

It is important to note that, strictly speaking, abstract justice applies primarily to lives as a whole. There is no way, I think, to create a rigorous and morally defensible general formula that equates particular fates with particular acts. There is something distinctly odd about asking whether cheating in a card game merits a severe headache, or whether a mere fleabite is adequate. Rather, abstract justice demands that, overall, the better a person is, relative to others, the better, overall, her life should be, relative to others. (Presumably, it also requires that good people lead good lives and not merely lives a little less horrible than the lives sinners lead. But I am uncertain about what such an "absolute" standard would look like. For most of our purposes, the relative standard is sufficient.) Sometimes, it is true, we talk about the abstract justice of a particular event. We might feel, for example, that the terrorist deserved to be blown up by the premature explosion of his bomb, just as we might say a pitcher deserved to lose a game because she allowed seven earned runs in the fourth inning. We say this, though, because however well she pitched in the other innings, her overall performance cannot be judged as exemplary if she pitches so badly in the fourth inning. Similarly, a single act may be so atrocious that the doer's life, overall, must be judged harshly, no matter what else he does. So, ultimately, abstract justice refers to the whole of a person's life, just as a pitcher's deserving to lose a game refers to the whole of her participation in the game.[16]

Unfortunately for my purposes, the law generally evaluates the moral heinousness of a single infraction of law, rather than the felon's life generally. So we will need some mechanism for judging, at least for the purpose of legal punishment, the extent to which a single particular violation of the law requires a worse fate. We will create such a mechanism by introducing some simplifying assumptions that serve as "legal fictions." The use of these fictions is justifiable insofar as the legal practice employing them is a justifiable practice. But, from a strictly moral point of view, they are merely fictions.

At this point, all I want to claim about abstract justice is that it is a good thing; it is desirable that people's relative life situations match their relative moral situations. I am not arguing that life is in fact abstractly just, or even that we ought to make it our goal to insure that the world is abstractly just. I am arguing only that abstract justice is, other things being equal, a good thing. We ought to value abstract justice. We ought to prefer, other things being equal, that abstract justice be served.

Certainly, most of us share this intuition. On the other hand, it is not incoherent to want everyone, saints and sinners alike, to lead happy and flourishing lives. For example, Peter van Inwagen has suggested to me (in conversation) that as long as no one gets less than she deserves, there is nothing undesirable about some people's getting more than they deserve. Yet most of us are distressed by a sinner's flourishing more than a saint; such a situation, we feel, is not fair. And that is not good.

I will not attempt to *prove* the truth of our intuition. Rather, I will argue for a weaker claim. Our feeling about abstract justice reflects many of our other views, and is embedded in important elements of our way of life, of the way we see the world. If I am right, the belief that abstract justice is desirable is not merely an isolated prejudice, but is part of a pattern of deeply seated attitudes we bring to the world.

Abstract justice is closely tied to the moral character of loyalty. Indeed, I will argue, our concept of friendship is unintelligible without something like a principle of abstract justice. This suggests two arguments for abstract justice: the argument from loyalty, and the argument from friendship.

The argument from loyalty suggests that if loyalty is a virtue, then abstract justice's being served is a good thing. Since viewing loyalty in this way is not only a deep moral feeling most of us share, but also very important to the way most of us look at and lead our lives, the intrinsic value of abstract justice is also important to the way most of us look at and lead our lives.

By "loyalty" to x I mean a strong and enduring attachment to, commitment to, and special preference for the flourishing and welfare of x; to be loyal to x is to be, in important ways, dedicated to the well-being of x. Loyalty to x might be expressed by making a sacrifice for the good of x, by working to x's benefit simply out of a desire to see x flourish, and so on. Now loyalty of this sort might be a "virtue," at least on some theories of virtue, just because being loyal usually has good *effects* (such as maximizing happiness), rather than because of any particular moral worth loyalty as such might have. But in calling loyalty a virtue I mean that appropriate loyalty has some intrinsic moral worth. I say "appropriate" loyalty because, as I will suggest, inappropriate loyalty, for example, loyalty to evil, is not good at all. I am claiming, in other words, that it is not attachment as such that is good, but rather standing by someone or something because that thing somehow calls for, deserves, or is worth standing by. Loyalty to the good, that is, commitment to the welfare of good things (at least in part) *because* they are good things, is the sort of thing that, by its nature, contributes to the goodness of a world. This is because it is only through this sort of loyalty that our moral values are realized in and expressed by our attachments. Only through loyalty of this sort do our attachments proclaim our moral commitments. Conversely, to be equally attached to goodness and to evil is to turn our backs on the moral realm, to refuse, in an important sense, to be a moral agent, because when I do so I refuse to make a crucial aspect of my life a reflection of my values, a realization and beacon of good according to my conception of good. Put another way, if I fail to distinguish between good and evil in my well-wishing, if I am indifferent as to whether a good or an evil person receives the better fate, then I divorce morality from my central commitments.

Now I suggest that it is an intrinsically good thing that people lead lives that express and realize commitment to the good, a good thing that people function as moral agents. Recall the discussion of the moral worth of persons in Chapter II: it is because I lead such a life that I have moral worth, and it is only because there are people who lead such lives that morality is applicable to the world at all. Without such a moral perspective, the world is just a meaningless chatter of events. And a significant world is better than a meaningless world.

In any case, the value of leading such lives does seem to be important to our way of looking at and leading our lives. So either our way of looking at and leading our lives is basically mistaken, or commitment to abstract justice is an intrinsically good thing. But commitment to abstract justice would not be an intrinsically good thing (as the above considerations show) unless abstract justice's obtaining were an intrinsically good thing. Thus, unless we are deeply mistaken in our basic outlook, abstract justice's obtaining is an intrinsically good thing.

We can formulate an argument of this sort as follows:

STEP 1. To be loyal to something is, in significant part, to wish well for it, to have a special commitment to its flourishing.

Comment: This claim is fairly obvious, since if I regard your flourishing as no more important than anyone else's, if I am indifferent to whether it is you or anyone else who receives a boon, then I am not loyal to you.[17]

STEP 2. If our loyalty is not given, at least in part, for moral reasons, that is, because we judge the thing to which we are loyal to be good, then loyalty is not a good thing. (Unless loyalty's appropriateness is at least partially dependent on the goodness of the thing to which one is loyal, appropriate loyalty is not a virtue.)

Comment: Being arbitrarily attached to any arbitrary thing is not particularly good. Indeed, it seems to be evil to be attached to evil. Moreover, to deny that our attachments are properly formed, at least in part, on the basis of goodness is to divorce our attachments from the moral realm.

STEP 3. Unless good people specially *deserve* to flourish, there is no (moral) reason to be committed to the welfare of good people and institutions rather than evil ones.

Comment: This claim requires some further argument. We may begin by asking about the moral basis of loyalty to good rather than evil. What is the reason why I should prefer the flourishing of something I find good (for example, Gandhi) over something I find evil (for example, the terrorist Evans)? The question here, of course, is not "what might *cause* me to feel this," but "what moral *justification* is there for this preference?" The only feasible answer, I will argue, is that it is a good thing that the good flourish more than others, and hence that a world in which the good flourish more than the wicked is, to that extent, a better world.

The argument is as follows: suppose, on the one hand, it is true that abstract justice is a good thing, that it is a better world insofar as the good fare better than the wicked. Then my hoping that Gandhi flourishes more than Evans is, at least in part, a hope that the world be a good world. And such a hope is not only justifiable, but a precondition of being a moral agent (being committed to the obtaining of states of affairs one thinks good, or at least acceptable, given the possible alternatives). Thus, if abstract justice is a good thing, there is a moral reason to prefer Gandhi's flourishing to Evans's.

On the other hand, suppose it is false that abstract justice is a good thing. Suppose, in other words, that morality is indifferent to whether it is Gandhi or Evans who flourishes, and a world in which Evans flourishes more than Gandhi is no worse than a world in which Gandhi flourishes more than Evans. There are then two possibilities: morality may require that *I* be indifferent to who flourishes, or it may not. In the first case, loyalty, whether to good or to evil, is always immoral. Thus loyalty is not a good thing. Suppose, then, that morality does not require me to be indifferent to whether it is Evans or Gandhi who flourishes. It follows that if I hope that Evans flourishes more than Gandhi, my hope would be in no way at odds with morality, since, *ex hypothesi*, morality itself is indifferent to whether Evans or Gandhi flourishes more. Similarly, my hope that Evans flourishes more than Gandhi is not inconsistent with wanting the world to be a good world, since, *ex hypothesi*, the world in which Evans flourishes more than Gandhi is no worse than the world in which Gandhi flourishes more than Evans. So on this hypothesis as well, it follows that there is no moral reason for being loyal to good rather than to evil. Thus, if morality itself does not prefer the flourishing of the good to the flourishing of the evil, there is no moral reason for me to be loyal to the good. Hence, unless abstract justice is a good thing, there is no moral reason for being loyal to the good rather than to the evil.

STEP 4. Therefore, unless abstract justice is a good thing, (appropriate) loyalty is not a good thing (not a virtue).

STEP 5. But (appropriate) loyalty is a good thing (appropriate loyalty is a virtue).

CONCLUSION: Abstract justice is a good thing.

Since loyalty of this sort is central to friendship, it is not surprising that we can also give an argument that abstract justice is crucial to the moral character of friendship. The argument is as follows:

STEP 1. Caring for someone is finding in him attributes that demand affection.

Comment: One can, of course, care *about* things without finding them good, worthy of affection, and so forth. The person who says "my country, right or wrong" cares about the welfare of his country, that is, the welfare of his country makes an important difference to him. Caring about someone is not necessarily personal, in the sense that my concern for her may have little to do with her intrinsic character, with the person she is. Caring *for* something, however, is a more personal relationship. To care for something is to have an affection for something that stems from the character of that thing, to care for a thing because of what it itself is.[18] It is not just that x's nature *causes* my affection. If, for example, you have strange psychic powers that allow you to command others to sacrifice their welfare for yours, they do not thereby care for you, and their relationship to you is not a personal one. Nor is my caring about a brother whom I have never met a personal affection; that care stems from the fact of our biological relation, rather than from the sort of person he is. Rather, I care for you if my affection is (in my view) an appropriate or fitting response to your character, much as anger might be the fitting response to an act of injustice, or sympathy to an undeserved hardship. Now it is appropriate to say that my affection for x stems from x's nature or character in this way only if there is something about x, some attribute it has, to which (in my view) affection is the appropriate response. Thus caring for someone is finding in him attributes that demand affection.

STEP 2. Part of feeling affection for a friend is wishing him well, hoping that he flourishes, hoping that his life is a happy one.

STEP 3. Unless attributes demand affection at least in large part because they are good, caring for someone is not a (morally) good thing.

Comment: Here again, to deny that our affections are properly given (at least in part) on the basis of a recognition of goodness is to divorce affection from the moral realm.

STEP 4. Caring for someone is a morally good thing.[19]

STEP 5. Therefore caring for someone is hoping he flourishes because he is good.

STEP 6. Thus to care for someone is, in part, to express a commitment to abstract justice.

A third line of thought deserves mention. To be a moral being is, in part, to want the world to be a good world. Now to be good is not

only to conform to moral standards, but to make moral discrimina-
tions, to mark and respect moral values. So moral beings should desire that the world not only be good, but mark and respect moral
values. Moral beings should desire that the world, in the fate it accords individuals, should be a respecter of goodness. For such a
world is a moral world, a world that reflects, is imbued with, morality. Now the obvious way for the world to reflect moral distinctions
is for good to flourish and evil to fare poorly. That is the world, one
might say, that a morally discriminating creator, one who wished her
creation to mark moral distinctions, would create. So if there are evil
people in the world, it is better that the universe mark out evil with a
harsh fate, rather than treating good and evil people alike.

In sum, to be loyal to someone, care for someone, or wish a friend
well, ideally, is to think his particular virtues deserve good fortune.
Without a conception of abstract justice, there is no reason for loyalty of this sort. Unless good people specially deserve to flourish,
there is no reason to be committed to the welfare of good people and
institutions rather than evil ones. And if our loyalty, friendship, and
care is not given, at least in large measure, for moral reasons, that is,
because we deem it a thing good, then loyalty, friendship, and care
are divorced from the moral realm. Thus to deny the intrinsic goodness of abstract justice's being served is to sever the link between
morality and some of our crucial practices. And to do that is to im-
poverish our conception of ourselves as moral beings. It also under-
cuts an important aspect of human life. If abstract justice is desirable,
to be committed to good is also to care for good, and also to hope
for a world that respects goodness, to desire that fate reflects moral
distinctions. And in fact, for most of us, these elements are inextrica-
ble. But if abstract justice is not desirable, this element of human
experience is a mistake, an unfortunate trait we happen to have.

But perhaps I have been too hasty. The issue between my view of
responsibility and the traditional view depends on the contrast between abstract justice and absolute justice *ab initio*. We should ask,
then, whether friendship, loyalty, and the like should be based on
absolute justice *ab initio* rather than upon abstract justice. Should I
withhold my loyalty from someone who, though evil, could not help
being evil, or who started life at a disadvantage? The answer is "yes"
if loyalty should be based on abstract justice, "no" if loyalty should
be based on absolute justice *ab initio*.

Should I base my friendships only on traits within a person's control, as absolute justice *ab initio* would suggest? Here the obvious
answer is that friendship and loyalty should be based on abstract

justice. We do not befriend people who are disagreeable or cruel, whether or not they could help being disagreeable or cruel. This is not just self-interest on our part. If John, although pleasant to me, beats his wife and is a cheat in business, I do not wish to be his friend, whether or not he could help beating his wife or being a crook. Rather, the basis of friendship, namely the affection based on my values, is missing. Nor, conversely, do I withhold friendship from a person I admire simply because his admirable traits are due to a genetic or environmental advantage. After all, to base friendship on absolute justice *ab initio* is to base human relationships not on what people are, but on the persons they would have been under other circumstances. And that is absurd, because I cannot have any substantial human relationship with a counterfactual person (a person who would have been). Perhaps Mike's conversation would have been intellectually stimulating had his genetic endowment or early childhood history been different, but that fact does not enable me to have an intellectually worthwhile discussion with Mike, and so it is just fatuous to spend hours seeking out Mike's views on quantum physics, while away my evenings trying to get Mike to produce a new solution to the liar paradox, and so on. Mike is the person he is and should be treated as such. Mike is not the person he would have been under very different conditions, and it is not that hypothetical person whose traits should dictate my dealings with the real Mike. For similar reasons, it seems absurd to insist that I may not prefer, even a tiny bit, the flourishing of a saint to the flourishing of a cruel and stupid person who could not help being cruel and stupid. Surely the fact that the saint *is* extremely good (given my criteria for goodness) entitles him to some loyalty on my part. My values commit me to some degree of loyalty to those things that realize and express my values, not to things that cannot help violating those values.

Thus our conceptions of friendship and loyalty include a commitment to the importance of abstract justice's being served, and disregard the dictates of absolute justice *ab initio*.

Obviously, I have not proven that abstract justice's being served is desirable merely by showing that a belief in abstract justice enriches our conception of ourselves as moral beings, is important to our conceptions of loyalty and friendship, and links morality with important human practices. It could be that our conceptions of friendship and of ourselves as moral beings are mistaken. True, these conceptions are central to our way of life. But our basic outlook on the world may be mistaken. However, to show that a given belief P is crucial to and deeply embedded in a viable way of life is to give *a* reason (though not an absolutely conclusive one) for believing P. Moreover, in the absence of a powerful argument that P is false, it is rational to adopt P on this basis. Thus I have given a strong reason (though not a conclusive one) to trust our intuition that abstract justice is desirable.[20]

A THEORY OF RETRIBUTION

The outline of my account of retribution should now be clear. In this section, I detail that account and try to make it plausible. But first it is important to stress that retribution is only one aspect of punishment. There may be reasons other than retribution for modifying fines or imprisonment, such as the deterrent effect of a lengthy prison sentence or the hardship that imprisoning the defendant would cause her dependents. In this discussion I am considering only the retributive aspect of punishment. Keep in mind, therefore, that our results must be modified by whatever other considerations are relevant. When I say, for example, that latitude in prison sentences should reflect only the moral turpitude of the felon, I mean that this is the only consideration relevant to *retribution*.

Desert

Since most theories of retribution employ, explicitly or implicitly, the notion of desert, it will be useful to begin with a few words about the concept of desert.[21] There are, of course, several different ways in which I may be said to "deserve" something. The two senses of "deserve" relevant to our purposes are *overall desert* and *specific desert*.

Overall desert is based on abstract justice, on a moral fit between a person and her life. I deserve a harsh fate if I am an evil person and a pleasant fate if I am a good person. There should be a "fit" between the entirety of a person's moral situation (the sum of her moral merits and demerits) and the entirety of her life situation (all the good and bad things in her life). Someone may be said to deserve a specific result (*specific desert*), such as having a vase fall on her foot, when that event would bring about such a fit. In other words, she deserves to have the vase fall on her foot because that would balance the books, bring into agreement her "moral credits" column and her "life situation" column. But there is more to specific desert than mere balancing of the books. The specific result must be an *appropriate* way of balancing the books.

For example, overall desert suggests that the dedicated, unselfish AIDS researcher deserves to flourish. But when it comes to specific desert, we want to say not just that the AIDS researcher deserves to flourish in ways unrelated to AIDS research, but that he deserves to succeed at finding a cure for AIDS. When we say that the careless person deserves to be injured in an accident, we mean an accident resulting from his carelessness. We do not mean that he is getting what he deserves if an airplane falls from the sky into his living room. I would accommodate this perception by saying that there are two elements of what a person deserves: *merit* and *appropriateness*. Although the AIDS researcher may merit, by dint of his moral qualities, having a wonderful marriage, this does not seem as *appropriate* a reward as his finding a cure for AIDS. In ordinary speech, when we speak of "poetic justice," we mean that an outcome is not only just, but particularly appropriate in this way. There is no single criterion for appropriateness, of course, since what is appropriate depends upon how we conceive the moral point of the event, which aspects we pick out as most salient. And there is often more than one legitimate way of conceiving of the moral point of an event or situation. On the other hand, we generally regard the goal or aim of a morally significant activity as morally salient. Thus it is not surprising that we tend to agree that someone who works hard and intelligently toward a worthwhile goal, for no reason other than because it is a worthwhile goal, deserves to succeed.

So far, we have distinguished between overall and specific desert, and between merit and appropriateness. A third distinction is necessary for a theory of desert. Desert comes in different strengths: not only may an agent deserve more or less hardship or reward, but she may deserve it more or less *strongly*. It is sometimes convenient to speak as if there were a dividing line between those whose harsh fates are required by justice and those to whom abstract justice permits a particular harsh fate. We may define *strong desert* as follows: a strongly deserves x when, because of A's moral situation, abstract justice requires that A receive x; it is morally unfortunate if A does not receive x. We may define *weak desert* thusly: A weakly deserves x when, because of A's moral situation, A is subject to x; there are no grounds for moral complaint if A receives x.

It is instructive to contrast the dangerous driver with the person who refuses to wear a seat belt. Arguably, the person who habitually endangers others by his reckless driving, in full knowledge of the danger but uncaring of the peril he poses to others, deserves to die young in an auto accident: it would be unfair if he lived to a ripe old age. The dangerous driver merits death. This is because our dangerous driver flaunts objective morality in such a way that his flourishing constitutes a kind of moral blemish on the world state. Such a flagrant and serious flaunting of correct values calls out for retribution.

By contrast, the person who habitually drives without a seat belt does not merit death. She is guilty of putting a minute's inconvenience ahead of safety, and this is a morally incorrect ranking of priorities. But this is a minor evil. Since, overall, she is not an evil person, it would ordinarily be unjust for her to die young: she would ordinarily deserve to live to a ripe old age. However, she habitually shows disdain for such protective strategies as wearing seat belts. Because she flaunts the protective strategy of seat belts, the ordinary rules of abstract justice do not apply to her being harmed in an auto accident.[22] She has, as it were, waived her ordinary moral immunity from dying young. That is, although it is not the case that she deserves to die young in an auto accident, it is not unjust if she does. True, the minor evil involved in scorning seat belts is not a capital offense, and so it does not violate abstract justice if she does, in fact, live to a ripe old age. But if, in fact, she dies young as a result of not wearing a seat belt, she has nothing to complain about. She is not getting less than she deserves. For although her moral status indicates that she deserves to live to a ripe old age, her disregard of safety means that being killed in an auto accident is removed from the realm to which abstract justice applies (she has only herself to blame.)[23] I express this by saying that the reckless driver strongly deserves to die in an auto accident, while someone who fails to wear a seat belt weakly deserves to die in an auto accident.[24]

The difference here is not in the degree of forseeability (probability of harm resulting), nor in the fact that harm from an accident is an unintended side effect. After all, the dangerous driver strongly deserves some misfortune, even though harm to others is an unintended side effect, and people may strongly deserve harsh fates for negligently causing unlikely harms, if the harm is sufficiently great (starting a nuclear war, for example). What matters is the moral character of the shortcoming. We place moral stances along a continuum stretching from horrific, evil, bad, and indifferent to good, excellent, and extraordinary. Where we place an agent's attitude is a complex judgment involving the entirety of the moral story concerning her (remember the complexity of the cases discussed earlier). There are several dimensions involved. One dimension is the nature of the values violated. For example, respect for life is a more central value than is the value of industry. Similarly, placing a minute's inconvenience above personal integrity is worse than placing losing one's sight and legs above another's right to life. Thus the decision to perjure oneself to avoid a moment's inconvenience is worse than the decision to kill someone when threatened with blindness and amputation. Another dimension is the proclamative character of the action or situation. The more the situation calls for making a moral stand, the more serious it is. Sometimes it is the agent himself who turns an action into the taking of a public stance. For example, a fraternity at Louisiana State University flew a Confederate flag on Martin Luther King Day. What makes this action particularly egregious is the proclamative character of the act: it constitutes a public proclamation of disdain for the values Martin Luther King Day celebrates. There is no simple formula for assessing an agent's desert. However, the more flagrant the violation of correct values, the more strongly deserved is the harm. Parallel remarks apply to reward, *mutatis mutandis*.

In short, strong desert is governed by moral appropriateness of harsh fate for an egregious moral flaw, while weak desert is governed by causal appropriateness of harsh fate for a flaw which, while not morally egregious, removes the agent's normal (moral) immunity from a harsh fate.

In the law, weak desert plays an important role in civil actions, especially tort law. Criminal law is generally based upon strong desert. There are, of course, exceptions, and any detailed treatment of criminal liability would have to take account of them. For the most part, however, punishment is based on strong desert.

The Theory

Generally, retribution is a mechanism for establishing overall desert. A person deserves or merits retribution insofar as, and to the extent and manner in which, his life situation is better than his moral situation.[25] Retribution calls for specific punishments when those punishments are specifically deserved: an individual deserves a particular punishment when that punishment would be an appropriate means of bringing about a "fit" between the entirety of his moral situation (the sum of his moral merits and demerits) and the entirety of his life situation (all the good and bad things in his life).

This principle, which I will call the principle of "general retribution," tells us who deserves punishment and just what sorts of punishments are appropriate. However, general retribution evaluates not just particular acts or traits, but the whole of a person's moral situation, and not just particular punishments or harsh treatment, but the whole of a person's life. We are rarely in a position to make this kind of judgment, nor should the law be expected to do so. Rather, the law must make judgments about penalties for particular evil traits or actions. Thus, for practical application, we need a "spin-off" theory that will link particular acts or traits to particular punishments (for example, incarceration for ten years). We need, in other words, a principle of specific retribution. As we will see, the principle of specific retribution is only an approximation of the general principle of retribution. It is, we might say, a necessary compromise. However, I will suggest, the general principle should sometimes be used to mitigate the results of the specific principle.

The *principle of specific retribution* I propose is that a person deserves or merits punishment for x insofar as abstract justice demands that his fate be worse than it otherwise would be because of x. Put another way, if x is an evil characteristic, then, according to abstract justice, one who has x should have a worse fate than someone otherwise like him who does not have x. Thus we may view x as a "vector" contributing to the moral situation of the agent; x contributes n degrees of badness to the overall moral situation of the agent. The appropriate punishment, therefore, is a punishment that contributes n degrees of badness to the overall life situation of an agent.

We might arrive at such a calculation in several ways. We might imagine the "standard agent," who does not have trait x, and ask how much worse a person she would be if she were otherwise the same, but evidenced trait x. We might then ask ourselves how much better the standard person deserves to fare in life than does someone who is like the standard person but with trait x. This thought experiment is, in important ways, a fiction. It is meant, however, only to be suggestive, a way of helping to bring out our judgments of relative abstract justice. Alternatively, we might gauge our principle of specific retribution according to the context of punishment. I will suggest below a general framework the criminal law might use for evaluating the relevant sort of moral turpitude of an offender.

Notice that if the principle of specific retribution, coupled with a corresponding principle of specific reward, were applied to *all* of an agent's traits, the result would be the general principle of retribution. The specific principle is thus a compromise to the extent that its application is limited in practice to only some of an agent's traits or characteristics. (The situation is analogous to vectors of force in classical mechanics.)

Unfortunately, however, the specific principle still requires us to make impractical judgments. Ten years in jail may prove a greater hardship for one person than it does for another. Clearly, it is not reasonable to ask the law to determine, about each felon, just how much of a hardship it is for her to spend a year in jail. As a practical matter, therefore, we have to adopt a simplifying assumption, which I will call the *assumption of uniformity:* a punishment inflicted on one person has the same degree of harshness as the same punishment inflicted on anyone else. This assumption is not in fact true, and thus it is sometimes important to modify that assumption. I suggest, thus, that the principle of uniformity be taken as defeasible—we adopt the assumption of uniformity except when strong evidence is presented that it is appropriate to modify the assumption in a particular way. We sometimes do this in assessing fines. Since a hundred-dollar fine might be a severe hardship to a poor person and a trivial hardship to a rich person, we sometimes give judges latitude to impose a fine of not less than x and not more than y. This permits the judge to lessen or magnify the fine depending not only on the moral turpitude of the offending act, but also upon the harshness of the fine for the particular defendant. We do not, generally, modify the uniformity assumption when levying prison sentences. The use of judicial discretion in meting out prison sentences is generally intended, at least in our legal system, to reflect only the moral turpitude of the offense.[26]

How the turpitude or viciousness of the offense is measured depends somewhat on the context. In most nonlegal contexts, the viciousness of the offense is judged by the extent to which it evidences contempt for the correct conception of human goodness, to the extent that it reflects evil commitments and an evil worldview. Here my account of moral responsibility is quite helpful. As I pointed out, Abner, who kills in the belief that he is saving his victim's immortal soul, deserves praise for his concern for others' well-being, blame for his contempt for others' rights, and so on. In addition, if Abner is aware of the need to respect others' rights, and does not do so, he is blameable for the additional trait of displaying contempt for moral obligation. That is, he not only fails to do what he is in fact obligated to do, but also gives little regard to the very notion of a moral obligation. In short, the theory of responsibility detailed earlier in this work gives us a powerful tool for making such assessments.

In law, however, we are not always concerned with moral turpitude as such. I will discuss, briefly, tort law and criminal law. The nature and moral underpinnings of tort law have been changing, and the basis for retribution in tort law is correspondingly being affected. Since my purpose is not a full and adequate account of tort law, I will, for the sake of simplicity, discuss retribution as it applies to the earlier, simpler conception of tort law.

Historically, the special province of tort law was harm caused by failure to live up to the obligations of care and fair dealing implicit in belonging to a *polis*, a civic community. Thus, historically, special weight was given to the obligations of due care and fair dealing. Thus the retributive element in tort law consists mostly in matching the relevant aspects of the tortfeasor to the degree to which he shows contempt for the duties of due care and fair dealing. More precisely, the court matches those aspects of the life situation of the tortfeasor that are directly affected by both the court's decision and the tort situation, such as the amount of the court's award and the benefits the tortfeasor obtained by her wrongful action, against the degree to which the tortfeasor's action may rationally be construed as evidencing disregard for, contempt of, or failure to live up to the duties of due care and fair dealing. The law generally takes an "objective" view of wrong (that is, it assumes that the tortfeasor evidenced the disregard that most people who acted as the tortfeasor did would be evidencing). It is open to the court, however, to modify the "objective" degree of wrong by considering evidence concerning the tortfeasor's actual state of mind. It is important to note that the retributive element of tort law applies not only to punitive or exemplary damages, but to the award for damages as well. For example, even for a highly culpable act, if the hardship caused by paying damages is great enough, retribution may require no exemplary damages (though, again, deterrence may require more hardship than retribution alone demands).

Punishment in the criminal law, I suggest, aims at implementing the rule of law. Thus the relevant criterion in criminal law is the extent to which the offense shows contempt for the rule of law. Since, I would urge, the law must be understood as expressing the public morality of the community, the centrality and importance of the values toward which the offense shows contempt is a relevant factor. Thus, since the sanctity of life is a deeper and more central value in our law than is regimentation of traffic, murder shows greater contempt for the rule of law than does jaywalking. The character of the offense is also relevant: keeping sloppy records shows some contempt for the legal duty to keep accurate records, but less than does deliberately falsifying them. Here again, the techniques employed by my theory of responsibility are helpful in assessing precisely the degree of contempt for the rule of law shown by an offense.

Finally, the criminal law generally makes the simplifying assumption that the felon's situation is, apart from his offense, already abstractly just. Thus the courts, in assessing the retributive element of punishment, need only consider the extent to which the turpitude of the offense requires the felon's life situation to be worsened. However, when this simplifying assumption would create too much of an imbalance between moral situation and life situation, the courts may modify the assumption ("the defendant has already suffered enough"). Here again, the pattern is that in making judgments of specific retribution a simplifying assumption is made, subject to modification in order to bring the results of applying the judgment of specific retribution in line with the general principle of retribution.

Retribution and Abstract Justice

The moral justification of this theory of retribution is fairly straightforward. We have already seen reason to think that abstract justice's being served is a good thing. Thus it is a good thing, it is morally desirable, if a person's life situation matches her moral situation. The theory of retribution given above simply articulates what is involved in a person's life situation matching her moral situation. Thus it is a good thing, a morally desirable outcome, if the retributive principles spelled out above are reflected in people's fates.

Now it does not follow, of course, that any action designed to bring about a morally desirable outcome is justified. It may be, for example, that we are not entitled to act in that way, or that our acting in that way may also bring about morally undesirable outcomes that outweigh the good for which we are striving. Thus it does not follow that our meting out a punishment in line with my theory of retribution is justified.

But that is not the question at issue. The justifiability of punishing in accordance with principles of retribution pertains to a different issue, namely the relationship between retribution and punishment. Explaining that relationship requires a full theory of punishment, a task that must await a future work. Our concern is only with moral responsibility. The point is that insofar as moral responsibility is a precondition for justified punishment, it is because someone not morally responsible for an offense is not intrinsically subject to punishment. But if, indeed, abstract justice's being served is a good thing, then someone whose life situation is better than her moral situation is intrinsically subject to punishment. That is, there is a moral demand that, as a result of her offense, her life be made worse. This moral demand may be overridden by other factors. But to the extent that abstract justice is not served by her remaining unpunished, there is *a* moral reason why she ought to be punished (even if not by us), *a* moral reason why her fate should be worse than it is. And so, to the extent that morally meriting a worse fate is a necessary condition for punishment, my principles of retribution indicate when that condition is fulfilled. Any other conditions there might be for inflicting punishment stem from factors other than moral responsibility (for example, serving an important social goal, or the point and/or moral authority of the law the offender violated). Similarly, there may be good moral reasons for punishing people who are not morally at fault, or for punishing them to an extent greater than their moral culpability would warrant. For example, the reasons generally given to justify making selling adulterated milk a crime of strict liability include the facts that the vendor of the milk is generally better able to bear the risk than is the consumer, that the extra deterrence gained by strict liability is worth the (relatively) small fines to which the vendor might be subject, and so on. The point, once again, is that none of these reasons bear upon the moral responsibility of the seller.

Abstract Justice and Responsibility

It is also relatively easy to show that my theory of responsibility is enough to assess abstract justice. My view of responsibility, after all, gives a detailed account of how good or bad a person is, of the moral merits and demerits of that person's moral situation. I have argued at length that, however she got to be that way, a person with an evil worldview is an evil person, since what she is, as a moral agent, is precisely that worldview as it operates in her behavior, circumstances, thoughts, feelings, and the like. Charlie is a worse person insofar as he enjoys the suffering of animals, and thus his moral situation is not as good as Ellie, who is otherwise like Charlie but does not enjoy the torments of animals. Thus, insofar as it is a good thing that abstract justice reign, it is a good thing if Ellie's life is better than Charlie's. Thus, if Charlie's and Ellie's life situations are comparable, there is a moral reason why Charlie's life should be worse as a result of his enjoyment of the suffering of animals. (That is, Charlie's enjoyment of the suffering of animals is a vector pushing toward badness in determining the morally appropriate life for him.) And so Charlie is intrinsically subject to punishment for his evil emotion. Thus the retributive requirement for punishing Charlie for his emotions is satisfied. I would suggest that there are good reasons why it would nonetheless be inappropriate to punish Charlie. But these reasons have to do with factors other than moral responsibility. For example, I would argue, a practice of punishing those who enjoy seeing animals suffer would hamper more than it would serve the state's goal of making feasible the rational pursuit of the correct conception of human goodness. There are many reasons for thinking this, most of which would take too long to articulate and defend.

I will mention but one reason, which, though not the most powerful reason, is perhaps the easiest to state. I suggested that the aim of law is to make feasible the rational pursuit of the correct conception of human excellence and flourishing. I will argue in a later work that the lawfulness of punishment, that is, administering punishment in a lawlike way, is crucial for such an aim. And so, I would argue, the state may justly punish Charlie only if it has a lawlike procedure for punishing others who share Charlie's delight in animal anguish. In other words, punishing for emotions, if done at all, must be a general and lawlike practice. Now, provided Charlie keeps his feelings to himself, his feelings do little to hamper citizens in their pursuit of excellence. I am not saying they have *no* effect, but rather that the impediment Charlie's feelings pose is a small one. By contrast, suppose the state routinely inquired into a person's emotional response to bestial suffering and punished those who enjoyed it. The time and effort devoted to this task, the invasion of privacy required, and the risk to the innocent of being wrongly convicted, would significantly impede citizens in making rational plans to pursue excellence. Thus no licit social purpose would justify inflicting legal harm on Charlie for his evil emotion. Thus it would be wrong to punish Charlie for his emotions, even though he is morally responsible for them, and even though he is intrinsically subject to punishment for them (that is, the retributive requirement is satisfied). And so we do not need the traditional account of responsibility to explain why it would be wrong to punish Charlie.

In sum, the traditional account of moral responsibility is not needed to explain the moral basis of punishment.

GRATITUDE AND RESENTMENT

I feel some gratitude toward a stranger who gives me directions, thus enabling me to arrive at my dentist's for a checkup, though I feel none toward a drought-ending rain, though it save my crop and perhaps my very life. I resent those who subject me to minor ridicule, though I feel no resentment toward a strong wind that topples the walls of the public outhouse in which I am seated. This is not because I value the dentist's probe above my life, nor because I enjoy giving public demonstrations of sanitary techniques. It is because rain and wind bear no responsibility for their effects; gratitude and resentment are personal feelings, appropriate only when merited by good or ill for which the recipient of our feeling is accountable.

In this section I will give an account of gratitude and resentment, by which I mean an explanation of how personal feelings of gratitude and resentment can be understood as appropriate, using only my sense of "moral responsibility." I wish to show that we do not need to invoke the traditional notion of responsibility in order to make intelligible (justifiable) personal feelings.

The basic idea can be simply stated, though it will require considerable explication. Gratitude and resentment are personal analogues of approbation and disapprobation. We would expect to find, thus, that in certain respects gratitude and resentment are mirror images of each other. What makes gratitude *personal* is its relationship to solidarity, to the expression of concern and respect for us as fellow moral agents. What makes gratitude *approbatory* is its relation to goodwill. What makes resentment *personal* is its relationship to betrayal and rejection, to the breaking of a trust. What makes resentment *disapprobatory* is its relationship to ill will, to unfairness. Roughly, gratitude is the appreciation of goodwill that reflects concern and respect for us as fellow seekers of the good, comrades in the joint moral project, based on values and attitudes appropriate to the moral project. Roughly, resentment is anger at ill will that reflects a betrayal, an unfair rejection of us that violates a trust. Before explaining these points in detail, it is necessary to make two preliminary comments about the kind of explanations of emotions I am giving.

Two Preliminary Remarks

What should this sort of explanation of an emotion do? It is important to understand that I am giving an account of the moral appropriateness of gratitude and resentment. I am not trying to account for *all* of the ways in which we use the words "gratitude" and "resentment" in English. After all, the English language, like any natural language, is quite flexible. This flexibility is the drug of poets and the bane of philosophers. Philosophers try to define the boundaries of gratitude, punishment, justice, and such. To their dismay, words are easily pressed into new service. Usage tramples over boundaries, setting up new camps in foreign climes. So we should expect to find nonstandard uses of words such as "gratitude" and "resentment." In addition, since human beings are less than perfect, we sometimes feel resentment inappropriately (unfairly), as when we resent a colleague for a promotion, or because she is a better surgeon. So I will try to articulate the central or paradigmatic kind of gratitude and resentment. Nonstandard and inappropriate resentments are extensions of paradigmatic resentment. For example, paradigmatic resentment includes a judgment of moral accountability. When I resent a colleague for her promotion, she is, I know, not morally accountable for any wrong. What happens is that I inappropriately extend to her case the attitudes and feelings appropriate to paradigmatic cases: I respond to her as if she deserved my ill will, though, in some sense, I know she does not. Not all extensions are inappropriate. An atheist might feel, when considering her lot in life, a deep appreciation of her good fortune, fortune that she does not regard as merely her due, but as a "gift of fate." She might properly express what she feels by saying "I feel grateful." Here she means that she feels something akin to what would be gratitude were her boon given her by a person. She feels *as if* the world treated her with goodwill, though she does not really attribute any sort of will or consciousness to the world. And she feels that some of the acts and responses linked to gratitude are appropriate. She may, for example, recognize a moral directive to reciprocate by contributing to the well-being of other moral agents.

Such extensions of paradigmatic gratitude and resentment are psychologically fascinating and important. However, they are conceptually parasitic upon paradigmatic resentment, and it is only the element of paradigmatic resentment and gratitude that relates to valid judgments of moral responsibility. So I will limit my discussion to paradigmatic resentment and gratitude. When I speak of "gratitude" and "resentment," I will mean paradigmatic gratitude and resentment.

The alert reader may prickle at my cavalier way of treating nonstandard cases. It may seem that I have made my view trivially immune to counterexamples, or, indeed, falsification of any sort. Any time we encounter a case that does not fit my account of gratitude, I can simply say "that is not *paradigmatic* gratitude." So nothing could count against my view. I do not mean to rely on such shady tricks. The plausibility of my view rests on three things: (a) the plausibility of what I say as an account of *most* feelings of gratitude, (b) the plausibility of my distinctions as *crucial,* central to the way our emotional lives work, and (c) the plausibility of explaining what goes on in nonstandard cases as an *extension* of what I am calling paradigmatic gratitude and resentment.

An example of each sort might help. If what I say about gratitude does not seem to capture what we usually feel when we feel gratitude, my account is inadequate on count a. If the distinctions I use in defining gratitude and resentment do not explain the role that gratitude and resentment play in our emotional lives, my account fails on count b. For example, it is important that gratitude brings with it a justified impulse toward reciprocating the benefit received. And it is a vice not to feel gratitude when gratitude is due. So my characterization of gratitude must make it clear why it is a vice not to feel gratitude when appropriate, and why gratitude should bring with it an impulse to reciprocate. Finally, unless we can really see the troublesome case as a plausible operation of extension upon what I am calling resentment, then the troublesome case *is* a counterexample. Suppose I resent a colleague for her promotion. There are several ways in which I might resent her, each of which requires its own story. I might actually resent the institution for which we both work, or even fate itself, and transfer my resentment to the promoted person. (I discuss a case of this sort later on.) Another possibility is that in resenting my colleague, I am responding to her *as if* being promoted were an act of betrayal on her part, as if being promoted were somehow an unfair rejection of me that violates some sort of trust. Perhaps she is my friend, and I feel she is showing me up. Or I feel that a friend would not "take" the promotion away from me. There are many such stories to tell. If none of these stories is a plausible description of what is going on when I resent a colleague for her promotion, if this does not seem to capture what I feel, then my account of resentment is flawed on count c.

Nonetheless, it must be admitted that, in some extreme cases, I might have to say "what you are feeling is not really gratitude at all." This move is acceptable, however, only when the reader to whom it is addressed finds it plausible. For example, Gabriele Taylor, discussing pride, considers the case of a guest who claims to be proud of a feast he attended. "The guest maintains that he is proud of the feast's occurring on the grounds that he was present at it. He is not in any way responsible for the occasion, nor does he claim responsibility." She concludes that "we cannot in this case make sense of what he says and will conclude that whatever his feelings about the matter may be, they can hardly amount to feeling proud of *the feast,* though this guest may still be proud of having attended it."[27] She is entitled to her conclusion to the extent that the reader is not tempted to say "but I do understand what the guest is saying. His feeling is similar in crucial respects to feeling pride in the accomplishments of one's child or in having done a difficult and good deed. The role that 'pride' plays in our emotional life applies equally well to what the guest feels. For example, if indeed pride is a vice, the guest is guilty of a vice in the same way, and for the same reasons, that Oedipus is guilty of a vice." So there is a check on the appropriateness of this technique of dealing with counterexamples as well. Due to limitations of time and space, I will not consider all the counterexamples and nonstandard cases that might arise. Nor will I touch on what be called the affective flavor of gratitude and resentment.

I am giving what might be called a cognitive account of gratitude and resentment. That is, I explain these emotions in terms of attitudes and judgments. But I do not mean to say that an emotion is just a judgment. Gratitude, on my account, is an "appreciation of" something, and "appreciation," denotes more than a judgment of approbation. It has links to action, and is associated with a variety of appropriate "raw feels." As noted in Chapter II, if I had no such raw feels associated with my approbation and no links to appropriate action, I could not be said to have an emotional life and so could not feel gratitude. But it does not follow that appreciation consists in any particular raw feel or disposition to act. Gratitude, for example, is often linked with the warm fuzzy feeling of being cared about. But certainly I can feel gratitude toward someone without experiencing this warm fuzzy feeling. The point is that (a) that warm fuzzy feeling is *an* appropriate human response to the relevant cognitive judgment or perception, and (b) for me to be a human emoter, I must have some appropriate human responses to my cognitive judgments or perceptions. Similar points might be made about the "anger" involved in my account of resentment.

There is much more to be said about the character of gratitude and resentment and about their role in human life. It is worth noting that situations that call for gratitude often produce resentment instead. It is worth noting that resentment has a "bitter taste." My account is meant to supplement, not replace, observations of this sort.

Gratitude

What is gratitude? It seems safe to say that gratitude is appreciation of the goodwill of another from which one has benefited. The obvious next questions are is "what is 'goodwill'?" and "what is a 'benefit'?" One tradition insists that goodwill is limited to compassion or caring that goes *beyond* the requirements of obligation, and that "benefit" is a positive good, not just a refraining from harm. Now it is true enough that we do not feel gratitude to a passerby for not mugging us. But this is not because she has a duty not to mug us. It is also not because a benefit is a positive boon rather than the absence of a negative harm. Indeed, we may appropriately feel gratitude toward someone who is in a position to harm us illegally, but refrains from doing so.

Consider the case of Nimbia, a witness at my trial, who is asked a question by opposing counsel. It is tempting for her to tell a lie that would harm me, since answering the question truthfully would cause her personal embarrassment, and, if she lies, she will not be found out. Nonetheless, she tells the truth. Had Nimbia not been called to the stand, my case would be no better or worse off than it is after her answer. (In other words, her answer does not help my case, though the lie would have hurt my case.)

I might well feel gratitude toward Nimbia. If I do, my feeling is not inappropriate. Suppose, for example, that my wife says "I am grateful to Nimbia for telling the truth." I respond "Grateful? Why should I feel grateful? She only did her duty, and I received no more than my due. I don't feel grateful at all." Is there not something wrong with my attitude—am I not, in fact, guilty of being ungrateful?

Now it is surely more appropriate to say that Nimbia refrained from harming me than to say that she benefited me. The net result of her answer is not that my case is stronger, but that my case is not harmed.[28] Nimbia was under oath and had to answer the question or face contempt of court. She merely refrained from lying, that is, from committing perjury. It would have been both wrong and illegal to do otherwise. So here is a case of my feeling gratitude toward someone for not harming me, even though her refraining from harm is no more than morality and the law require.

So a "benefit" or "boon" here means anything that supports my projects (advantages me), including someone's refraining from harming me. We still lack, however, an account of "goodwill." I will provide one, with the help of four "clues." One clue comes from that fact that gratitude can be felt only *by* someone who has moral commitments, *to* someone who has moral commitments. This suggests that goodwill is something like "acting out of moral commitment, out of a vision of and concern for the good."

A second clue comes from that fact that gratitude includes not only appreciation and approval of the donor for conferring the benefit, but also being touched in some way by the fact that goodwill is directed toward me. I feel gratitude only when I feel that the conferring of the benefit shows some sort of concern and respect for me. The respect may be for my moral agency generally, rather than for my specific characteristics. Nimbia shows respect for me as a fellow citizen under the law—she may know nothing about me individually. Nonetheless, her act shows respect and concern for me, for in telling the truth she shows a recognition of the fact that my rights are worthy of sacrifice on her part.

The third clue is that I do not feel gratitude toward those who confer a benefit out of *improper* regard for me. Jones may confer a benefit upon me because of his like for me, but if that like is suspect, I may not feel gratitude at all. Suppose Jones thinks me "cool" because of my new sportscar and feels what I regard as a kind of craven hero-worship of me. I may feel contempt or annoyance for Jones rather than gratitude. (Actors and other celebrities sometimes feel this way about some of their fans.) Note that Jones is acting on the basis of a pro-attitude toward me, his act is not motivated by personal advantage or a desire to use me, and his act shows regard for me. But it is the wrong sort of regard and the wrong sort of pro-attitude for gratitude. So this is not an example of what I will mean by "goodwill."

The fourth clue consists of the connection between gratitude and solidarity. I feel closer to, feel a kind of bond with, someone to whom I feel grateful. The reason, I suggest, is that goodwill involves recognition of fellowship in the moral community. What I am appreciating when I feel gratitude is (in part) my benefactor's affirmation of our common commitment to the good. Moreover, my appreciation itself is also a recognition of that fellowship.

A few words on moral fellowship must suffice. (It should be noted that the main arguments of this section would survive even if all reference to moral community were excised.) Let us view the moral community as the collection of moral agents. Since to be a moral agent is to have values, and since everyone thinks his values are the right ones, every moral agent is committed to the project of realizing the good in life. My argument for two points I will assume here, namely the importance of community in human life, and that to have values as such is also to have an investment in others' moral flourishing, must await a later work. But, given these assumptions, to be a moral agent is at the same time to be embarked upon a common moral project, such that one has regard for and a commitment to one's fellow good-seekers.

We can now say what goodwill is: goodwill is impetus toward action[29] reflecting respect and concern to a fellow member of the moral community, either insofar as he is a member of that community, or as a response to the particular manner in which he is a member of that community, where both the impetus and the concern are based on a commitment *to* the common moral project *as* a common moral enterprise. It is, thus, an impetus toward realizing the common moral project *as* a common moral project.

The last piece of the puzzle can be extracted by looking back at the case of Nimbia. It is tempting to say that gratitude is appropriate when the benefit conferred exceeds one's expectations. But I may appropriately feel gratitude toward Nimbia even if I know that most witnesses in this situation would tell the truth, even though it is a sacrifice and hard for them to do. Hence I would *expect* a witness in Nimbia's position to tell the truth. Perhaps, therefore, it is better to say that one feels gratitude for a benefit when there are circumstances that make the conferring of the benefit seem a *noteworthy* example of goodwill. Although by not mugging me a passerby does show some degree of goodwill, this is not a *noteworthy* example of goodwill, so I feel no gratitude.

What makes Nimbia's act noteworthy and the passerby's not? Well, refraining from mugging me should not be a hardship for the passerby. If the passerby really had to make a big effort in order to keep from mugging me, if it was a great sacrifice, then there is something wrong with her. Put another way, a good person would not be attracted by the prospect of mugging me. By contrast, Nimbia, by telling the truth, subjected herself to personal humiliation. And there is nothing wrong or unusual in wishing strongly to avoid personal humiliation. Good persons will be attracted by the prospect of avoiding humiliation, even if this attraction is always outweighed by a desire to tell the truth. Let Nimbia be as saintly as you like, she would still consider being publicly humiliated a sacrifice she (gladly) makes for the sake of telling the truth. In other words, morality and the law required Nimbia to make what most people, reasonably and justly, would deem a sacrifice. So I may properly feel grateful to someone for doing her duty, even if that is the norm, when (a) doing her duty costs her a lot, and (b) there is nothing wrong or unusual with that being a cost. This, then, is one way goodwill might be noteworthy. In addition, goodwill may be noteworthy if it goes far beyond what morality requires. For example, when I was in Munich, I asked a passerby where a certain street was. He did not know, but pulled out a map and ran down the street to glance at the street sign, so that he could help answer my question. The sacrifice he made was not great. Still, since morality did not require him to interrupt what he was doing to march down the street and help me, I (appropriately) felt grateful to him. Third, goodwill may be noteworthy simply because, in context, it is rare (for example, one might feel gratitude for the honesty of a used-car salesperson). Finally, goodwill might be noteworthy for the size of the benefit it confers. If a benefit that results from goodwill makes me feel that life is working out well, strongly reinforces my sense that I am flourishing, I might well feel grateful, whether or not the benefit was required by morality, was unusual, or required a large sacrifice. (Her act, after all, strongly reinforced my sense that the common moral project, so far as it directly affects me, is going well.) So there are at least four ways in which goodwill might be noteworthy.

We are now in a position to say what gratitude is. My feeling gratitude is my feeling appreciation and approval for the noteworthy goodwill shown by someone's conferring a benefit upon me, where I view the goodwill as expressing concern and respect for me as a member of the moral community, based on (what I consider) morally cogent reasons. My gratitude is *appropriate* when the person to whom I am grateful does confer a benefit upon me, the conferring of the benefit does show goodwill, does express concern and respect for me, and when that concern and respect reflect attitudes, values, and commitments that are in fact morally cogent. I ought to feel "indebted" to such a person, in the sense that some sort of appreciation and reciprocation are called for. That is, (a) the appreciation I feel is warranted, and should (circumstances permitting) be expressed, and (b) appropriate matching acts of goodwill on my part are an indicated response. The reciprocating act of goodwill on my part need not be specifically to the person to whom I am grateful. Since her act was a contribution to and affirmation of the common moral project, a similar act on my part supports the project to which my benefactor was committed in helping me, and so "benefits" her by helping to realize her project.[30]

A few remarks may show why feeling gratitude, so defined, is morally justifiable. Someone whose values, attitudes, and the like are appropriate and are realized in noteworthy actions that benefit and show respect and concern for me, helps make the world more hospitable to my values, a place in which I, as a moral agent, feel at home, have a place. It is not merely that she is (in this regard) a good thing toward which I ought to feel some affection or loyalty. It is also that her act helps me to see myself as having a place in this world as a moral agent, helps me both to be and to see myself as a valued contributor to the common moral project. It is an act directed toward me as a moral agent. A special kind of appreciation is appropriate for her as a comrade in the moral struggle. Her act affirms a kind of moral solidarity between us, a care and respect based on our joint moral commitment to the good. This solidarity exists not because she is a free chooser, not because her acts are uncaused, but because we in fact share a deep moral commitment to the good, a commitment that recognizes our importance as comrades in these commitments. Thus the basis of the solidarity is quite independent of how she came to have her views and feelings. It is quite independent of the cause of the benefit I received. Nonetheless, it seems quite clear that the solidarity is real, it is important, and it is worth appreciating, caring for, and showing loyalty to. Hence gratitude, as I have described it, is a justifiable emotion.

It is also clear why gratitude and Evaluation Responsibility are tightly connected. Evaluation Responsibility is accountability for one's worldview. Gratitude is appreciation for some aspect of that worldview as realized in one aspect of the benefactor's life, namely conferring a benefit upon me. The conditions for Evaluation Responsibility and for appropriate gratitude are also parallel. Gratitude is due when the benefit conferred does reflect the appropriate values, attitudes, and commitments. An agent is Evaluation Responsible for a trait when it does indeed reflect her values, attitudes, and commitments. Again, one is Evaluation Responsible for a trait T only if it is sufficiently specific. A similar point applies to attributing the attitudes and values upon which gratitude is based. Suppose Jones shows concern for me because of my honesty, but Jones likes honesty only because he thinks he can use honest people. Then gratitude is not appropriate, because Jones has not shown goodwill. In this case, the description "Jones has a pro-attitude toward honesty" is insufficiently specific; it leaves out a key moral factor. Finally, Jones may not be Evaluation Responsible for a trait if he is not a full moral person while instantiating it. Now if Jones is not a full person while conferring a benefit upon me, this is either because he does not have the sort of developed values required for my feeling gratitude to him, or because his values are not properly reflected in his behavior, including conferring the benefit. In either case, gratitude is not appropriate, by our account of gratitude. In sum, one can feel gratitude toward someone who confers a benefit when and only when the benefactor is Evaluation Responsible for certain kinds of traits instantiated by conferring the benefit.

In this discussion of gratitude and moral responsibility, we did not need to call upon the traditional view of moral responsibility, or such notions as free choice, voluntarity, the cause of an action, and so on. Rather, the key notions in explaining and justifying gratitude are precisely those upon which my account of moral responsibility is based (for example, fit with a worldview in operation). I conclude that my account of responsibility is sufficient to explain and justify gratitude.

Resentment

Resentment is a kind of anger. For simplicity, we will think of anger toward or about something as violent nonacceptance of it, although there are more complexities and nuances than this simple formulation suggests. Much of the cognitive complexity of anger will be captured by the rest of what I say about resentment. For example, I would suggest that anger is a condemnatory response appropriate to a moral outrage. We do not need to include this in our description of anger, however, since what I say about resentment will entail that the emoter is condemning a moral outrage. Still, it must not be forgotten that much of the raw feel and behavior-disposing force of resentment resides in the fact that it is *anger at* (rather than merely a *noticing of*) a certain kind of betrayal.

What kind of anger, then, is resentment? Well, resentment is a kind of mirror image of gratitude. Gratitude recognizes goodwill. So we might expect resentment to recognize ill will. For the sake of symmetry, it is convenient to speak of "ill will" as impetus directed toward action that derives from ignoring or having contempt for morality, values, and the moral project generally.[31]

It is only anger at particular sorts of ill will that constitutes resentment. To resent someone is to feel that, in some sense, he has *betrayed* one. Now to feel betrayed is always to feel *rejected*. In betraying me, Liebowitz rejects me for someone or something else— money, another person, whatever. Liebowitz finds something else to be more important, desirable, or commanding of loyalty than I am. To be an instance of betrayal, however, the rejection must show ill will. If, after all, Liebowitz is entirely correct in putting the need to tell the truth ahead of helping me defraud an innocent person, then he has not betrayed me. So to count as betrayal of me, Liebowitz's rejection of me must be unfair or unfounded, show a kind of contempt for morality, in the wide sense of "morality" that includes appropriate values, defensible goals, rules and attitudes, character traits, and ways of viewing and conducting a life.

Finally, to be a betrayal, a rejection that shows ill will must also be a violation of *trust*. Now trust can be construed *subjectively* or *objectively*. That is, Liebowitz's act may be counter to the trust I in fact placed in him. Or it may be counter to an objective trust that attaches to his situation, role, or circumstances. For example, a corrupt sheriff may be elected by apathetic voters who know he is corrupt.

No one, subjectively, trusts the sheriff. Nonetheless, the sheriff occupies a position of trust—an objective trust attaches to one who occupies the office of sheriff. Violation of either sort of trust may give rise to a perception of betrayal. It should be noted that just as concern and respect may be shown me personally, as a particular moral agent, or formally, merely for being a member of the moral community, so trust and betrayal may be personal or formal. For example, anyone who is a moral agent might be viewed as objectively trusted not to do gratuitous harm. Thus I might feel that a bully, though a stranger to me, has betrayed a trust by going out of his way to humiliate me pointlessly. If I resent him for pointlessly humiliating me, it is because I view his act as a violation of the (objective) trust I place in persons *qua* members of the moral community. His rejection of me for the gratification of his ego violates what he owes me by virtue of the confidence that all members of the moral community are objectively entitled to have in one another's goodwill, as comrades in the moral struggle.[32]

Here, then, is the account of resentment I offer. Resentment is violent nonacceptance of an unfounded or unfair rejection of oneself that violates a trust, anger about ill will reflected in a betrayal. The betrayal shows contempt for me, for the common moral project, and for the solidarity of good-seeking. The betrayer thus proclaims herself an enemy of the good and of the common struggle to achieve it. To view such contempt for oneself, and for the good, with equanimity, is to give up one's passionate commitment to the good and one's role or task in achieving it. Thus anger is the appropriate response.

According to this account, resentment has an important role to play in human life: those who think it is never appropriate to feel resentment are wrong. Since the heart of my argument for this is a basic view of the human problem, I can but sketch out what I take to be the role of resentment.

The human task, I have suggested elsewhere, is to make peace with the fact that this is a flawed world, without betraying the strength of our standards.[33] We must, at the same time, show no disloyalty or lack of fealty to our values and standards, and yet find good and acceptable a world that is sorely lacking according to those values and standards. We must find a balance, a truce, between the push for moral excellence, which we never abandon, and loving acceptance of imperfection. Moral passion is a *sine qua non* for human moral commitment. If we ever become so reconciled to injustice that we cease to feel anger when we encounter it, if we ever so slacken our commitment to morality that we can view its flagrant violation with contentment or equanimity, we betray our moral commitment to justice, values, and the good. Thus one who does not, generally, feel resentment and anger when resentment and anger are appropriate, has gone some good way toward abandoning the human task. On the other hand, dwelling in resentment and anger makes impossible the sense of solidarity with the world in which we find ourselves, renders impossible the peace of acceptance that is also a condition of human flourishing. Thus resentment and anger should grow, as circumstances permit, into a resolve to work for a better outcome coupled with acceptance of the limitations of those around us. In other words, the process of resentment turning into peace is crucial to human life as we understand it, to the precarious balancing act that constitutes human well-being, namely balancing moral fervor and calm acceptance of failings.

Armed with this account of paradigmatic resentment, we can now say a bit more about nonparadigmatic extensions of resentment. Suppose I resent the president of the university for his salary, which is ten times greater than my own. Now, there are several different ways in which I might resent him for the size of his paycheck. I will discuss two of the possible stories to be told.

I might resent the president because I feel that I deserve a greater share. It is unfair, some injustice is done me, when the president is paid ten times more than I am. A fair distribution, I think, would be $55,000 for each of us, rather than $10,000 for me and $100,000 for the president. I feel that the university has betrayed me, has unfoundedly rejected me by giving the $45,000 in question to the president instead of to me. And I feel that in doing so, the university has violated the objective trust attached to its position—the university should be fair, and it is not. I am treating the university, in other words, as a moral agent. And I resent the university for its betrayal, for the violation of objective trust that its rejection of me evidences. It is not surprising, however, that I locate that resentment in the president, as if it were her betrayal, not the university's. The money that provokes my ire goes to the president, and she is a more direct and less abstract object of resentment than is something as abstract as a "university." It is not hard to give a psychological explanation of the transference of my resentment to the president herself.

A further extension of resentment may occur if I feel that what the president does is worth ten times what I do, but that had I had her opportunities, I would also be worth that much.[34] Here I resent fate, as it were. I feel that fate has betrayed me, that the finger of fate has unfairly passed over me and pointed to the president instead. If I do not have an objective trust in fate to be fair, I do not feel resentment, I just feel envy. Why should I feel trust in fate to be fair? One possibility is that I anthropomorphize fate; history shows that human beings are avid anthropomorphizers. No doubt this is why many people resent fate. A more interesting and complex possibility stems from the nature of the human task. It is, I suggested, a precondition of moral agency to view and evaluate the world, to evaluate the world about me in terms of my moral framework. So I must look at fate to see if it is fair. (Here the connection between resentment and abstract justice becomes clear.) Now if the result of my evaluation is "the world is rotten," then I will not flourish. So, to flourish, I must try to find a way to see the world as acceptable, as *my* world, as a world I can care for. This may be an impossible task, in which case I am bound to fail, doomed not to flourish. But the only way to find out if it is possible is to try to do it. So it is appropriate to try to find a way of seeing the world as acceptable without betraying my values. Thus I place objective trust in the world and try to view that trust as somewhat well-placed (without betraying or cheapening the correct values). If the world shows contempt for that trust, then I feel betrayed: the world has rejected me, for reasons that show contempt for morality, for the values and standards I deem correct, and in so doing violates, in my eyes, the objective trust attaching to fate to be just. I feel betrayed by the world because it is a bad world. When I feel this, I am treating the world as if it were a moral agent, as if the way fate plays itself out reflects a set of values. I do this because I cannot help but look at fate in terms of my values and cannot help but demand of fate that it conform. (I cannot help but wish for abstract justice.) In this case as well, it is easy to explain how my resentment at fate might be transferred to the president of the university.

It should be clear that the range and complexity of stories to be told is vast. Human emotions are varied and complicated. These two brief examples, however, suggest the sort of account I might give of a specific case of nonparadigmatic resentment.

It remains only to show that this account of resentment is both justifiable and compatible with my account of moral responsibility.

Resenting someone presupposes not that she has free will, but rather that she has a developed worldview in operation. After all, to resent someone is precisely to see her as a moral agent, as subject to the demands of loyalty and fairness that the moral realm imposes, to see her as a member of the same moral task force as oneself. And this is true of her to the extent that she views and responds to the world with a set of concepts developed and coherent enough to make room for a moral dimension. If her way of making sense of the world, in her thoughts, acts, and the like includes such concepts as the idea of reciprocity, the notion of other beings with complex subjective lives, and so forth, then the world as she sees it is a moral world, that is, a world to which morality is applicable. Her decisions, acts, feelings, and thoughts are thus moral decisions, acts, feelings, and thoughts, in the sense that they take a position with respect to morality. If indeed the concept of trust is applicable to the world as she understands it (whether she sees this or not), and if how she lives violates that trust, then the position her life takes (whether or not this position taking is conscious or free) is contemptuous of morality, and she is indeed an enemy of (and not just an impediment to the realization of) that moral framework to which my loyalty is pledged. And so, when she really does unfairly and unfoundedly reject me by betraying a trust, she merits the anger that my moral passion, my commitment to the common moral project, demands. She embodies a kind of evil to which violent nonacceptance is the appropriate human response.

Hence this account of the nature and justification of resentment accords nicely with my account of moral responsibility. Someone whom I justly resent is morally responsible, in fact, blameworthy, for the traits upon which my resentment is based. To resent someone I must be a moral agent, in my sense, and I can only resent those who are moral agents, in my sense. Voluntarity, control, free will, and causation play no important roles in this explanation and justification of resentment.

We have before us, thus, plausible accounts of resentment and gratitude that make no use of the traditional notion of responsibility. It is inappropriate to resent or be grateful to the weather not because the weather lacks free will, but because it lacks a worldview. A hurricane's destroying your house does not reflect hurricane values, and so it cannot be said to reject you, much less reject you for reasons that constitute taking an adverse position toward morality. It is inappropriate to resent a colleague for her promotion, not because she could not help being promoted, but because her promotion is not a betrayal of trust, is not a rejection of you, and so on. The personal animus in my resenting someone stems not from her free will, but from the fact that what I resent her for is a rejection of me (personally or as a member of the moral community), and for a stance of enmity to the values and moral project to which I am passionately committed. Resentment, as I understand it, is a personal emotion on both ends. It is a response to the personhood, the worldview in operation, of another, as her personhood is reflected in her response to my personhood. Resentment is a necessary expression of moral commitment in a flawed world, and so an essential facet of the emotional life of human beings, just as gratitude is a necessary expression of moral commitment in a world not wholly evil. To be human is to be grateful, and to resent.

Appendixes

A. A VARIANT OF PAP

Several variants of the Principle of Alternate Possibilities have been advanced since Frankfurt's paper appeared, of which, perhaps, the most important are Peter van Inwagen's "prevention principles," articulated in his *Essay on Free Will*.[1] Van Inwagen distinguishes between two principles. PPP1 asserts that "a person is morally responsible for a certain event-particular only if he could have prevented it" (p. 167). In applying this principle, van Inwagen uses a modification of Davidson's criterion for event-particular identity; x and y are the same event-particulars if and only if x and y have the same causes. PPP2 maintains that "a person is morally responsible for a certain state of affairs only if (that state of affairs obtains and) he could have prevented it from obtaining" (p. 171). Both principles, according to van Inwagen, are immune to Frankfurt-style counterexamples. (Van Inwagen himself, it should be said, prefers PPP2 to PPP1, since he thinks we are responsible not for event-particulars but for generic states of affairs.)

Now PPP1 is indeed immune to Frankfurt-style counterexamples, but only because, given van Inwagen's criterion for being the same act, I would not be responsible for having done any act x given *any* significant counterfactual variations. For example, even if determinism is false, I would not be responsible for having done x had I acted from a different motive. For then the causes of my action would have been different, and so the action I would have performed would not have been x, however similar to x it might have been. Indeed, as I argue at length, we are responsible, strictly speaking, not for acts as such but for the properties we instantiate by performing those acts. If I am right, PPP1 is true for the trivial reason that we are *never* responsible for event-particulars as such. Hence PPP1, though true, does not establish the necessity of alternate possibilities.

What van Inwagen must argue for is not PPP1, but rather the claim that we are not responsible for instantiating a property P unless we could have failed to instantiate P. And this principle *is* susceptible to counterexamples. A brief example will suffice. Suppose that Bill decides to give me a particular set A of beliefs, attitudes, dispositions, and so on. He performs neurosurgery, altering my brain so that I have set A. Now by chance I happened to have set A before Bill began his procedure. Thus my brain after the procedure is no different than it was before Bill began. As a result, my subsequent actions are no different than they would have been without the procedure. I am just as susceptible to rational persuasion as I was before, and so forth. Does Bill's procedure make any difference to my moral status? Am I henceforth absolved of all moral responsibility?

PPP2 raises similar problems. Van Inwagen imagines that A witnesses a brutal assault occurring outside her window, but decides not to call the police. Unbeknownst to her, her telephone is out of order. Van Inwagen claims that A is responsible, perhaps, for *deciding* not to call the police, but not for failing to call. And she is certainly, avers van Inwagen, not responsible for the fact that the police were not called.

Van Inwagen's claim is not as unproblematic as he seems to think it is. Suppose, for example, that a law, known to A, requires citizens witnessing an assault to call the police. Suppose as well that the *mens rea* requirement for this crime of nonreportage is that it be committed intentionally. Are we to say that A is not guilty, either legally or morally, of violating the law of nonreportage, that she is morally or legally guilty only of *attempted* nonreportage?

The drawbacks of holding individuals responsible for actions now become evident. If instead we hold individuals responsible for (sufficiently specific) properties they instantiate, such difficulties do not arise. A is morally responsible for the disregard for the law evidenced by her nonreportage. For whatever the *causes* of her failure to call the police, her inaction did *evidence* disregard for the law.

But now the inability to have done otherwise does not seem to obviate A's responsibility, except insofar as inability counts as *evidence* that A did not fail to take her legal duties seriously.

It is also worth noting that my version avoids some of the objections raised against other versions. For example, the case of Harry, unlike Frankfurt's cases, involves what John Martin Fischer calls "actual-sequence" compulsion.[2] Robert Audi's objection in "Moral Responsibility, Freedom and Compulsion," so telling against some versions, does not tell against mine.[3] Audi points out that "if x does A at t for reasons of a kind that make him morally responsible for doing it, the fact that if he had not had those reasons and did not intend to do A, he would have been compelled to do it . . . for other reasons, does not entail that he could not have done otherwise at t" (p. 5). In my example, the actual cause of A's slap was something beyond A's control, and one that the traditional view does not recognize as generating responsibility. Yet A is nonetheless responsible.

B. OBJECT-STAGES

Since some philosophers have expressed skepticism about object-stages, let me give a brief argument that we must admit them into our ontology. The reader not convinced by my argument can view my talk of object-stages as a slightly odd way of phrasing the problem; the most important claims and arguments I make about persons do not depend on the reality of object-stages.

Socrates as a young man was not bald, but hirsute. As an old man, Socrates was completely bald. Now if young Socrates is the same thing as old Socrates, it would seem that one and the same thing is both bald and not bald (hirsute). And that is a contradiction. Now the obvious answer to this problem is that Socrates is bald at one time and hirsute at another. But how are we to construe "being bald at one time"? There are several possibilities. First, we could introduce time-indexed properties. We could say, in other words, that there is a property of being bald-at-t_1, and a different property of being bald-at-t_2. Socrates has one of these properties and lacks the other. Hence contradiction is avoided. A second way is to index the copula. Socrates is-at-t_2 bald, we might say, though it is false that Socrates is-at-t_1 bald. (More colloquially, we use tenses: Tom Stoppard was a baby, but is an adult.) We can also construe predication as a relation between a thing and a time: Bald(Socrates, t_2) and not Bald(Socrates, t_1). In other words, Socrates bears the relation of baldness to one thing, t_2, but not to another, t_1. Finally, we can index the object, Socrates. Socrates-at-t_2 is bald, but Socrates-at-t_1 is not. Notice that this last option amounts to introducing person-stages: Socrates-at-t_1 *just is* an object-stage. Each of these methods solves the problem about Socrates.

However there is a problem that can be solved only by indexing objects. Suppose that at time t_1, the young Dante loved the young Beatrice. By t_2, however, both have grown considerably older. Beatrice has become irascible and wicked. Now the older Dante does not love the older Beatrice. However, let us suppose, he still loves the younger Beatrice; he still feels romantic urges when he thinks of her, and so on. (If the reader feels that one cannot "love" a past stage, then change the word "love" in what follows to whichever word expresses what Dante feels toward the young Beatrice.) We can capture without contradiction the difference between Dante's love (at time t_2) for the Beatrice of t_1, and his failure at t_2 to love the Beatrice of t_2, by indexing Beatrice:

> Dante loves Beatrice-at-t_1, and
>
> Not: Dante loves Beatrice-at-t_2.

Here there is no contradiction. Dante loves one thing and fails to love another. But indexing properties merely gives us:

> Dante loves-at-t_2 Beatrice, and
>
> Not: Dante loves-at-t_2 Beatrice,

which is a contradiction. Similarly, indexing the copula gives something like:

> Dante is-at-t_2 in love with Beatrice, and
>
> Not: Dante is-at-t_2 in love with Beatrice,

while treating predication as a relation yields:

> Loves (Dante, Beatrice, t_2), and
>
> Not: loves (Dante, Beatrice, t_2),

both of which are contradictory. Thus only by indexing objects can contradiction be avoided. Hence it is necessary to admit object-stages into one's ontology. (For a more detailed discussion of object-stages, see my doctoral dissertation, *Objects and Necessity*, University of Chicago [1978]).

C. PERRY ON PERSONAL IDENTITY

Some mention should be made of John Perry's famous paper, "Personal Identity, Memory and the Problem of Circularity."[1] Perry is concerned with avoiding the claim that it is circular to insist that for n to be the same person as a past stage q is for n and q to share a memory. (The same problem applies to more complicated versions; for example, there is a series of stages between q and n such that every pair of those stages share at least one memory.) The difficulty is that we have not only real memories, but apparent ones as well. Let us express this by saying that only some recollections are true memories, where a recollection is anything that seems, correctly or incorrectly, to be a memory. The problem is that I might recollect inventing the slogan used in an advertising campaign, when it was actually my subordinate who first proposed it. That does not make me identical with (the same person as) an earlier stage of my subordinate. Only real memories count toward personal identity. But the difference between a real memory and an apparent memory is that the real memory is of something that happened to *me*. So construing personal identity in terms of memory seems to beg the question.

Perry's solution makes two assumptions. First, there is some type of causal link, M, that characterizes true as opposed to apparent memories. Since we are not identifying M, we are not begging the question here. We are assuming only that real and apparent memories are characterized by different causal processes. Second, Perry assumes that most recollections are true memories—true memory is more common than apparent memory.

The stage is now set for Perry. Suppose q witnesses an event e (for example, he sees it happen). A later stage, n, recalls seeing e occur. N's recollection of e is a true memory if and only if q's witnessing of e is M-related to n's recollection of e, where M is the type of causal relation most frequently productive of recollections. Put another way, n is the same person as q when there is a series of stages linking p and n such that for any two stages in the series, the latter has a recollection R of an event witnessed by the earlier stage, such that R is produced by the type of causal mechanism that produces most cases of recollection. (Actually, what is needed is a slightly more complicated variant of this formulation, to account for certain versions of the brave-soldier paradox.) This formulation is not circular, since nothing in it presupposes that q and n are the same person.

Now there are several problems with Perry's account. For example, if the physiological process of memory differs greatly between individuals, it is not clear that there is anything common to all cases of real memory, except those factors that presuppose real memory. There are further problems concerning personal identification (though not personal identity). It is not clear that we could discover what M is without making assumptions about the veridicality of the recollections of the subjects investigated, nor is it clear what grounds we would have for our judgments about personal identity now, lacking, as we are, knowledge of M and access to the brain physiology of most persons about us. But the problem I wish to focus on is of a different character.

How on earth, one wants to ask, can one justify incarcerating n for the crimes of q simply because a recollection of n's is M-related to a witnessing of q? The fact that n's recollection of an event witnessed by q is produced by the same type of mechanism that produces most recollections hardly seems morally relevant to guilt. It seems an irrelevant basis for insisting that n is married to p that n has a recollection that is M-related to q's witnessing of q's undergoing a ceremony to a stage k, and that p has a recollection that is M-related to a witnessing of k. These facts have little to do with the marriage relation and seem an arbitrary and trivial reason for insisting, for example, that it is immoral for n to have sex with someone other than q (if adultery is indeed immoral). Whether or not Perry's criterion is circular, it misses the point. Put another way, if the basis of personal identity were indeed what Perry indicates, then personal identity would provide no basis for marriage relations, punishment, and the like. The fact that it was (an earlier stage of) n who committed the crime could play no role in justifying punishing n. The fact that it was (an earlier stage of) n who married an earlier stage of q could play no role in justifying n's marital duties toward q. And this is clearly wrong and absurd.

Thus what *constitutes* personal identity cannot be what Perry says it is. At best, Perry's criterion gives us a way of picking out a relationship that is based on entirely different concepts than the causal mechanism linking one's recollections to past witnessings. In that case, even if Perry is right, he has left the nature of personal identity entirely unexplained.

D. VAN INWAGEN'S ARGUMENT

An interesting argument of Peter van Inwagen's deserves mention. In "The Incompatibility of Responsibility and Determinism," van Inwagen purports to prove formally that responsibility and determinism are incompatible.[1] The crucial assumptions of his argument are (1) that if no one is responsible for p, or, more precisely, "no human being, or group of human beings, is even partly responsible for the fact that p," (p. 32), and if no one is responsible for p's implying q, then no one is responsible for q, and (2) that no one is responsible for a logically necessary state of affairs. Now, claims van Inwagen, if determinism is true, it is logically necessary that the laws of nature together with the state of the world, p, at some time in the remote past before human beings existed, implies that I light my pipe. Since that is a logical necessity, no one is responsible for it. Using his two assumptions and basic modal logic, van Inwagen proves that no one is responsible for p's implying that I light my pipe. Clearly no one is responsible for p (the state of the world long before there were human beings). So I am not responsible for lighting my pipe.

The problem with his argument is that, in order to make his assumptions plausible, van Inwagen must construe "even partly responsible for" very broadly. But then his assumption begs the question. For example, if my view is correct, then I am partly responsible for p's implying that I light my pipe, necessary as that implication is. After all, p implies that I light my pipe only because p implies that I have a certain moral outlook. Thus, since p's implying that I light my pipe shows something about my worldview, I am partly (in this broad sense) responsible for p's implying that I light my pipe. True, I could not help p's implying that I light my pipe. But that, on my view, is not a reason for thinking that I am not responsible for it. Again, it may be that in some sense my lighting my pipe was necessary. Why should this mean that I am not responsible for it? Only because necessary truths are beyond our control to change. But that, on my view, does not mean that we cannot be responsible for them. So although van Inwagen's argument may succeed against traditional construals of responsibility, it does not succeed against mine.

Van Inwagen merely comments that the validity of the assumption "seems to . . . be beyond dispute. No one is responsible for the fact that $49 \times 18 = 882$" (p. 32). And of course no one is responsible for *that* logically necessary truth, nor for the others he mentions (that is, that arithmetic is incomplete and that the atomic number of gold is 79). But it does not follow that no one is responsible for *any* logically necessary truth.[2]

E. THE NATURE OF EMOTIONS

A few remarks about the nature of emotions seems appropriate. Feeling an emotion is not like feeling a twinge. Let us use the word "feels" to describe occurrent inner sensations, such as twinges and the felt flush that sometimes accompanies anger. I want to say that one can feel anger without having any particular feels.

I will give three arguments that emotions are not simply "feels." First, there are examples of emotions that involve no particular feels. Second, one often does not determine which emotion one is feeling by examining one's feels. Third, one can have emotions of which one is unaware.

Consider the case of two judges who sentence a criminal. The judge who finds the defendant's crime to be outrageous may act no differently from the judge who merely notes that it is illegal. He may not even have different inner sensations. He might, of course, become excited, feel flushed, and so on. But such internal events are not necessary components of moral outrage; it is enough that one have a certain attitude. Indeed, the outraged judge may not have any prominent feels at all while sentencing the felon. His outrage may consist not in his feels, but in the attitude he has toward the defendant. He may see the sentence as vengeance visited upon a vicious and despicable felon. He may take personal satisfaction in pronouncing the sentence. He might deem it intolerable that the criminal go free. The other judge may believe that she is merely doing her job in pronouncing the sentence mandated by law. She may not care whether the felon ultimately goes free, so long as she, the judge, has done her work efficiently. On the basis of these beliefs, one may properly call the first judge "outraged" and the second not. Thus the two judges, who have different emotions, may not have different interior sensations. But they do have different attitudes. So no particular inner sensation is necessary to feel moral outrage.

Again, as Frithjof Bergmann points out, to find New York depressing is not necessarily to have any particular sensations. It is enough to perceive New York in a certain way, to see it as a gray, dirty city instead of seeing it as a vital, heady place with a sense of history. Moreover, Bergmann asks, how do we determine whether what we feel is embarrassment or shame? Not, says Bergmann, by applying a magnifying glass to the feels swimming in the fishbowl of consciousness. Nor, for that matter, do we look more closely at our present behavior or dispositions to behave. (Although, *contra* Bergmann, this is sometimes helpful.) Rather, one evaluates the event or situation that is the object of the emotion. One asks oneself "how bad was it, and how much am I to blame?"[1]

The third argument rests on the fact that one can have an emotion without being aware of it. Someone who says "I did not realize it, but I have been angry at John for years" is not committing a solecism. People often rightly say such things. But it is quite implausible that the speaker had a flush, twinge, or whatever, lasting several years, that he somehow missed. On the other hand, one can quite easily have an attitude without being aware of it.

Again, although we understand the claim that someone was angry without knowing it, we should not know what to make of someone who said "I was angry that the terrorists killed the group of children, though I entirely approved of what they did." We can make sense of this peculiar assertion only by taking the speaker's approval to be mixed; there are ways in which she did not approve. (For example, she wished they had invited her to join them.) Thus one can feel anger or outrage without having any particular interior sensations, but one cannot feel anger or outrage without having the relevant attitudes.

These considerations strongly suggest that an emotion is not a "pure" sensation caused by an attitude, but essentially includes the attitude. It does not follow, of course, that an emotion is *nothing but* an attitude or judgment. Indeed, we would not know what to make of the claim that someone feels emotions, but *never* had the kind of flushes, queasiness, and so forth that we often have.

In sum, emotions, although they may include feels, are not *merely* feels; emotions of any complexity essentially involve or include attitudes, values, and so forth. Hence many of my emotions are part of my moral personhood.

F. GEORGE SHER ON DESERT

George Sher's book, *Desert* is perhaps the most sustained and detailed theory of desert in print.[1] As such, it deserves more than a quick mention. Sher suggests that different aspects of desert, such as retribution and reward for hard work, require different justifications. I will discuss the two sorts of desert most relevant for this work, namely retribution (deserved punishment) and what we might call "achievement desert."

Sher's theory of retribution is a variant of the familiar view that the point of punishment is to erase an unfair advantage gained by the felon.[2] According to Sher, the felon has enjoyed a freedom from the dictates of morality, dictates to which the rest of us conform. Since the deliberate harming of another is against the dictates of morality, if the victim deliberately harms the felon, the victim has gained a comparable freedom from the dictates of morality.

Sher points out that his variant avoids some of the problems of Morris's version. For example, it would seem to follow from Morris's view that someone who lived a disadvantaged life deserves a "free crime."[3] On Sher's view, he states, this does not follow, since what is at stake is not hardship but freedom from the dictates of morality. Sher is correct about this, but his view faces a precisely parallel problem for the sinned-against. Sher's response is that the burden is nontransferrable: "the original unfairness is not removed but merely displaced" (p. 85). Of course, this response is equally available to Morris.

Another criticism of the "balancing" view is voiced by Richard Burgh,[4] who points out that rapists and embezzlers may not have benefitted from others' restraint in not raping and embezzling. As Sher points out, however (p. 79), they have benefitted from others' restraint in obeying other elements of the law. Burgh's response is that all wrongdoers have enjoyed this general benefit, and so, on the balancing view, all crimes deserve the same punishment. This does not follow, Sher correctly notes, since the advantage gained by the rapist's lack of restraint is presumed to be greater than that gained by the jaywalker's.

Sher's view does mitigate a third criticism of Morris's position. A jaywalker who jaywalks in order to be in time to pull off a million-dollar sale derives greater advantage from his crime than does a murderer who kills merely to pass a dull afternoon. It would appear to follow from Morris's view that the jaywalker deserves a much harsher sentence than does the whimsical murderer. This absurd consequence does not follow from Sher's view, since sentencing should be based not on the advantage gained, but on the degree of freedom from moral dictates, and jaywalking is less of a departure from morality than is murder. It does follow from Sher's view that an evil but relatively harmless violation of law deserves a harsher sentence than, say, negligence that causes great harm. But this is a bullet Sher can safely bite, as long as Sher does not insist that his version of the balancing theory is the only goal or justification of punishment. Sher, after all, is speaking only of retribution. And while it is absurd to say that the jaywalker is morally worse than the whimsical murderer, it is plausible that the bus driver who falls asleep at the wheel, and is convicted of negligent homicide, is less morally heinous than the con artist who defrauds elderly women of small amounts of money by playing on their emotions, leaving them hurt and humiliated. If retribution is but one of the factors influencing the sentencing of felons, then such factors as deterrence and social interests may make it reasonable to give the former a harsher sentence than the latter.

Perhaps the deepest problem with Sher's view is that the kind of "compensation" the victim receives is not very satisfying. Sher claims that punishment "does go some way toward restoring a benefit that [the victim] but not [the felon] has foregone" (p. 87). But why should the victim of a felon particularly desire a "symbolic lifting of the corresponding moral restraints on his behavior" (p. 87)? I cannot, after all, use this symbolic lifting to achieve any goal other than vicarious revenge. After all, the removal of moral bounds is not itself desirable: doing wrong with impunity is only a benefit if the wrong done advances my goals in some way. This was true of the felon, since the felon got to do what he wanted. It is not true of the victim, since the symbolic lifting of moral restraints does not particularly allow the victim to do what she wants. Moreover, the felon's freedom from moral bounds set back the victim's ability to pursue her aims, and the "symbolic lifting" achieved by punishing the felon does nothing to make up this setback. Thus the "restoring" of which Sher speaks is trivial. More generally, the symbolic equalizing of which Sher speaks does not seem to be of sufficient moral importance to justify inflicting the harm that punishment inflicts. It is too slight a reason to justify the practice of punishment.

Sher provides a different ground for desert for one's achievements, whether good or ill.[5] One source of desert, Sher thinks, is justified by the value of autonomous action: "Desert is grounded in the value of freedom" (p. 41). Autonomous acts, says Sher, have value, and the value of the autonomous act carries over to the predictable consequences of the act. Thus it is good that people get the predictable consequences of their autonomous acts: "Because . . . consequences are part of what an agent chooses, it would be quite arbitrary to say that it is good that the agent perform the act he has chosen, but not good that he enjoy or suffer that act's predictable consequences" (p. 39).

I am not sure I follow Sher's reasoning here. Two problems should be raised. First, there are many reasons why it might be good that Jones get a raise, only one of which is that Jones merits the raise. (For example, Jones's getting an undeserved raise may have a variety of good consequences.) Thus from the fact that it is good that Jones get a raise, it does not follow that Jones deserves a raise. Thus even if Sher is right that the value of autonomy means that it is good that agents enjoy or suffer their acts' predictable consequences, it does not follow that agents deserve to enjoy or suffer their acts' predictable consequences. Second, it is not clear why Sher thinks it is good that people suffer their acts' predictable consequences. On my view, because people's life situations should match their moral situations, it is not necessarily best that people get more than they deserve. By contrast, it is not clear why the value of freedom means that it is not good that people get more than they can reasonably expect. That is, Sher's opponent might insist that the best situation is one in which people choose freely, and their choices always work out splendidly. After all, although most people want to be able to do what they have chosen, most people would choose to get more than can reasonably be expected. Thus, it might be argued, although Jones's not doing what he has chosen to do mitigates his freedom of choice, his getting more than can be expected does not interfere with or undermine his freedom of choice. Hence, it might be argued, it is good that agents perform what they choose to perform, and good that what they get is always better than the act's predictable consequences. Thus the value of choice does not entail the value of people getting no more than they can reasonably expect. And so it does not seem to follow from the value of autonomy that "the individual's own purposes, goals, intentions and judgments should determine his or her fate,"[6] in the sense that one deserves the predictable consequences of one's actions.

The same two problems apply to the justification Sher offers, in a later section, for desert for diligence. Sher suggests that a desire confers value on what is desired. Hard work confers greater value than desire. Because "our time and energy are . . . the very stuff of which we fashion our lives," it follows that "any agent who devotes a major portion of his time and energy to achieving a goal is quite literally making that goal a part of himself" (p. 61). Thus the value of persons transfers to the value of their goals. Again, while it may follow from this that we ought to treat people's goals with respect, it does not follow that people deserve to obtain the fruits of their diligence.

Sher recognizes five types of troublesome cases for his view: "Expected consequences seem undeserved when they are: (1) very easily acquired, (2) the disastrous results of merely careless acts, (3) the spoils of wrongful acts, (4) the harmful effects of self-sacrificing acts [and] (5) the results of choices made under threat, or in some other illegitimately structured choice situation" (p. 45).

Sher has a response to each type of case. In case 1, says Sher, the choice "though not unfree . . . is also not a meaningful expression of his will" (p. 45). It is not clear why Sher thinks this, because it is not clear what makes a choice "significant" for Sher. On my account, what makes a choice "significant" is the extent to which it reflects an agent's worldview, and easy choices can certainly reflect important aspects of a person's worldview.

In cases 2, 3, and 4, according to Sher, there are other negative factors, and "the value [autonomous acts] inherit from the agent's exercise of freedom is outweighed by their disvalue" (p. 46). I do not see how Sher can say this. On Sher's view, what makes me deserving of passing the test is that passing the test is a predictable consequence of my studying. Going through the windshield is a predictable consequence of not buckling one's seatbelts, and thus, on the predictable-consequence view, the person who freely chooses not to buckle his seatbelt deserves to go through the windshield. Of course, the disvalue of dying in an automobile accident may outweigh the good of someone's getting what he deserved. Thus Sher is entitled to say that although the careless person who does not buckle his seatbelt deserves to die in an automobile crash, it is not a good thing for him to get what he deserves. But, since the driver freely chose not to wear seatbelts, and flying through the windshield is a predictable consequence of not wearing seatbelts, Sher must admit that the beltless driver deserves to die. After all, desert must often be weighed against other goods. For example, we have to weigh the fact that Smith deserves the job against the utility of giving the job to Jones instead. It would be misleading to say that Smith does not deserve the job, though he is more qualified, has worked harder, and has seniority over Jones, because the job would mean more to Jones than to Smith. But if we conflate desert with what would be good for someone to get in other ways, then desert can no longer function as a counterweight to other goods. Similarly, it seems to follow from Sher's view that the self-sacrificer ought to get more than he deserves. True, "it is bad that the price of virtue is harm or injury to a good man" (p. 47), "it is bad that [the person] has freely chosen to do what is wrong," and "it would also have been better if the consequences of the choice had not played themselves out" (pp. 46–47). But what this must mean, on Sher's account, is that it is a bad thing if the evil-doer and the self-sacrificer get what they deserve.

Put another way, someone who cheats at poker does not deserve to win, even though winning is a predictable consequence of cheating, just as someone who works hard at finding a cure for AIDS may deserve to succeed, even though he knew succeeding was a long shot. (Indeed, Sher recognizes effort that does not lead to success as one sort of desert not justified by the expected consequence view.) For Sher, these cases are quite different in character. In fact, what these cases seem to show is that desert is based not on expected consequences, but on moral status: the cheater is evil and does not deserve to thrive, while the AIDS researcher is working for the good and deserves to succeed. Similarly, Sher argues that the diligent thief does not deserve to succeed because "the value conferred by their efforts is offset by the [moral] disvalue . . . of their projects" (p. 67). Here again, it seems more appropriate, given Sher's account, to say that although the thief deserves to succeed, it is not good that the thief get what she deserves.

Notes

CHAPTER I

1. P. F. Strawson, "Freedom and Resentment," *Proceedings of the British Academy* 48 (1962): 195. See also James Rachels, "What People Deserve," in *Justice and Economic Distribution*, ed. John Arthur and William H. Shaw (New York: Prentice-Hall, 1978), p. 159: giving people "what they deserve is one way of treating them as autonomous beings, responsible for their own conduct. . . . Recognition of deserts is bound up with this way of regarding people."

2. Cf. Roderick Chisholm, "Freedom and Action," in *Freedom and Determinism*, ed. Keith Lehrer (New York: Random House, 1966), p. 12: "If the man was responsible for what he did, then, I would urge, what was to happen at the time of the shooting was something that was entirely up to the man himself. . . . If a man is responsible for a certain event or state of affairs . . . , then that event or state of affairs was brought about by some act of his, and the act was something that was in his power either to perform or not to perform."

3. See, for example, Anthony Kenny, *Freewill and Responsibility* (London: Routledge and Kegan Paul, 1978), p. 30: "In order to do X freely one must have both the ability and the opportunity not to do X." See also Brian Barry, *Political Argument* (Atlantic Highlands, N.J.: Humanities Press, 1965), p. 108: "A person's having been able to have done otherwise is a necessary condition of ascribing desert"; and Richard Sorabji, *Necessity, Cause and Blame* (Ithaca, N.Y.: Cornell University Press, 1980), p. 251: we could not be deserving of praise or blame "if it had all along been necessary that we should act as we did."

4. When I first presented these views, in the fall of 1979, I was told that no one thought as I did. Since then several philosophers, including Daniel Dennett and Robert Merrihew Adams, have published work agreeing with some of the more controversial claims in this book.

5. Richard Brandt, "Determinism and the Justifiability of Moral Blame," in *Determinism and Freedom*, ed. Sidney Hook (New York: New York University Press, 1958), p. 149.

6. *Oxford English Dictionary* (Oxford: Oxford University Press, 1933), vol. 12, p. 326.

7. *Ibid.*, vol. 1, p. 898.

8. Since it is only in Chapter III that I provide a rigorous account of what it means to say that A is responsible for x, my remarks here must rely, more

or less, on some rough intuitions about responsibility. This reliance limits the discussion a bit. But then the purpose of this section is merely to raise doubts about (rather than refute) the traditional view. If one keeps in mind some of the points made in Chapter III (for example, the limited sense in which I use the term "responsibility"), it becomes even clearer that William and Harry, in the stories I will tell about them, are responsible in the way I say they are.

9. The words "are properly reflected" are a bit vague. In Chapter II this notion is discussed more fully. As we will see, the relation between having attitudes and acting is even closer than my comments here suggest, since to have an attitude is just for the whole of one's circumstances, acts, and occurrent feels and thoughts to be best understood in terms of that attitude.

10. Lon Fuller, *The Morality of Law* (New Haven, Conn.: Yale University Press, 1964). Many others, of course, have drawn similar distinctions.

11. This is true despite the fact that Aristotle, whose moral philosophy is a prime example of a "virtue" theory, is sometimes interpreted as holding the traditional view.

12. For example, Daniel Dennett points out in "I Could Not Have Done Otherwise—So What?" *Journal of Philosophy* 81 (October 1984): 557, that we never inquire whether a person could have done otherwise before praising her. Moreover, if "responsibility really did hinge" on PAP, argues Dennett, "it would be unlikely in the extreme . . . that anyone would ever know whether anyone has ever been responsible, [since] it is possible for all we know that our decisions and actions truly are the magnified, macroscopic effects of quantum-level indeterminacies occurring in our brains."

13. Peter van Inwagen, "Ability and Responsibility," *Philosophical Review* 87 (April 1978): 201–224.

14. Harry Frankfurt, "Alternate Possibilities and Moral Responsibility," *Journal of Philosophy* 66 (1969): 829–839. For a discussion of Frankfurt's own view, as proposed in his "Freedom of the Will and the Concept of a Person," *Journal of Philosophy* 68 (January 1971): 5–20, see *Moral Responsibility*, ed. John M. Fischer (Ithaca, N.Y.: Cornell University Press, 1986), pp. 43–51; Gary Watson, "Free Agency," *Journal of Philosophy* 72 (April 1975): 205–220; and Michael Slote, "Understanding Free Will," *Journal of Philosophy* 77 (March 1980): 136–151.

15. Of course, it is physically possible for him to break the law. But the compulsion of law is precisely the kind of thing for which we use the excuse "I could not have done otherwise." After all, people are not usually given credit for generosity because their tax dollars are used, in small part, to feed the hungry. (On my view, the explanation is that, for most people, paying their taxes reflects a commitment to staying out of jail rather than to feeding the hungry.) Nor are people generally blamed for doing what the law requires, except when the law requires such gross immorality that one ought to prefer imprisonment to obeying the law. (On my view, the explanation is that one ought, generally, to obey the law: one is responsible, but not blameworthy.)

16. See Daniel Dennett, *Elbow Room: The Varieties of Free Will Worth Wanting* (Cambridge, Mass.: MIT Press, 1984). Dennett correctly points out

that we ask whether someone could have done otherwise to decide "what meaning we should attach to" the person's action. Unfortunately, he identifies this with "what conclusions to draw from it about the future" (p. 142). As a result, Dennett thinks that "Jones could have done otherwise" means "Jones 'might, for all anyone could know for certain beforehand, have done something different'" (p. 148, quoting J. L. Austin, "Ifs and Cans," in his *Philosophical Papers* [Oxford: Oxford University Press, 1961], p. 207). But this is not right. Suppose no one knows that Smith has a brain tumor. Recently, the tumor has grown sufficiently to interfere slightly with Smith's neural processing. Neither Smith nor anyone else has noticed the effect, since it is slight at this point and arises only when Smith is attempting complex hand-eye coordination tasks. Today Smith and Jones play Pacman. Smith's score is several points lower than Jones's. Smith says, "I could have won had I pushed myself more." Now, as a result of the brain tumor, Smith could not have done otherwise (in the relevant sense) than lose. But he could have done otherwise in Dennett's sense, since the existence of Smith's tumor is not known to anyone. Some things about which we are ignorant nonetheless insure that we could not have done otherwise than we did.

Moreover, as Milbur's case shows, we can be responsible for things even when we could not have done otherwise in Dennett's sense: Milbur is praiseworthy even though he and we know that he could not have done otherwise than visit the sick once a month.

17. There is a second advantage to my version. Sorabji, in *Necessity, Cause and Blame*, objects that in Frankfurt's counterexamples, the factors that make it impossible for the agent to do otherwise "are not the ones [that] explain" what the agent does, and so Frunkfurt-style inability to do otherwise is relevantly different from the inability to do otherwise occasioned by determinism (p. 254). This response does not apply to my counterexample, since Bill's pressing the button does (causally) explain what Harry does.

18. Note that since the cause of the slap was external to Harry, it was, according to Aristotle's definition, involuntary. Moreover, this case is also a counterexample to Fischer's "actual-sequence" view, since the actual causal sequence was not, in fact, within Harry's control. (See John M. Fischer, "Responsibility and Control," *Journal of Philosophy* 79 (January 1982): 24–40.)

19. Consider also the case of White and Green, described by John M. Fischer in "Introduction: Responsibility and Freedom" in *Moral Responsibility*, p. 41. Green and White both save a drowning child, but White's action arose from electronic stimulation of his brain by a group of California scientists. Green has the same device planted in his brain, but the scientists do not turn it on while Green is saving the child. Had Green chosen not to save the child, the scientists would have forced him to. Green freely rescues the child, even though he could not have done otherwise, yet "it would be ridiculous," says Fischer, "to praise White." Thus, concludes Fischer, having the actual sequence of events under one's control is what is necessary to moral responsibility.

As I mentioned earlier, the case of Harry's slapping his landlord seems to be a counterexample to Fischer's view, since the actual sequence was not in Harry's control. Does the case of Green and White tell against my view? I suggest it does not. If White would have saved the child anyway, that is, if the scientists prodded White to do exactly what White would have done anyway, then White still deserves praise. It does not much matter what actually caused White's muscles to move, as long as their movements fit perfectly White's values, choices, and so on.

For a discussion of blame and brain tampering, see the case of Brian in Chapter IV.

20. See Appendix A for a discussion of some variants of PAP advanced since Frankfurt's paper appeared.

21. According, at least, to Davidson and Prichard. To the extent that one adopts a more "liberal" account of actions, such as Goldman's, acts become increasingly similar to instantiations of traits. For example, if one holds that an action is any instantiation of any property (in the widest sense) by an agent for any duration of time, then an action *just is* an instantiation of a trait.

22. Moreover, Teri's failure to give to charity is just the sort of thing that most moral theories evaluate. Unless the relevant moral theory is quite bizarre (nonstandard), Teri's failure to give to charity does have moral import. So Teri's not giving to charity meets the two criteria for moral responsibility set forth in Chapter II.

23. For example, Michael J. Zimmerman, in *An Essay on Moral Responsibility* (Totowa, N.J.: Rowman and Littlefield, 1988), suggests that people are not substantively responsible for omissions, but rather for the direct acts they perform. That is, on Zimmerman's view, Teri is only indirectly responsible for not giving to charity, and indirect responsibility is empty: with the possible exception of "intentional omissions," "the question of appraisability for an omission arises only when there is an initial volition of which the omission in question is itself a consequence" (p. 93). But which of Teri's initial volitions over the last twenty years are the culpable ones? The answer must be "all of them," since any one could have been replaced by a volition to give money to charity. But surely there is nothing culpable about Teri's volition to buy a loaf of bread for her dinner.

24. To use the language of George Bealer's intensional logic, Teri is within the extension of the intensional abstract [not: x gave to charity within the last twenty years]. See his *Quality and Concept* (Oxford: Oxford University Press, 1982).

25. Note, by the way, that there is a difference between situationally specific omissions, such as not pulling out a drowning man at a particular time in a particular place, and failing to give to charity for the last twenty years. Since no particular situation called for giving to charity, there is no particular answer to the question "Well, what did she do instead?" Act and choice analyses can treat failures to perform particular acts in particular situations much more easily than they can nonspecific omissions, such as failing to give to charity.

26. As Hobart points out, actions are significant only insofar as they reveal one's character. (R. E. Hobart, "Free Will as Involving Determinism and Inconceivable Without It," *Mind* 43 [January 1934]: 1–27.)

27. Cf. Stephen David Ross, *The Nature of Moral Responsibility* (Detroit: Wayne State University Press, 1973): An act "is mine only insofar as a determinable relation can be found between my character and the act" (p. 215).

28. See Susan Wolf, "Asymmetrical Freedom," *Journal of Philosophy* 67 (1980): 151–165: "An agent can be both determined and responsible only insofar as he performs actions that he ought to perform. If an agent performs a morally bad action, on the other hand, then his action can't be determined in the appropriate way" (p. 163). The opposite view is held by Zimmerman, in *An Essay on Moral Responsibility*. According to Zimmerman, one is "directly culpable" for x if one "strictly willed it in the belief that one would thereby do wrong," while one is "directly laudable" for x if "one strictly willed it for the sake of doing right, but not in the belief that one would thereby do one's duty," and so doing one's duty in very difficult circumstances is not, according to Zimmerman, something for which one is directly laudable (p. 8). I hold, with common sense, that agents can be responsible both for evil actions and for doing their duty, since one who performs a morally bad action may be a worse person than someone otherwise similar who does not perform that action, and one who does her duty in a difficult situation may be a better person than one who does not.

29. You might think that the traditionalist has a way of avoiding this consequence. She might distinguish between culpable and nonculpable error and insist that when people act wrongly through culpable error they are responsible for their misdeeds. This only postpones the problem, however, since a culpable error, on the traditional view, must be a freely chosen error as well as an example of wrongdoing. Since, *ex hypothesi*, people choose to do wrong only through error, it would follow that culpable error itself is the result of a prior error. Ultimately, thus, the chain must end in nonculpable errors that are the cause of the wrongdoing. My view, by way of contrast, avoids the problem, since it does not require that culpable errors be freely chosen. Thus even if people choose to do wrong only through error, it does not follow that culpable errors are the result of prior errors.

30. A third possibility is so-called "agent-causation"; my acts are caused, but by me, not by prior events. (See, for example, Roderick Chisholm, *Person and Object* [Peru, Ill.: Open Court Publishing, 1976].) What this "agent-causation" is supposed to be remains a mystery.

31. For a somewhat longer discussion of the dilemma, see Frithjob Bergmann, *Being Free* (Notre Dame, Ind.: University of Notre Dame Press, 1977), pp. 231–238. John Thorp, in his *Free Will* (London: Routledge and Kegan Paul, 1981), tries to resolve the apparent dilemma that actions are either caused or random by appealing to the notion of "hegemony." One description of an event has hegemony over a second description if the first is causally explained by another event at its level while the second is not. A mental description, such as "deciding to flip the light switch," may have

hegemony over its physical analogue (neuron 241 firing) when it "makes sense" for me to turn on the light switch, while neuron 241's firing involves quantum indeterminacy. According to Thorp, in such a case my turning on the light switch is not random (the decision "makes sense"), but neither is it strictly determined (there is only a certain statistical probability of neuron 241's firing). However, this will not fly. My turning on the light switch is explained by my desire not to bump into the furniture. Now Thorp seems to be committed to a mysterious occasionalism here. My deciding to turn on the light cannot cause neuron 241 to fire, since *ex hypothesi* these are two descriptions of the same event. If there is no causal chain linking my desire not to bump into furniture with neuron 241's firing, then Thorp seems to be reduced to a perplexing sort of occasionalism: it is just good luck that the neuron appropriate to my desire fired, since there is, say, a 20 percent chance that it will not. So it looks as if the desire must *cause* the neuron to fire. Not only is this cross-level causation mysterious, but it defeats Thorp's project: my action is still determined, though on the intentional rather than the neurological level.

32. For example, some have tried to avoid the problem by suggesting that "Jones could have done otherwise" just means "Jones will act otherwise, if he wants" or "he could have done otherwise, if he had wanted to do otherwise." (See G. E. Moore, *Ethics* [Oxford: Oxford University Press, 1912]; C. L. Stevenson, *Ethics and Language* [New haven: Yale University Press, 1944]; A. Kaufmann, "Moral Responsibility and the Use of 'Could Have,'" *Philosophical Quarterly* 12 [1962]: 120–128; and James Lamb, "On a Proof of Incompatibilism," *Philosophical Review* 86 [1977], 20–35.) This construal, however, does not sit well with the traditional emphasis on voluntarity. Sorabji, for example, in *Necessity, Cause and Blame*, claims that the ability to do otherwise had the agent wanted to do otherwise cannot ground responsibility unless the agent could have *wanted* something other than what she wanted.

CHAPTER II

1. Since, I will argue later, beliefs, emotions, and the like cannot be instantaneous like this, this bit of science fiction rests on a confusion. But it will serve to make the point.

2. If thoughts and other mental states are not properties of the body, then they will have to be included as well in the description of a person-stage. We merely add to the collection of subatomic particles the particular thoughts, and so on, occurring at that moment.

3. See Appendix B for a fuller discussion of stages and identity over time.

4. See, for example, the discussion of John Perry's paper in Appendix C.

5. Although, I would argue, this is not quite true; it is not always illicit to punish those who are not morally responsible.

6. For example, George Sher, in *Desert* (Princeton, N.J.: Princeton University Press, 1987), points out that desert claims "presuppose a single concep-

tion of the self. On that conception, persons are both constituted by their preferences and abilities and extended over time" (p. 169).

7. Cf. Locke's distinction between "man," "soul," "body," and "person"; I am arguing that the terms "legal person," "biological person," and such are similarly divisible.

It should be said that my claim here is not an example of Geachean relative identity. (See, for example, Peter Geach, "Identity," *Review of Metaphysics* 21 [September 1967].) My claim that A and B are the same legal person but not the same biological person should be construed as the nonrelativistic claim that A and B are constituents of one temporal complex, C, but are not both constituents of a different temporal complex, D. (Cf. David Wiggins, *Identity and Spatio-temporal Continuity* [Cambridge, Mass.: Basil Blackwell, 1967].) More precisely, it is a feature of certain (momentary) quarks and electrons, existing at different times, that they constitute a legal person, that they can be understood in terms of a continuing legal standing. However those same quarks and electrons cannot be understood as constituting a continuing organism of the species Homo sapiens; that is, they do not exhibit continuity of the requisite biological functions. Thus no nonstandard use of "identity" is required by my account.

8. We must distinguish, in other words, between what a term attributes and the conditions under which we can use it. Since, were it not for physics departments, laboratories, and the like, I would have no notion of what an electron is, I can say that an electron has a negative charge only because of the existence of the social institution of science. In fact, if language is essentially social, then every word's application depends upon social institutions. But the mere fact that a term's application requires human intentionality is not enough to make the term "intentional." What makes a term intentional is the *semantic content* of what it attributes, not the *conditions of usage* (the various constraints upon *making* the attribution). What it means to say that something is a weapon, what we are saying about something by calling it a weapon, is that we tend to use it a certain way. But what it means to say that something is an electron, what we are saying about it by calling it an electron, *pace* certain philosophers of science, has nothing to do with human institutions, practices, predilections, or habits.

9. The distinction I am drawing is similar to that drawn by the ancient Greeks between *physis* and *nomos*. There is, of course, much debate about whether the fundamental objects are subatomic particles, macroscopic objects such as icicles, or even, as Quine has suggested, abstract mathematical objects. For the sake of convenience, I will assume that the fundamental objects are subatomic particles.

10. A "count noun" is a noun that individuates. For example, "water" is not a "count noun" but a "mass term," for one cannot ask, "How many waters are there in Michigan?" as one can ask, "How many bachelors are there in Michigan?" One can only ask, "How much water is in Michigan?" and an appropriate response would be given in terms of bulk (so many tons, gallons, or whatever). Bachelors are discrete individuals (even if sometimes

given to indiscretion), while "water" is so much stuff of a certain sort (H_2O). Bachelors are counted by number, water by quantity; there are *fewer* bachelors and *less* water in Nevada than in Michigan.

11. Two things determine the truth of intentional assertions. First, the physical facts must be favorable; the spatial disposition of matter in a room is not *irrelevant* to its neatness. Second, it must be part of a rational way of viewing the world. In general, an intentional assertion is correct if and only if (1) all its dependency relations on nonintentional facts are satisfied (the facts are favorable) and (2) the process of rational inquiry, ideally followed out, would lead to (in the case of objective truths) or permit (in the case of relative truths) the adoption of the assertion. Here "rational inquiry" is used in a very broad sense. It includes such things as giving a fictional depiction of what a certain kind of life is like. Moreover, rational inquiry always begins with one's present convictions and predilections; by "rational inquiry" I do not mean a Cartesian inquiry *ab nihilo*.

12. Kripke, of course, does not say that taxonomists must or should base their taxonomies on natural kinds, and he says little about what makes a natural kind "natural." Thus it would be unfair to attribute to Kripke any particular view about taxonomy.

13. This is not really circular. By "human respiration" I mean a particular mechanism for respiration, which we could describe without any reference to "human." I call it "human respiration" only for ease of description, as it would take many pages to describe the particular lung structure, biochemistry of oxygen transfer, and so forth to which I am referring.

14. Such cases shed some light on the nature of taxonomy. When confronted with a puzzling case, the biologist must weight biological functions; continuity of some functions will count more than continuity of others. (In practice, of course, the situation is quite complex. For example, combinations of functions may be more important than each function considered separately.) This process of weighting biological functions reflects the aesthetic and explanatory goals of the biologist: what does she wish to explain, and what constitutes a good explanation? Moreover, although species terms define the relevant biological functions, we choose a taxonomy that matches our conceptions of important biological functions. The function of reproduction, for example, plays an important role in modern taxonomy. Conversely, whether the splitting of one organism into two constitutes reproduction or the death of an organism of one species and the birth of two organisms of another species can only be settled by appealing to an already established taxonomy.

15. Differences between them, in other words, are due to differences of circumstances, not differences of status. For example, Joe Smith does not have the liabilities to which car manufacturers are subject, because he does not manufacture cars.

16. I say "is applicable" rather than "applies," because intervening circumstances can annul one of A's claims or obligations. For example, a person against whom A has a contractual claim might die, or the statute of limitations on A's crime may excuse B.

17. After all, as F. H. Bradley points out in *Ethical Studies*, 2d ed. (Oxford: Oxford University Press, 1927), personal identity is a precondition for answerability.

18. Mill, I would argue, held that pleasure is the enjoyment of happiness and that to be fully happy is to lead an ideal human existence (of which there may be more than one variety), to fully instantiate the (or a) correct normative picture of human excellence. It is in this sense that Mill is an Aristotelian: the happy person is the person who fully realizes human nature. Unlike Aristotle, Mill held that the method of discovering human nature is empirical. Just as the nature of an elm is discovered by seeing what the elm does under ideal growing conditions, human nature is discovered by seeing what people choose under ideal conditions, that is, what is chosen by autonomous agents, familiar with a broad range of lifestyles, who engage in free and informed debate and experiment. This interpretation also explains why Mill thought that the harm principle is justified by utility and renders the much-maligned "proof" of the principle of utility plausible, rather than a simple logical error. (That is, on this view, it is straightforwardly true that the only proof that something is desirable is that it is in fact desired by people under ideal conditions.) A defense of this interpretation of Mill is, of course, beyond the scope of this work.

19. Sartre, Jean-Paul, *L'Existentialisme est un humanisme* (1946), translated by Philip Mairet as *Existentialism and Humanism* (London: Methuen and Co., 1973). It should be said that Sartre later expressed reservations about this claim.

20. Of course, by regarding the latter choice as nonproclamative, I express a moral judgment, namely that no general values, no moral desiderata, are involved. In that minimal sense, all choices are proclamative.

21. Of course, the links between preferences and values are generally much more complex and individual than my comments above suggest. And I do not want to say that my preference for blue is *caused* by any particular value I possess, nor that to choose blue is to *assert* a moral judgment. My claim is simply that even mere preferences do not occur in a moral vacuum. Preferences often *reflect*, perhaps in complex and convoluted ways, one's moral vision. That is, there is some story to be told about me that "makes sense of" my preferences in terms of my values, attitudes, goals, and such.

22. In fact, Bernard Gert, in *The Moral Rules* (New York: Harper and Row, 2d Torchbook ed., 1973) goes so far as to insist that "the moral philosopher ought to be concerned only with that code of conduct of which the moral rules form the core" (p. 5). And although a few pages later he admits to morality what he calls "moral ideals" and devotes a full chapter to them, moral ideals turn out to be slight modifications of moral rules: "the moral ideals can be summarized as 'Prevent evil'. . . . Substituting 'prevent' for 'don't' and changing the wording slightly generates a moral ideal from each of the moral rules" (p. 128).

23. Peter Glassen, "'Charientic' Judgments," *Philosophy* (April 1958): 138.

24. A further complication is that many of our choices reflect conditional

judgments. In deciding that I should not wear a bathing suit because my legs are unattractive, I may not be proclaiming that bathing suits should be eschewed. Perhaps I am asserting only that if one has unattractive legs, one should not wear bathing suits. Or I may be asserting only that those who are sensitive to derisive looks and have unattractive legs should avoid bathing suits. Note that even conditional judgments are generally reflections of more general, nonconditional judgments (For example, one ought to act rationally in pursuing one's interests).

25. Examples of this view are, alas, not hard to find; one may find it in most Hollywood films aimed at persons over twelve.

26. Robert B. Zajonc, in "Feeling and Thinking: Preferences Need No Inferences," *American Psychologist* 35 (1980): 151–175, argues that emotions are precognitive, and hence independent of values. For a view closer to my own, see J. Sabini, and M. Silver, *Moralities of Everyday Life* (Oxford: Oxford University Press, 1982).

27. Robert Solomon, *The Passions* (Garden City, N.J.: Anchor Books, 1976), p. 194. As Joseph Margolis points out in "The Relevance of the Emotions for Medicine," in *Understanding Human Emotions* (Bowling Green, Ohio: Studies in Applied Philosophy, Bowling Green, 1980), ed. Fred D. Miller, Jr., and Thomas W. Attig, Solomon goes too far in his assertion that emotions "constitute" that framework. My feeling anger at terrorists involves beliefs that are manifested in other ways (for example, writing a paper arguing that killing is never permissible). Writing the paper is not itself anger.

28. In *What Is an Emotion?* ed. Cheshire Calhoun and Robert C. Solomon (Oxford: Oxford University Press, 1984), the editors identify five types of theories of the emotions: (a) "sensation theories" (for example, Hume's), (b) "physiological theories" (for example, Descartes's and James's), (c) "behavioral theories" (for example, Ryle's and Skinner's), (d) "evaluative theories" (for example, Sartre's and Solomon's), and (e) "cognitive theories" (for example, Errol Bedford's). The kind of interpretive account of emotions I give requires a "fit" with all five elements: it counts against my feeling anger that my sensations, physiology, or behavior is ill-explained by attributing anger to me, and any attribution to me of anger is also an attribution to me of certain sorts of cognitions and evaluations.

29. Irving Thalberg, in *Perception, Emotion and Action* (New Haven, Conn.: Yale University Press, 1977), distinguishes between those who think my emotional attitude toward someone *entails* a certain way of thinking about him, and those who hold that my thinking that way about him *causes* my emotional attitude toward him. On page 32, Thalberg cites the following as adherents of the entailment view: Errol Bedford, Gilbert Ryle, Bernard Williams, Terence Penulhum, Anthony Kenny, and himself in his earlier work. (Adherents of the causal view, such as Armstrong and Wilson, are discussed in Thalberg's "Review of Wilson," *Philosophical Review* 83 (1974): 115–132.) Against the entailment view, Thalberg correctly points out that there are descriptions of an emotional episode that do not entail

particular thoughts (pp. 34–36). Thalberg is right that if the entailment view is supposed to assert that every description of an emotion entails particular beliefs and attitudes, it is clearly wrong. But this is certainly not what I mean by suggesting that anger is inseparable from certain sorts of attitudes. (After all, although being an equilateral triangle entails being equiangular, the description "what I am holding in my hand right now" does not, though what I am holding is an equilateral triangle.)

30. This assumes, of course, that determinism is at least roughly true.

31. For an interesting discussion of the psychology of hitting in anger, see P. S. Greenspan, "Unfreedom and Responsibility," in *Responsibility, Character, and the Emotions: New Essays in Moral Psychology*, ed., Ferdinand D. Schoeman (Cambridge, England: Cambridge University Press, 1987), pp. 63–80.

32. It is worth noting here that the crucial point is not what caused his action, but whether his action accords with, suits, fits his attitudes.

33. Charles Taylor, *Human Agency and Language* (Cambridge, England: Cambridge University Press, 1985), p. 63.

34. So when I say that we are responsible, ultimately, for our (moral) personhood, I am not claiming, as Aristotle and Hume seem to claim, that only general and enduring traits are of moral interest.

35. First, there is no one-to-one mapping between a belief and a behavioral disposition, since how a belief disposes me to act depends upon my other beliefs and desires. For example, whether my belief that this table is heavy will dispose me to walk around it or push it out of my way depends upon whether I want to show off my strength, feign ignorance of the table's weight, avoid putting strain on my back, and so on. And those desires in turn may depend upon my other beliefs (for example, my desire to avoid putting strain on my back depends upon my belief that my back is injured and that strain will exacerbate the injury) and my other desires (for example, the desire to avoid pain). As I argue later, this network is an extensive one. So, at the very least, the correlation must be between the whole set of my beliefs and desires on the one hand and a large set of behavioral dispositions on the other. Second, that large set of behavioral dispositions is compatible with several very different sets of beliefs and desires if we do not also take into consideration such things as occurrent thoughts and feels. Recall the discussion of Hilary in Chapter I.

36. The simplest "functionalist" accounts of belief are thus mistaken. It is just wrong that the belief that smokers appear distinguished is just whatever plays a particular causal role. For there may be no unique causal role common to all instances of the belief that smokers appear distinguished. Yet if functionalism of this sort were correct, in the absence of such unique causal roles we could not have any beliefs at all.

37. See Daniel Dennett, *Brainstorms: Philosophical Essays on Mind and Psychology* (Montgomery, Vt.: Bradford Books, 1978). It should be noted that, despite some important disagreements, most of what I say about worldviews is consistent with Dennett's view. I differ from Dennett in at least two

crucial ways. First, my criteria for an adequate intentional explanation are *much* more stringent and comprehensive than his. The requirements of depth of explanation and fit to the entirety of an agent's life, to name just two, are quite foreign to Dennett's view. In general, Dennett overlooks the systematic character of intentional explanation. Indeed, Dennett is rather cavalier about adopting intentional accounts. Second, unlike Dennett, I not only think there are occurrent mental "feels" and thoughts but also deem them necessary for bona fide beliefs.

38. It is curious how readily some experimenters make claims about "speech centers" or "pleasure centers" of the brain. Much of the evidence for localization comes from removing areas of the brain and seeing which functions are impaired. This is a bit like removing the fuel line from a car and, when the car does not move, claiming that the car's motion occurs in the fuel line.

39. See also Dennett's remarks in *Brainstorms*. Of course, some features of the chess-playing machine's strategy may be readily locatable in a given subroutine. But with a complex program, much of the computer's strategy cannot be given a simple location in the program, for it is a feature of the whole of the program's operation. Similarly, *some* beliefs may be "brain-mapped" in the sense that some local area of the brain is primarily responsible for the aspects of behavior that justify ascribing the belief to the agent.

40. See Ronald Dworkin, *Law's Empire* (Cambridge, Mass.: Harvard University Press, 1986) for an illuminating and detailed discussion of legal and literary interpretation.

41. This is not to claim that psychology as a discipline is inherently "subjective." Intentional psychological theory need not replace or compete with physiological accounts of behavior; the two perform different tasks. And both may properly be called "psychology." There is no reason why an intentional psychological theorist need claim that intentional psychological theory provides the best or only account of human behavior.

42. Kelly Hite has objected (in conversation) that if beliefs do not come singly, it is difficult to see how we could acquire any. My answer is that children develop a continually more-sophisticated network of dispositions, preferences, expectations, memories of sense perceptions, and so forth, so that it becomes increasingly more appropriate to attribute a network of beliefs to them. Thus there is no "first" belief; rather, the entire mental life of small children becomes increasingly more "belief-like," if you will.

43. Since I first wrote these words some years ago, some functionalists have done just this.

44. In turn, although feeling relief is not a mere sensation, one cannot feel relief if one has *no* "inner feels," if everything is "dark inside." Again, one could always define the word "relief" so that computers feel relief (for example, they print the word "whew!" on the screen). But it would not matter that the computer felt relief in *that* way.

45. My realism about "inner occurrences" does not commit me to dualism or epiphenomenalism. It is, for example, consistent with dual aspectism and

with a doctrine of "emergent properties." In fact, my view about beliefs, pains, and such is a kind of functionalism, although "causal role" is replaced by "explanatory roles" (the plural is important), and the data to be explained include inner "mental" occurrences. Indeed, I am quite prepared to accept two "supervenience principles," that is, (1) that every mental change is also (reflected in) a physical change, and (2) that two bodies, all of whose physical states are exactly the same, have the same mental states (with the possible exception of historically defined states), as well as the determinist thesis that (3) every physical change falls under a universal, physical, causal law.

46. So this is not an argument that we are not machines. Rather, it is an argument that, for example, IBM PCs do not have beliefs and emotions in the robust sense relevant to morality. And to deny that persons have such inner occurrences is to deny them moral standing.

47. This is not an example of what Davidson calls "the logical connection fallacy"; my claim is not that the *description* of the action mentions the belief, but that the action (partially) *constitutes* the belief.

I should note that I think that there is *a* sense in which beliefs are causes of actions. Beliefs are what I call "immanent causes" of actions, much as being triangular is the cause of this figure's being trilateral, and the glass's crystal-line structure is the cause of its being hard. My claim is that, strictly speaking, beliefs are generally not *efficient* causes of actions.

48. I say "we can tell" rather than "a story could be told" only for simplicity of expression; A's being a moral person does not depend upon what kind of story *we* can tell, but upon what kind of story about A could be told, whether we can do it or not.

49. Peter K. McInerney writes, "What makes diverse psychological factors into one person-stage rather than many or none, is dependent upon the relations between person-stages that make them all into the stages of one person" ("Person-Stages and the Unity of Consciousness," *American Philosophical Quarterly* 22 [July 1985]: 197). In fact, McInerney does not go far enough; what makes something a psychological factor at all depends upon the unity of persons over time.

50. By "common core" I do not mean a set of properties each of which is possessed by every stage. What I have in mind is rather a Wittgensteinian "family resemblance." I discuss this below.

51. James Griffin, in *Well-Being* (Oxford: Oxford University Press, 1986), pp. 377–378, n. 3, suggests that the notion of psychological continuity is too vague to do much work. Griffin points out that people might most clearly see their lives as a whole immediately after a religious conversion or other radical change in personality. I suggest that to the extent this is true, it is precisely because they recognize a pattern of psychological *growth*, rather than an abrupt replacement of one personality by another.

52. For example, one can only apply the Nazi picture of the Jew to the neighbor one has known all one's life by allowing oneself to be blind to the obvious discrepancies between the neighbor's characteristics and the attrib-

utes attributed to all Jews by Nazi mythology. Similarly, any American slave-holder with intellectual honesty could not fail to see that his slaves were not animals incapable of human thought, or else it would not have been neces-sary to prevent his slaves forcibly from learning to read. Anyone proposing a law making it a crime for dogs to learn to read would be laughed at. It is a common human failing to tell oneself lies one believes, that is, to believe things one knows, in some sense, are false. To be a Nazi, one must have this failing to a more than usual extent.

53. I use the word "laws" loosely here. I do not mean exceptionless uni-versal generalizations, but general patterns or regularities.

54. See, for example, Michael Tooley, "Abortion and Infanticide," *Philos-ophy and Public Affairs* 2 (1972): 37–65 and Mary Anne Warren, "On the Moral and Legal Status of Abortion," *The Monist* 57 (October 1973).

55. I will argue, in a later work, that free will cannot be the basis of rights.

56. Some readers will immediately insist that there is no "correct" moral theory or perspective. I discuss this problem in the next chapter.

57. I am not alone, of course, in insisting that evaluation is what is central to moral agency. Harry Frankfurt, for instance, claims that what is central to human agents, as opposed to cows, is that we are able to form "second-order desires"; we desire to desire some things and desire not to want others. So we not only have desires but evaluate our desires. (Harry Frankfurt, "Free-dom of the Will and the Concept of a Person," *Journal of Philosophy* 67 (January 1971): 5–20.) Charles Taylor takes Frankfurt's point a step further. What is crucial to human agency, says Taylor, is that some of our second-order desires are "strong evaluations"; we prefer some desires and motives to others because they are morally better, are part of a better way of life. I might, says Taylor, desire not to want to run away from danger because I "value courageous action as part of a mode of life; I aspire to be a certain kind of person. This would be compromised by my giving in to this craven impulse" (Taylor, *Human Agency and Language,* p. 19). So "motivations or desires do not only count in virtue of the attraction of the consummations but also in virtue of the kind of life and kind of subject that these desires properly belong to" (p. 25). In fact, these general moral notions shape the way we view our desires. Without, for example, such notions as patriotism, we "would have no place in [our] vocabulary for physical courage"; any such act would be merely "foolhardy, mad, or moronically insensitive to reality" (p. 25, n. 8). In the prior two sections, I suggested that even Taylor does not go far enough: almost all of our thoughts, acts, and feelings express values.

58. Donald Davidson, "How Is Weakness of the Will Possible?" in *Moral Concepts,* ed. Joel Feinberg (Oxford: Oxford University Press, 1969). It is possible, of course, that Ann's action is due to a physiological "malfunc-tion," a quirky neurological event that defies intentional explanation. The principle of charity, however, requires that we say this only as a last resort.

59. Even the most extreme of hedonistic act utilitarians recognize this by considering the interests of persons but not stones. Of course, they will insist

that the capacity for pleasure is the key to moral agency, and so anything that can experience pleasure deserves special respect (has "rights," in this sense). I, of course, give a different answer.

60. Daniel Dennett, *Elbow Room: The Varieties of Free Will Worth Wanting* (Cambridge, Mass.: MIT Press, 1984), p. 23. Dennett's reminder that comatose persons can have interests does not tell against my point. Comatose individuals have interests, I would claim, only insofar as their precomatose or postcomatose stages do.

61. Griffin, for example, in *Well-Being*, when discussing the essence of personhood, suggests that "taking one's own course through life is what makes one's existence human" (p. 225).

62. I am not claiming that the extinction of a species of ferns is of no moral significance. I am only claiming that the extinction of those ferns in a universe in which there are not and will never be moral persons is of no moral significance.

63. This argument bears some structural similarities to a number of arguments for rights, such as Alan Gewirth's in *Human Rights* (Chicago: University of Chicago Press, 1982) and in *Reason and Morality* (Chicago: University of Chicago Press, 1978). My argument, of course, does not share Gewirth's analysis of the nature of rational agency.

64. After all, we feel quite justified in physically preventing someone from torturing a dog for sport. That is, not only do we feel free to prohibit it legally, but we feel free or even required to intervene physically when we chance upon someone in the act of wantonly torturing a dog. By contrast, no one would feel entitled, much less obligated, to wrestle a jaywalker to the ground to prevent him from jaywalking, though jaywalking is illegal. What this shows, I think, is that we regard torturing animals as a violation of rights (unlike jaywalking). We, as private citizens, feel entitled to use physical force to prevent someone from doing something only in extraordinary circumstances, namely when (1) we are certain that, if she knew the relevant facts, if she knew the relevant facts, she would *want* us to stop her physically (for example, she is, inadvertently, about to step in front of a moving truck), (2) the agent is not fully responsible at the time (for example, she is psychotic), or (3) someone's fundamental rights are about to be violated. Thus we may stop a murder or an assault.

Suicide raises an interesting question. Most people feel entitled to use force to prevent someone from committing suicide. Presumably, the justification is that either (a) we feel sure she will later thank us for our intervention, or (b) she is not, at present, a fully rational moral agent, or (c) that suicide violates a right of some sort. These justifications are consistent with my thesis. So, however, is the claim that we are *not* justified in preventing an adult from committing rationally considered suicide.

Note that it is not the gravity of the harm per se that justifies intervention; we may physically prevent someone from committing assault even if the damage caused by the assault would be minor. Rather, what justifies intervention is the belief that the injustice done to the perpetrator by using physical force against her is less important than the protection of the rights of the potential victim. Now it is clear that, in most cases, the use of force to stop the torture of an animal is not the result of a belief that the perpetrator would want to be stopped, nor need she be a child, mentally unbalanced, or ignorant of the consequences of her act. Hence our readiness to use force in such cases indicates a belief that the rights of the animal are being violated.

65. The story to be told about such a person is quite complex; his behavior and inner occurrences must be explicable in some way in terms of a story that attributes to him the belief that he is rowing a boat, despite the fact that he is firing the gun.

66. An interesting case is that of the completely paralyzed individual. Of course, if he can, say, flick his eyelashes, and so communicate with others, his worldview may be said to be in operation. But if he is *completely* immobile, then he is not a full moral agent. Indeed, in an important sense he is not an agent at all; he has no place in the world, cannot make a life for himself, and so on. (I owe this example to Kelly Hite.)

67. Thomas Reid, *Essays on the Intellectual Powers of Man* (1785).

68. H. P. Grice, in "Personal Identity," *Mind* 50 (October 1954), offers a solution to this problem. What is required for the general and the lad to be the same person, says Grice, is not that they share a common memory, but that they both belong to a series of stages, such that the series exhibits continuity of memory.

69. Grice's solution to the brave-officer paradox will not work here. For there are no stages that link the pre-t stages and the post-t stages in the manner required by Grice's account.

70. Of course, we are concerned not only with fairness to Ebeneezer, but also fairness to the person to whom the promise was made. In some cases, releasing Ebeneezer of the promise made to Jones might be more unfair to Jones than holding Ebeneezer now to the promise made by young Ebeneezer would be to Ebeneezer now. In that case, we might require that Ebeneezer now fulfill the promise.

71. Bernard Williams, "The Self and the Future," in *Personal Identity*, ed. John Perry (Berkeley, Calif.: University of California Press, 1975), pp. 185–186.

72. This presupposes that the supervenience principle is true; duplicating the body exactly also duplicates memories, characters, and so forth. But if this is not true, if I am a mental substance in addition to my body, then my identity rests on the continuity of that mental substance as well as my body. So the bodily-continuity criterion would be implausible on its face.

73. Bernard Williams, *Problems of the Self* (Cambridge: Cambridge University Press, 1973).

74. Note once more that sameness of person should not be confused with strict identity, which is fully transitive. No two person-stages are *identical*; rather, they are two numerically distinct stages. They may, however, both be elements of a single enduring person.

75. Actually the matter is complicated somewhat by the fact that the his-

torical Guy Fawkes was, no doubt, pronounced legally dead over three hundred years ago.

76. Wiggins discusses a variation on this theme; he supposes that my brain is divided, and each half is housed in a new body. Both surviving individuals have my character, memories, and so on. See *Identity and Spatio-temporal Continuity*.

77. Derek Parfit, "Personal Identity and Survival," *Philosophical Review* 80 (January 1971).

78. Bernard Williams, *Moral Luck* (Cambridge, England: Cambridge University Press, 1981).

79. The kind of "understanding" needed here is the Wittgensteinian one of "being able to go on." A full person need not be able to articulate these ideas. It is enough if her conceptual framework is rich enough to accommodate her participating in them when she encounters them.

80. Note that, because social practices, institutions, and models reflect central values, a widespread radical change in social concepts results in a sweeping moral make-over.

CHAPTER III

1. As J. R. Lucas points out in *The Freedom of the Will* (Oxford: Oxford University Press, 1970), the English word "responsibility" comes from the Latin word *respondeo*, meaning "I answer." R. L. Franklin, in *Freewill and Determinism* (Atlantic Highlands, N.J.: Humanities Press, 1968), suggests that responsibility is a defeasible concept: "A is responsible for x" means that no moral principle excuses A's guilt or carelessness concerning x. I take issue with this claim, since one can be responsible for an ordinarily blameworthy trait that is rendered morally neutral by a moral principle (for example, lying under duress). John Martin Fischer suggests that someone is "'morally responsible' insofar as he is accessible to such attitudes and activities [as] praise, blame, punishment and reward" (*Moral Responsibility*, ed. John M. Fischer [Ithaca, N.Y.: Cornell University Press, 1986] p. 12). Gabriel de Tarde, in *Penal Philosophy*, trans. Rapalje Howell (Boston, Mass.: Little, Brown, 1912), claims that "A is responsible for x" means "A was the willing and conscious author of the act." I suggest that we can be responsible for things of which we are not the willing and conscious author. More specifically, de Tarde suggests that A is responsible for x if (1) the causes of A's doing x were typical or normal ones (that is, A is similar to other people) and (2) A has a continuing personal identity. Jeffrie Murphy, in *Retribution, Justice and Therapy* (Dordrecht, Holland: D. Reidel, 1979), points out that on de Tarde's formulation, it is not only psychotics who are not responsible for what they do, but saints as well. I would add to Murphy's objection that were muscle spasms to become more common causes of behavior, we would not thereby blame people for their muscle spasms. Murphy suggests that what is needed for responsibility is not similarity to others *simpliciter*, but similarity in certain key respects, namely moral motivation, the ability to

conform to rules, and so on. After all, says Murphy, though Gandhi had greater courage, he was like others in having a moral sense (pp. 132–133). I find Murphy's remark puzzling, since Gandhi did seem to have a greater than normal capacity to conform to rules, which is one of Murphy's specific respects. What this suggests is that similarly to others does not play a key role here: what counts for moral responsibility is simply having a moral sense that is reflected in one's conduct (in short, being a worldview in operation). Moira Roberts's view is an example of a theory that tries to conflate two senses of "acting responsibly;" namely "being accountable" and "being morally mature." According to Roberts, people are responsible for what they do to those affected by their actions, because when we improperly harm another, we fail to allow for that harm in our mental construct of our situation, as if our actions occurred in isolation (we are "contracting out of [our] social relations"). In this sense, being responsible consists in "knowing what one is about," in having an appropriate mental construct of one's action situation (Moira Roberts, *Responsibility and Practical Freedom* [England: Cambridge University Press, 1965], pp. 232–233.) I am not sure this captures the laudatory sense of "responsible action," since one can be "irresponsible" in things that concern only oneself. We can fix this problem by broadening Roberts's definition a bit, defining responsible actions as those that accord with a morally and factually appropriate map of possible options and attitudes, whether conscious or not. (This definition suits well my worldview-based account of moral responsibility.) Nonetheless, there are "irresponsible actions" for which we are morally responsible.

2. For example, Michael J. Zimmerman, in *An Essay on Moral Responsibility* (Totowa, N.J.: Rowman and Littlefield, 1988), distinguishes between causal responsibility, prospective personal responsibility, and retrospective personal responsibility (p. 1). See also Kurt Baier, "Responsibility and Action," reprinted in *The Nature of Human Action* ed. Myles Brand (Glenview, Ill.: Scott, Foresman, 1970).

3. For example, as Myles Brand has pointed out to me, my assumption (in the section entitled "Hume and Motives") that enjoying the suffering of animals is the sort of thing that bears moral evaluation is not warranted by certain moral theories, for example, pure hedonistic egoism.

4. Because Alasdair MacIntyre, among others, has criticized so-called "analytic" philosophers for making detailed arguments whose premises are sweeping assumptions (*After Virtue*, 2d ed. [Notre Dame, Ind.: University of Notre Dame Press, 1984]), I feel it necessary to explain why I make these assumptions. A proper defense of the most obvious moral assertions would take too long, and it grows tiresome to keep adding a host of conditionals such as "if killing people for the thrill of seeing their blood flow is wrong." I make these assumptions in the belief that they are both true and defensible. In the unlikely event that it is not, in fact, wrong to kill people for the thrill of seeing their blood flow, then what I say about that case must be modified.

5. Ted Honderich, *Essays on Freedom of Action* (London: Routledge and Kegan Paul, 1973).

6. Cf. J.W.C. Turner, "The Mental Element in Crimes at Common Law," in ed. D. Seaborne Davies et al., *The Modern Approach to Criminal Law* (London: Macmillan, 1945).

7. Anthony Kenny, *Freewill and Responsibility* (London: Routledge and Kegan Paul, 1978), p. 38.

8. See *Abbott v. the Queen* [1976] 3 All E.R. 140 and *Regina v. Dudley and Stephens* 14 Q.B.D. 273 (1884).

9. That is, if one accepts Davidson's account of actions.

10. Of course, one might say that Mickey's act was involuntary because he had no *morally acceptable* alternative. But now voluntarity does not explain the moral difference between *having lied* and *having lied under threat of execution.* Rather voluntarity itself is explained by this distinction. (Robert Audi, in his "Moral Responsibility, Freedom and Compulsion," *American Philosophical Quarterly* 11 (January 1974): 1–14, stresses the role that moral evaluation plays in determining voluntarity.)

11. In Chapter V, I argue that there are three elements required for criminal liability: (1) the evil proscribed by law occurred, (2) the evil is assignable to the defendant, and (3) the defendant satisfies the appropriate *mens rea* requirements. (A parallel structure applies to tort liability.) Questions of moral responsibility center on the third element.

12. For that belief is a constituent of his worldview. For a rather different approach to responsibility for beliefs, see Michael Stocker, "Responsibility Especially for Beliefs," *Mind* 91 (1982): 398–417.

13. At best, control would be an "accidental" prerequisite; it just so happens that everything for which we are responsible is within our control. But even if we are not responsible for x, and x is not within our control, our lack of responsibility could not be *due to* our lack of control.

14. Cf. J. Sabini, and M. Silver, "Emotions, Responsibility and Character," in *Responsibility, Character and the Emotions: Essays in Moral Psychology,* ed. Ferdinand D. Schoeman (Cambridge, England: Cambridge University Press, 1987): "someone who does good works . . . in a generous spirit is a better person than" someone who does similar works without compassion (p. 169). Sabrini and Silver suggest that this is true because people can control their emotions, whereas my argument will suggest that it is true whether or not people can control their emotions.

15. J.E.R. Squires, in "Blame," *Philosophical Quarterly* 18 (1968), suggests that "to blame a person is to be of the opinion that he is responsible for an undesired upshot, that he has done what he ought not" (p. 60). William Lyons articulates four elements of blame: (1) responsiblity for an action or inaction, (2) a harmful or undesirable state brought about by the action or inaction, (3) lack of excusing circumstances, and (4) consequent disapproval (*Emotion* [Cambridge, England: Cambridge University Press, 1980], p. 195). I suggest that Squires is correct if we acknowledge that "ought" does not imply "can" and that an "upshot" may be a morally undesirable state of the agent, such as an attitude or a value. I disagree, of course, with Lyons's emphasis on the effects of actions, and I argue that excusing circumstances

generally change what one is responsible for, rather than eliminating one's responsibility.

16. Lyons, in *Emotion,* lists ten ways in which one can control one's emotions: (1) "inducing an emotion in oneself," (2) "avoiding" or (3) "aborting an emotion by manipulating the context," (4) "talking oneself" out of or (5) "allowing oneself to be talked out of" or (6) "talking oneself into a badly grounded emotion," (7) "keeping an emotion going," (8) "overcoming an emotion by shock tactics," (9) "controlling the behavior stemming from emotions," and (10) "controlling the non-purposive expressions of emotion" (pp. 196–202).

17. See, for example, A. M. Honore, "Can and Can't," *Mind* (1964); Keith Lehrer, "Preferences, Conditionals and Freedom" in *Time and Cause: Essays Presented to Richard Taylor* ed. Peter van Inwagen (Dordrecht, Holland: D. Reidel, 1980); Carl Ginet, "Might We Have No Choice?" in *Freedom and Determinism* ed. Keith Lehrer (New York: Random House, 1966); and Peter van Inwagen, "Ability and Responsibility," *Philosophical Review* 87 (April 1978).

18. Quotations are from David Hume, *A Treatise of Human Nature,* ed. L. A. Selby-Bigge (Oxford: Oxford University Press 1888; reprint, 1968), and David Hume, *An Enquiry Concerning Human Understanding,* in *Enquiries Concerning the Human Understanding and Concerning the Principles of Morals,* ed. L. A. Selby-Bigge, 2d ed. (1902; reprint, Oxford: Oxford University Press, 1955).

19. Cf: "An action, or sentiment, or character is virtuous or vicious; why? because its view causes a pleasure or uneasiness of a particular kind. . . . To have the sense of virtue, is nothing but to feel a satisfaction of a particular kind from the contemplation of a character. The very feeling constitutes our praise or admiration" (Hume, *Treatise,* III I ii, p. 471). "'Tis evident, that when we praise any actions, we regard only the motives that produced them, and consider the actions as signs or indications of certain principles in the mind and temper. The external performance has no merit. We must look within to find the moral quality. . . . The ultimate object of our praise and approbation is the motive, that produc'd them" (*Ibid.,* III II i, p. 477). "All virtuous actions derive their merit only from virtuous motives, and are consider'd merely as signs of those motives" (*Ibid.,* p. 478). "No action can be virtuous, or morally good, unless there be in human nature some motive to produce it, distinct from the sense of its morality" (*Ibid.,* p. 479). "No action can be laudable or blameable, without some motives or impelling passions, distinct from the sense of morals" (*Ibid.,* p. 483). "Actions are, by their very nature, temporary and perishing; and where they proceed not from some *cause* in the character and disposition of the person who performed them, they can neither redound to his honor, if good; nor infamy, if evil. [A] person is not answerable for [immoral deeds if] they proceeded from nothing in him, that is durable and constant" (Hume, *Enquiry,* VIII II, p. 98). "Men are not blamed for such actions, as they perform ignorantly and casually, whatever the consequences. Why? but because the principles of these actions are

only momentary, and terminate in them alone" (*Ibid.*). "For what is meant by liberty, when applied to voluntary actions? . . . By liberty . . . we can only mean a power of acting or not acting, according to the determinations of the will; that is, if we choose to remain at rest, we may; if we choose to move, we also may" (*Ibid.*, VIII I, p. 95). "Liberty, according to that definition above mentioned, in which all men agree, is also essential to morality, and that no human actions, where it is wanting, are susceptible of any moral qualities, or can be the objects either of approbation or dislike . . . it is impossible that [actions] can give rise either to praise or blame, where they proceed not from these principles, but are derived altogether from external violence" (*Ibid.*, VIII II, p. 99).

20. See, for example, John Hospers, "What Means This Freedom?" in *Determinism and Freedom* ed. Sidney Hook (New York: New York University, 1958). See also Thomas Nagel, "Moral Luck," in his *Mortal Questions* (Cambridge, England: Cambridge University Press, 1979).

21. Of course, one could argue that by "motive" Hume does not mean a cause of behavior, although his language suggests otherwise. If so, it is not clear what he does mean. If he meant "attitude or belief revealed by action," I rest content to have clarified Hume's position.

22. Honderich, "One Determinism," in *Essays on Freedom of Action*, p. 208.

23. C. A. Campbell, "Is Free Will a Pseudo-problem?" *Mind* 60 (1951): 441–465.

24. Paul Edwards, "Hard and Soft Determinism," in *Determinism and Freedom*, pp. 123, 125.

25. Richard Brandt, "Determinism and the Justifiability of Moral Blame," in *Determinism and Freedom*.

26. Honderich, *Essays on Freedom of Action*.

27. The case of sentient computers is much like the case of "mind tampering"; I discuss such cases in detail in Chapter IV.

28. Moritz Schlick, "When Is a Man Responsible?" in *The Problems of Ethics* (New York, 1939); and F. H. Bradley, *Ethical Studies*, 2d. ed. (Oxford: Oxford University Press, 1927). See also Audi's arguments against Schlick in "Moral Responsibility, Freedom and Compulsion." Judith Andre makes a parallel point about praise and reward. "In its central sense," she writes, "morality refers to excellence of character. Whenever we praise people as moral we mean they are worthy of praise and emulation; but only sometimes do we mean that they are worthy of reward" ("Nagel, Williams and Moral Luck," *Analysis* (1983): 205).

29. I would deny this. So does our legal system, which makes selling adulterated milk a crime of strict liability.

30. As Franklin argues on p. 164 of *Freewill and Determinism*, blame may be ineffective but deserved, and deserved but ineffective.

31. See also my "With Virtue for All: Against the Democratic Theory of Virtue," *Southwest Philosophy Review* 5 (January 1989): 71–76.

32. See also *ibid.*

33. A. John Simmons, *Moral Principles and Political Obligations* (Princeton, N.J.: Princeton University Press, 1979).

34. Hospers, "What Means This Freedom?" in *Determinism and Freedom,* p. 137.

35. Nagel, "Moral Luck," in *Mortal Questions,* p. 28.

36. Nagel's paper has generated quite a bit of comment. In particular, some of the views expressed by Andre, in "Nagel, Williams and Moral Luck," and by Henning Jensen in "Morality and Luck," *Philosophy* 59 (July 1984): 323–330, accord well with what I have to say, though in many ways we regard the matter of moral luck differently. Mention should also be made of the title essay in Bernard Williams's *Moral Luck* (Cambridge, England: Cambridge University Press, 1981).

37. This claim does not assume rigid determinism. Even the libertarian does not deny that we can make true statements about what people will or will not do in certain situations. He simply denies that they are *caused* to do it. Free choice does not necessarily mean unpredictable choice. Now it takes independence of mind to hold out against the social and psychological pressure Nazism exerted in Germany in 1940, and Beckmann1, as I have described him, is not an independently minded person (whether by choice, conditioning, or whatever). Thus we can truly assert that Beckmann1 *would* have become a Nazi had he remained in Germany, leaving open the question of whether he *could* have done otherwise.

38. Here, of course, I get moral brownie points for my horror at the attitudes I am developing, but moral demerits for having those attitudes. That is, my attitudes are conflicting; this story attributes to me both a positive and a negative attitude toward, for example, violence, and I am evaluable for both attitudes.

39. Cf. Bernard Williams, *Ethics and the Limits of Philosophy* (Cambridge, Mass.: Harvard University Press, 1985), pp. 195–196: "the ideal that human existence can be ultimately just," that morality "transcends luck," is "one of the most moving ideals." However, "the idea of a value beyond luck is an illusion."

40. See also my "With Virtue for All: Against the Democratic Theory of Virtue," in which I discuss both moral luck and the related thesis that some virtues may be beyond the reach of some people.

41. Cf. Daniel Dennett, *Elbow Room: The Varieties of Free Will Worth Wanting* (Cambridge, Mass.: MIT Press, 1984), p. 156: "a completely self-made self, one hundred per cent responsible for its own character, [is] an impossibility."

42. See also Charles Taylor's discussion of "radical" moral choice in chapter 1 of his *Human Agency and Language* (Cambridge, England: Cambridge University Press, 1985).

43. For example, the argument of the Wanter shows that it is not free will but having a worldview that is the basis of moral personhood. And since being a moral person means having rights and responsibilities, it seems to follow that it is having a worldview, rather than having free will, that is at

the core of moral responsibility. That is, normal adult human beings have a special moral status precisely because their choices, acts, feelings, and thoughts are *moral* choices, acts, feelings, and thoughts; they express a moral perspective. To the extent that a person's moral perspective accords with the *correct* moral perspective, her attitudes are good ones. And because she (*qua* moral agent) just *is* those attitudes, actualized in a life, *she* is good. Again, since morality is concerned not with neural firings as such, but with moral judgments, values, and attitudes, and, I argued in Chapter II, attitudes and the like are not causes of actions, what morality must judge are not the causes of action, but the worldviews of agents.

CHAPTER IV

1. It should be noted, however, that, as Dennett points out, the threat to responsibility is not so much Laplacian determinism, "but science itself, or the 'naturalism' that is its enabling world view." *Elbow Room: The Varieties of Free Will Worth Wanting* (Cambridge, Mass.: MIT Press, 1984), p. 170.

2. One sort of worry, in addition to those discussed below, is illustrated by Jennifer Trusted's remarks in *Free Will and Responsibility* (Oxford: Oxford University Press, 1984). Trusted claims that for determinists, "no judgment and no action can be caused by ratiocination, they are caused by neural events in the brain" (p. 134). This distinction is one that reductive physicalists and functionalists deny, since they define "judgments and actions" as physical states or features of physical states. (Trusted's formulations in the book generally ignore the possibility that there are nonphysical, "mental" properties or events that are nonetheless lawlike, that is, follow "laws of thought.") In any case, it is not clear why Trusted thinks that determinism entails that "any internal debate . . . [is] of no consequence," (p. 132), and that "for determinists any belief must be non-rational in the sense that it must be entirely determined by physical events and hence the only justification possible is a pragmatic justification" (p. 78). As long as the internal debate is properly matched to the physical states that are causally efficacious, physical determinism does not mean that our behavior is not governed by rational considerations. After all, it is absurd to insist that my inputting "2 + 465" to my calculator is of no consequence, since it is the closing of the keyboard switches that caused the calculator to print "467."

3. One of the most interesting of these, due to Peter van Inwagen, is discussed in Appendix D.

4. P. F. Strawson, "Freedom and Resentment," *Proceedings of the British Academy* 48 (1962).

5. For a more detailed discussion of Strawson's argument, see Paul Benson, "The Moral Importance of Free Action," *Southern Journal of Philosophy* 28 (1990): 1–16.

6. In a footnote on page 199, Strawson seems to recognize this point. "Might it not be said," he asks, "that we should be nearer to being purely rational creatures in proportion as our relation to others was in fact domi-

nated by the objective attitude?" His answer, however, is that "it would not necessarily be rational to choose to be more purely rational than we are." In other words, irrationality might be useful.

7. This distinction is illicit only if one adopts the principle that what is true is what it is most useful to believe. Many have argued, however, that this view of truth is incoherent. Indeed, it seems to presuppose an objective truth about what is useful.

8. *Daniel M'Naghten's Case* 8 Eng. Rep. 718 10 Cl. and Fin. 200 (1843).

9. *United States v. Brawner* 471 F.2d 969 (D.C. Cir. 1972). This test is also used by the *American Law Institute Model Penal Code* (1962).

10. *Durham v. United States*, 94 U.S. App. D.C. 228, 214 F.2d 862 (1954).

11. I should state that I do not hold this view.

12. Keith Lehrer, "'Can' in Theory and Practice: A Possible Worlds Analysis," in *Action Theory*, ed. Myles Brand and E. Walton (Dordrecht, Holland: D. Reidel, 1976).

13. Isaiah Berlin, *Four Essays on Liberty* (Oxford: Oxford University Press, 1969), pp. xx–xxi.

14. See also John M. Fischer, "Introduction: Responsibility and Freedom," in *Moral Responsibility* ed. John M. Fischer (Ithaca, N.Y.: Cornell University Press, 1986), p. 20.

15. Of course, Brian is not morally responsible for instantiating the trait *having killed five people;* that trait is insufficiently specific. Surely it is morally relevant that Brian acted in accordance with what he (incorrectly) believed to be a moral imperative.

16. It must be said that there is a tradition that denies that inculcated beliefs count as "beliefs" at all, or at least not as "rational" beliefs. Melden, for example, says that if I cause someone to believe that he is Napoleon by implanting an electrode in his brain, "that surely is not a rational belief that he has, nor is he responsible for what he does in consequence of his belief, however convinced he may be that he is fully justified in acting as he does" (A. I. Melden, *Free Action* [London: Routledge and Kegan Paul, 1961], p. 214). And MacIntyre states that drugs, electrodes, and such cannot produce something properly called a "belief"; "the concept of causing people to change their beliefs, or to make moral choices, by brain-washing or drugs, for example, is not a possible concept" (quoted by Dennett in *Brainstorms: Philosophical Essays on Mind and Psychology* [Montgomery, Vt.: Bradford Books, 1978], p. 250, citing Anthony Flew, "A Rational Animal" in *Brain and Mind*, ed. J. R. Smythies [London: Routledge and Kegan Paul, 1968], p. 118).

I suggest that such claims are misguided. To have a belief is to adopt a certain cognitive stance toward the world. Beliefs characterize the ways in which we respond to and give significance to the world about us. How we came to adopt a stance is not relevant to its being a belief. And whether a belief is rational has to do with my evidence for it, not how I happened to come by it. This, I think, is the point of Kant's insistence that rationality functions *as if* it were causally free. Rationality gives a *reason* for holding a belief. And whether the reason is a good or bad one does not depend on what caused me to have the belief. It is a question not about the causal history of my belief, but about, for example, the *logical* connections between my beliefs and the information available to me. So the rationality of my beliefs is independent of the causes of those beliefs. As Dennett points out, were a benevolent neurosurgeon to implant the belief that honesty is the best policy in the minds of hardened criminals, we should not on that account "deny these people status in the society as responsible agents" (*Elbow Room*, p. 249).

17. A crucial thing to examine, of course, is the current attitude of a Nazi to the past atrocities committed by the Nazis. One has only to view Claude Lanzmann's film *Shoah* to see the pride with which the former Nazis Lanzmann interviewed still view their past operations. Similarly, Mrs. Michelson, the wife of a German schoolteacher in Chelmo, revealed something of her attitudes when she said that what was terrible about the atrocities was that a whole town should not have to be exposed to such misery. The misery of and injustice to those exterminated seem to count, in her eyes, only insofar as it distressed the non-Jewish residents of Chelmo. A third example comes from a PBS documentary entitled "Hitler's Night of the Hummingbird." On June 29, 1934, Hitler ordered the murder of most of the leadership of the SA, including Ernst Roehm. Some remarks of Roehm's sister are quite revealing. The murder of Roehm during "Operation Hummingbird," she said, was the beginning of the breakdown of justice. Prior to Roehm's murder, Dachau, under Roehm's control, already housed over twenty thousand inmates.

18. Note, by the way, that Brian's case is very much like the case of the computer with bona fide emotions and beliefs. My remarks about Brian apply, *mutatis mutandis*, to the feeling computer.

CHAPTER V

1. True, on some accounts of punishment, punishment inflicts harm only to bring about some other end, for example, to rehabilitate someone, or to deter others. Still, in punishment the harm inflicted is not a byproduct of pursuing the end. Rather, incarcerating a felon is a means of deterring others only insofar as and only by virtue of the fact that incarceration is a harm. It is precisely the harmfulness as such of incarceration that makes incarceration a means of deterring or rehabilitating. Thus punishment is radically unlike, say, taxing the rich to feed the starving, or cutting off a gangrenous hand to save the patient's life. (It is not the unpleasantness of being taxed that makes taxing the rich a means of feeding the starving.)

2. Briefly put, punishment should be regarded as legal deterrence, that is, as the instantiation of the rule of law as law. Legal deterrence aims not only at insuring that citizens' behavior conforms to the law but is a public proclamation of a community's commitment to the rule of law. The law is a set of

mechanisms that makes it feasible for citizens to undertake the rational pursuit of the correct conception of human flourishing. The rule of law is itself a crucial element of human flourishing. When law rules, citizens respect the law as a coherent and intelligible network of legal rules, maxims, and principles that publicly express the values of the community. The rule of law means not only that legal mechanisms in fact settle most disputes, but also that the law has integrity as a public artifact that expresses the public life and values of the community. Punishment is justifiable for precisely the same reason that law has authority, namely, it is required to make feasible the rational pursuit of the correct conception of human goodness. And it is precisely the rational pursuit of the correct conception of human goodness that grounds the moral status of persons, that makes harming them wrong. Thus punishment is justifiable.

These few sketchy remarks hardly do justice to the topic. A full theory of punishment and political authority is the subject of a future work.

3. I say blameworthiness "may well be" (rather than "is") irrelevant to punishment because the utilitarian might claim that the best balance of good over evil results when one incarcerates only those who are blameworthy.

4. Actually, I would argue that the connection between practical judgment and morality is much closer than these remarks suggest. All practical decisions are, in an important sense, moral ones. Jones chooses shoes to "match" his suit, and he tries to wear matching clothes because he wants to impress his boss, and he wants to impress his boss because he wants her to give him a raise, and he wants a raise because. . . . At the end of all such chains of practical reasoning is a vision of the good life, of what is good and valuable in human life, of what is worth committing oneself to as a moral agent. True, there are some choices about which morality is silent. Whether I choose blueberries or strawberries to go on my crepe is such a decision. But notice that, if blueberries would give me marginally more pleasure than strawberries, this is not a moral choice only because stringent act utilitarianism is false. In other words, I call this a nonmoral choice only by virtue of having made a variety of moral judgments. In this sense, every choice is a moral choice, and so "advisability" a moral predicate.

Nonetheless, some choices are more directly moral than others. Moreover, some moral directives are aspirative, while some are obligatory. The distinction I am making here between advisability and permissibility should be construed as a rough, not a rigorous one, concerning the obligatoriness of the moral prompting involved, as well as the directness of morality's involvement with the matter. This rough distinction is sufficient for our purposes. There is still a licit distinction between the extent to which an individual's moral demerits *warrant* punishment and the *usefulness* of inflicting that punishment, even if "usefulness" is, ultimately, also a moral notion.

5. An interesting case is self-punishment for evil thoughts. Suppose Ghermann, a religious ascetic, punishes himself for his longing for a slice of Sacher torte. Is Ghermann entitled to mete out the punishment? Generally, the

answer is "yes," though some would say "sometimes not." Locke, for example, insists that our lives belong to God, and hence Ghermann is not entitled to mete out to himself a death sentence, whether or not he deserves it. If Ghermann is wrong that his sybaritic desire merits whipping, or if he is wrong that whipping serves a valid, cost-effective purpose, his self-inflicted punishment is *unwarranted*, though he may nonetheless have the *right* to impose it.

6. This claim, of course, requires some argument. Since my argument for the claim depends upon my theory of political authority, I cannot give it here in any detail. My view, roughly, is that the justifying aim of a legal system is to make feasible the taking of rational steps (by those affected by the legal system's mechanisms) in pursuit of the correct conception of human goodness and flourishing. Now, whereas some commitment to abstract justice is called for, I would argue that a legal system that took upon itself the task of seeing that abstract justice is universally served would hinder, rather than facilitate, the feasibility of citizens' taking rational steps in pursuit of the correct conception of human goodness and flourishing. Hence, although punishing people for evil emotions would do some good, namely helping to see that abstract justice is instantiated, the project of "playing God" in this way is not a licit task for a legal system to undertake.

7. Herbert Morris, "Persons and Punishment" in his *On Guilt and Innocence* (Berkeley, Calif.: University of California Press, 1976).

8. Immanuel Kant, *Metaphysical Elements of Justice: Part I of the Metaphysics of Morals,* trans. John Ladd (London: Macmillan, 1965).

9. James Sterba, *The Demands of Justice* (Notre Dame, Ind.: University of Notre Dame Press, 1980), especially pp. 75–83.

10. David A. J. Richards, *The Moral Criticism of Law* (Evanston, Ill.: Dickerson Press, 1977), p. 240.

11. Robert Nozick, *Philosophical Explanations* (Cambridge, Mass.: Harvard University Press, 1981).

12. Richard Wasserstrom, *Philosophy and Social Issues* (Notre Dame, Ind.: University of Notre Dame Press, 1980).

13. Hyman Gross, *A Theory of Criminal Justice* (Oxford: Oxford University Press, 1979), p. 391.

14. I call it this because it bears some resemblance to Hegel's theory, though it is not really a fair representation of Hegel's complicated and somewhat unclear view, which rests on his not unproblematic metaphysics.

15. David Lyons, *Ethics and the Rule of Law* (Cambridge, England: Cambridge University Press, 1984), p. 150.

16. Some perplexities about abstract justice arise in an imperfect world. For example, suppose that during his first twenty years, Mitchell is an exemplary person who leads a hard life. (That is, his life is not abstractly just.) During his next twenty years, Mitchell is a thriving reprobate. Are the demands of abstract justice satisfied? One wants to say "in a sense they are, but in a sense they are not." Rather than complicate the discussion of ab-

stract justice, I try to deal with such problems in other ways: for example, by introducing a principle of specific retribution into the theory of retributive punishment.

17. This is why, although utilitarianism may deem it good that individuals show loyalty (if the effect of individuals' being loyal to each other is to produce more overall happiness), the utilitarian standpoint itself is incompatible with loyalty. Similarly, some construals of the universalizability principle are incompatible with loyalty, while more sensible versions recognize some loyalty-promoting maxims, such as "give preference to the good" or "accord some degree of special consideration to your family," as universalizable maxims.

18. This is a stipulative definition; that is how I am using the term. The stipulation is appropriate, however, because what I am calling "caring for" x captures the kind of affection that is a response to the person herself, as opposed to a general feeling of which I make x the object (in the way, for example, that a teenager might fix his general romantic yearnings upon a movie star).

19. Human error complicates the situation here. It is, as such, good to care for someone, since moral commitment is itself a good. However, if one is mistaken about what is good, one's caring for someone will also be mistaken. Thus caring for someone who is *in fact* evil is a moral error, and is, in that respect, not good. So although the argument is sound as it stands, an even stronger version is produced by replacing "caring for" with "appropriately caring for," and making the necessary modifications.

20. James Griffin, in *Well-Being* (Oxford: Oxford University Press, 1986), argues on pp. 258–264 that failing to recognize merit is not a moral wrong. His argument, however, is somewhat unclear. He seems to argue that Oxford University is not more unjust than American universities in paying professors on the basis of seniority rather than merit, and thus failing to recognize merit is not unjust. Of course, many do not share Griffin's intuition about this point. Griffin says that "rewards need not be money," and so, he seems to be saying, Oxford's policy is not injust, since Oxford might recognize merit in other ways. I find this puzzling, since, if Oxford's system is not unjust because merit is recognized in other ways, then the case of Oxford does not show that failing to recognize merit is not unjust, since, *ex hypothesi*, Oxford does not fail to recognize merit. Perhaps this is not the point of Griffin's remark that rewards need not be money: perhaps Griffin is merely assuming that there is no injustice at all in Oxford's policy. He may be right, but, given the widespread rejection of this view, some argument is needed. Griffin's second argument seems to be that since it undermines gratitude to feel it from a sense of duty, it is not wrong to fail to feel gratitude when gratitude is appropriate. This simply does not follow. It may undermine integrity to be honest only from fear of going to Hell, but it does not follow that people without integrity should not be sent to Hell. Griffin seems to be conflating the appropriate *motivation* for a feeling or action with the appropriate *evaluation* of the feeling or action.

21. See also Appendix F for a discussion of George Sher's insightful book about desert.

22. Of course, what is at stake are her attitudes, rather than a particular action. If she habitually wears seat belts, but forgets to buckle them only once, and that very time has an accident, we feel this is unfair, since fate did not respond appropriately to her general attitude to safety as expressed in her life.

23. Thus the expected-consequence account of desert is mistaken, for, as Robert Goodin points out, on the expected-consequence account, the person who fails to wear a seat belt is taking (say) a one in ten thousand risk of crashing, and thus deserves only a ten thousandth of the pain inflicted by going through the windshield. Robert E. Goodin, "Negating Positive Desert Claims," *Political Theory* 13 (November 1985): 584–585.

24. It should be stressed that, strictly speaking, strong and weak desert are part of a continuum, rather than a divide. Hitler more strongly deserves ill fortune than does an ordinary murderer, because it is more of a moral blemish on the face of the world if Hitler flourishes. There are also borderline cases where an agent is so much subject to a harsh fate that we feel some degree of moral discomfort when that harsh fate is not forthcoming, though we hesitate to say that he merits it. Consider a driver who falls somewhere between the dangerous driver and the driver who fails to wear seat belts. Although he is not an egregiously irresponsible driver, he generally drives ten miles per hour over the speed limit, habitually follows a bit too closely, never wears a seat belt, does not check his brakes sufficiently often, and so on. We may say, "There is no justice in the world" when learning that in twenty years of driving he has never had an accident. Yet we do not quite mean that it is morally unfortunate that he has not had an accident. This case seems to be on the borderline between strong and weak desert.

25. This claim commits me to saying that a moderately good person who has a spectacular life situation merits punishment. I accept this: we might well say, "She does not deserve her good fortune." But intrinsic subjection is only one of the necessary conditions for legal punishment. Surely it would not serve a licit, cost-effective social purpose to punish her, nor, it seems clear, are we entitled, in this case, to mete out abstract justice.

26. In fact, there is some disagreement about whether the sentence should fit the offense or fit the offender. Due to limitations of space, I gloss over this question here.

27. Gabriele Taylor, "Pride," in *Explaining Emotions*, ed. Amelie Rorty (Berkeley, Calif.: University of California Press, 1980), p. 389.

28. Joel Feinberg, in his discussion of good samaritans (*Harm to Others* [Oxford: Oxford University Press, 1984], vol. 1 of *The Moral Limits of the Criminal Law*), suggests there is some concept of an appropriate "baseline" from which benefiting and not harming is measured. Perhaps one might claim that my case is stronger after her answer than it was at the moment just after the question was asked, but before she answered. My welfare at the moment the question is asked is the appropriate baseline. Thus Nimbia bene-

fited me. But this is stretching a point—my case is weakened by the question's being asked only because the question's being asked provides an opportunity for Nimbia to harm my case by lying.

29. It is important to realize that "impetus toward action" should not be taken too literally as a cause or determinant of behavior. What I mean is really a bit more complicated. Goodwill is part of the attitudinal framework in terms of which my life is understood by me and is best intentionally explained by others. The point is that I have goodwill when I have a strong commitment toward realizing the good in my life in a way that shows respect and concern for others as fellow moral agents. Goodwill is a commitment to having my acts, circumstances, feelings, thoughts, relationships, and the like embody the good in this way. I am still speaking, in other words, not so much of causes of actions, but of the realization, embodiment and reflection of a worldview in the life one leads.

30. See Larry Becker's helpful and insightful discussion in *Reciprocity* (New York: Routledge, Chapman, and Hall, 1986).

31. It is useful to distinguish between two kinds of ill will. Ill will$_1$ shows contempt for the *correct* moral framework. Ill will$_2$ shows contempt for the *actor*'s moral framework. In other words, a sincere Nazi shows ill will$_1$ but not ill will$_2$ in murdering Jews. He believes, mistakenly, that he is acting with respect for the correct moral framework. (In other words, there are two ways to show ill will: by not caring about what the moral truth is, or by being mistaken about what the moral truth is.) As our treatment of moral responsibility shows, someone who shows ill will$_1$ but not ill will$_2$ is praiseworthy for the trait of showing moral concern (trying to do what is right) and blameworthy for his evil moral views. Accordingly, there is resentment based on someone's showing ill will$_1$, and resentment based on someone's showing ill will$_2$. The former is generally stronger, since the resented person lacks the mitigating trait of moral concern. Indeed, in some cases we feel no resentment at all for a betrayal showing ill will$_2$. ("What he did was wrong, but I understand his point of view, and so do not resent him for it." The idea here is that we appreciate the betrayer's moral concern and think his moral framework, though mistaken, is sufficiently plausible that we feel no anger, no outrage, at his having held it. We distinguish, in ethics, "intelligent" mistakes from "dumb" or "sloppy" and "ignorant mistakes," much as a mathematics teacher does in assessing her pupil's homework.) In the ensuing discussion I will not generally, distinguish between ill will$_1$ and ill will$_2$. The reader should keep in mind, however, that the difference is sometimes important.

32. This is not merely an ad hoc device to save my account. I am suggesting that one who feels this kind of resentment really does have a sense of violated trust, really does feel a violation of the trust appropriate to solidarity in the community of moral agents. This sense may be barely articulated, but, I suggest, it is there. This is a psychological claim that invites reflective introspection, and the reader who does not find this sense within

him, when he resents a bully in the circumstances I describe, should reject my claim.

33. See, for example, "On Being Responsible for Everything."

34. I am indebted to John Baker for this example.

APPENDIX A

1. Peter van Inwagen, *An Essay on Free Will* (Oxford: Oxford University Press, 1983).

2. See John M. Fischer, "Responsibility and Control," *Journal of Philosophy* 79 (January 1982): 24–40.

3. Robert Audi, "Moral Responsibility, Freedom and Compulsion," *American Philosophical Quarterly* 11 (January 1974): 1–14.

APPENDIX C

1. John Perry, "Personal Identity, Memory and the Problem of Circularity," in John Perry ed. *Personal Identity* (Berkeley, Calif.: University of California Press, 1975), pp. 135–155.

APPENDIX D

1. Peter van Inwagen, "The Incompatibility of Responsibility and Determinism," in *Action and Responsibility* (Bowling Green, Ohio: Bowling Green Press, 1980), 30–37.;

2. See also Michael Slote's review of van Inwagen's *Essay on Free Will* in *Journal of Philosophy* 82 (June 1985): 327–330, for a discussion of a variant of this argument.

APPENDIX E

1. Frithjof Bergmann, "Monologue on the Emotions," in *Understanding Human Emotions* (Bowling Green, Ohio: Bowling Green Press, 1980). Bergmann's main argument that emotions are not sensations is that "there are relatively few sensations, which . . . are easily recognized and not at all difficult to describe." Yet "there is an enormous variety of emotions." Thus "the difference between two emotions must not necessarily correspond to a difference between two sensations" (p. 4). But Bergmann seems to move from this formulation to the claims that "emotions are not merely sensations" (p. 5), and that "emotions have an additional component" or "additional ingredient" (p.7). Now these latter assertions are at best misleading. If his two premises are correct, Bergmann has shown that emotion words are not mere labels for discrete sensation-types (that is, sensations distinct in how they feel), and so he is correct that when we distinguish between fear and anxiety, we are not merely distinguishing between sensation-types. But it

does not follow that fear is not "merely" a sensation, that it has another component or ingredient. Four different emotion words may all describe the very same sensation-type, felt under different conditions. But the conditions are not extra ingredients or components of the thing we feel, any more than tallness is an extra "ingredient" of tall men, or shortness an extra ingredient of "shorties." It would be an obvious error to insist that because there is only one species of human being, "tallies" and "shorties," or "sailors" and "tenants," cannot be merely human beings but must have some extra component or ingredient. Again, if I am both the oldest and the wisest person in the room, "the oldest person in the room" and "the wisest person in the room" both name me. The fact that there are two distinct descriptions does not mean that they describe two distinct things, nor that they name a curious compound consisting of me plus some additional ingredient or component.

Yet this is exactly Bergmann's argument. Bergmann's premises, in other words, are compatible with the claim that every emotion is a sensation, though two different emotion words may describe the same sensation felt under different conditions. (Just as "tenant" and "sailor" may both describe the same person.) In other words, one could claim that "shame" denotes a certain sensation, when felt after doing something wrong. "Embarrassment" denotes the *same* sensation when felt after doing something awkward. But there is no curious entity consisting of that sensation plus its occurring after having done something wrong. There is just the sensation.

APPENDIX F

1. George Sher, *Desert* (Princeton, N.J.: Princeton University Press, 1987).

2. See, for example, Herbert Morris, *On Guilt and Innocence* (Berkeley, Calif.: University of California Press, 1976).

3. See also Gertrude Ezorsky, "The Ethics of Punishment" in her *Philosophical Perspectives on Punishment* (Albany, N.Y.: SUNY Press, 1972), especially pp. xxii–xxvii.

4. Richard W. Burgh, "Do the Guilty Deserve Punishment?" *Journal of Philosophy* 79 (April 1982), pp. 193–213.

5. Actually, Sher argues that "the value of freedom is one genuine source of desert [that] justifies only a small subset of the corresponding desert claims" (p. 49). He does not explicitly characterize this subset. The examples he gives seem largely to fall under the rubric "achievement desert," though this is not his term. I apologize if my way of putting the matter does violence to Sher's view.

6. Robert Simon, "An Indirect Defense of the Merit Principle," *Philosophical Forum* 10 (1978), p. 237.

Index